Fashion and Textiles

Fashion and Textiles

Colin Gale
Head of the School of Fashion and Textiles
University of Central England
Birmingham, UK

Jasbir Kaur
School of Fashion and Textiles
University of Central England
Birmingham, UK

CBSPD

CBS Publishers & Distributors Pvt Ltd

New Delhi • Bengaluru • Chennai • Kochi • Kolkata • Lucknow • Mumbai
Hyderabad • Jharkhand • Nagpur • Patna • Pune • Uttarakhand

Fashion and Textiles

ISBN: 978-81-239-1956-0

CBS Edition: 2011
Reprint: **2024**
First published by Berg, Oxford, UK

This edition has been published in India by arrangement with AC Black Publishers Ltd, London, for Berg Publishers

Published by **Satish Kumar Jain** and produced by **Varun Jain** for
CBS Publishers & Distributors Pvt Ltd
4819/XI Prahlad Street, 24 Ansari Road, Daryaganj, New Delhi 110 002, India.
Ph: 011-23289259, 23266861 Website: www.cbspd.com
e-mail: delhi@cbspd.com

Corporate Office: 204 FIE, Industrial Area, Patparganj, Delhi 110 092
Ph: 011-4934 4934 Fax: 011-4934 4935 e-mail: publishing@cbspd.com; publicity@cbspd.com

Branches

- **Bengaluru:** Seema House 2975, 17th Cross, K.R. Road, Banasankari 2nd Stage, Bengaluru 560 070, Karnataka, India
  Ph: +91-80-26771678/79 Fax: +91-80-26771680 e-mail: bangalore@cbspd.com
- **Chennai:** 7, Subbaraya Street, Shenoy Nagar, Chennai 600 030, Tamil Nadu, India
  Ph: +91-44-26680620, 26681266 Fax: +91-44-42032115 e-mail: chennai@cbspd.com
- **Kochi:** 42/1325, 1326, Power House Road, Opp KSEB, Ernakulam 682 018, Kochi, Kerala, India
  Ph: +91-484-4059061-67 Fax: +91-484-4059065 e-mail: kochi@cbspd.com
- **Kolkata:** 147, Hind Ceramics Compound, 1st Floor, Nilgunj Road, Belghoria, Kolkata 700 056, West Bengal, India
  Ph: +91-33-25633055/56 e-mail: kolkata@cbspd.com
- **Lucknow:** Basement, Khushnuma Complex, 7-Meerabai Marg (Behind Jawahar Bhawan), Lucknow 226 001, UP, India
  Ph: +0552-4000032 e-mail:tiwari.lucknowi@cbspd.com
- **Mumbai:** PWD Shed. Gala no. 25/26, Ramchandra Bhatt Marg, Next to JJ Hospital Gate no. 2, Opp. Union Bank of India, Noorbaug, Mumbai 400 009, Maharashtra, India
  Ph: 022-66661880/89 e-mail: mumbai@cbspd.com

Representatives

- **Hyderabad** 0-9885175004
- **Patna** 0-9334159340
- **Jharkhand** 0-9811541605
- **Pune** 0-9664372571
- **Nagpur** 0-8692091830
- **Uttarakhand** 0-9716462459

Printed at: Printed in India

Fashion and Textiles

Colin Gale
Head of the School of Fashion and Textiles
University of Central England
Birmingham, UK

Jasbir Kaur
School of Fashion and Textiles
University of Central England
Birmingham, UK

CBSPD

CBS Publishers & Distributors Pvt Ltd

New Delhi • Bengaluru • Chennai • Kochi • Kolkata • Lucknow • Mumbai
Hyderabad • Jharkhand • Nagpur • Patna • Pune • Uttarakhand

Fashion and Textiles

ISBN: 978-81-239-1956-0

CBS Edition: 2011
Reprint: **2024**
First published by Berg, Oxford, UK

This edition has been published in India by arrangement with AC Black Publishers Ltd, London, for Berg Publishers

Published by **Satish Kumar Jain** and produced by **Varun Jain** for
CBS Publishers & Distributors Pvt Ltd
4819/XI Prahlad Street, 24 Ansari Road, Daryaganj, New Delhi 110 002, India.
Ph: 011-23289259, 23266861 Website: www.cbspd.com
e-mail: delhi@cbspd.com

Corporate Office: 204 FIE, Industrial Area, Patparganj, Delhi 110 092
Ph: 011-4934 4934 Fax: 011-4934 4935 e-mail: publishing@cbspd.com; publicity@cbspd.com

Branches

- **Bengaluru:** Seema House 2975, 17th Cross, K.R. Road, Banasankari 2nd Stage, Bengaluru 560 070, Karnataka, India
  Ph: +91-80-26771678/79 Fax: +91-80-26771680 e-mail: bangalore@cbspd.com
- **Chennai:** 7, Subbaraya Street, Shenoy Nagar, Chennai 600 030, Tamil Nadu, India
  Ph: +91-44-26680620, 26681266 Fax: +91-44-42032115 e-mail: chennai@cbspd.com
- **Kochi:** 42/1325, 1326, Power House Road, Opp KSEB, Ernakulam 682 018, Kochi, Kerala, India
  Ph: +91-484-4059061-67 Fax: +91-484-4059065 e-mail: kochi@cbspd.com
- **Kolkata:** 147, Hind Ceramics Compound, 1st Floor, Nilgunj Road, Belghoria, Kolkata 700 056, West Bengal, India
  Ph: +91-33-25633055/56 e-mail: kolkata@cbspd.com
- **Lucknow:** Basement, Khushnuma Complex, 7-Meerabai Marg (Behind Jawahar Bhawan), Lucknow 226 001, UP, India
  Ph: +0552-4000032 e-mail:tiwari.lucknowi@cbspd.com
- **Mumbai:** PWD Shed. Gala no. 25/26, Ramchandra Bhatt Marg, Next to JJ Hospital Gate no. 2, Opp. Union Bank of India, Noorbaug, Mumbai 400 009, Maharashtra, India
  Ph: 022-66661880/89 e-mail: mumbai@cbspd.com

Representatives

• **Hyderabad**	0-9885175004	• **Jharkhand**	0-9811541605	• **Nagpur**	0-8692091830
• **Patna**	0-9334159340	• **Pune**	0-9664372571	• **Uttarakhand**	0-9716462459

Printed at: Printed in India

Contents

List of Figures

Plates

For Our Parents

Preface

Fashion and textiles are profoundly linked. In this book we have investigated the way each currently depends on the other and how the relationship between them is played out. Fashion and textiles are two great industries and while one, textiles, might be seen as simply providing raw material for the other, fashion, in reality the story is much more complex. Each industry stands in its own right as a major force in the contemporary world, each industry relates in various ways to many others: interiors, the media, cosmetics, agriculture, retailing, manufacturing and so on. Both industries have individual strengths and interests as well as a traditional common purpose. The bond between fashion and textiles is thus one of mutual dependency and reciprocal influence; a shared destiny based on our need for clothing. Together the scope and variety of our clothing needs, coupled with the diversity of fabrics used for clothing, provide an amazing set of stories and issues. The story of fashion and textiles draws in all of humanity and provides the basis for this book.

As with our previous *The Textile Book* this volume has been developed, in part, to fill a perceived gap in educational literature. The incentive for this text is based on our experience with students of textiles and of fashion. Fashion and textiles are often taught in close proximity around the world, existing in the same academic departments, schools or faculties. In varying degree they may be taught together. More often than not they are taught separately as there is insufficient time or opportunity for a student to learn both. As a result many students feel they have insufficient knowledge or understanding of subjects which may prove very significant in their future employment. For example design students often wish to focus on activities and issues that arise in what might seem a continuum: designing and using fabrics for fashion. However, often in education, the *design* and the *use* of fashion-fabrics are treated as independent and unrelated skill sets. Fabric design being the preserve of the textile specialist, while its use is a subject for the fashion specialist. This division of fashion and textiles at an educational level can also extend to associated industrial, managerial, business and retail studies. Hopefully this book demonstrates how useful it can be to think of fashion and textiles together. Such thinking can provide powerful insights and a strategic awareness of economic issues. For the general reader and those lucky enough to have had a more integrated experience, the book addresses some very current issues and provides many leads for further study.

We are aware that terminology for fashion and textiles, is often neither exact, nor the same around the world. We have tried to adhere to certain rules but often the context of a word will need to be considered. This will apply to, for example, *fashion* (*the trend*) as opposed to *fashion* (*the industry*). Equally *textiles* (*the subject*), as opposed to *textiles* (*the plural of textile*). Our use of the words *clothing*, *apparel* and *fashion* follows the principle that fashion is a part of apparel, and apparel a part of clothing. In general we take fashion to be the very style-driven consumer garments sector. Apparel we take to be the entire range of consumer garments and clothing accessories, with varying elements of style. Clothing we take to be the generic term for all garments including entirely functional items. In a sense the three words represent the level of perspective being adopted. Often through the book it has proven useful for us to employ apparel or clothing as more appropriate perspectives for topics under discussion.

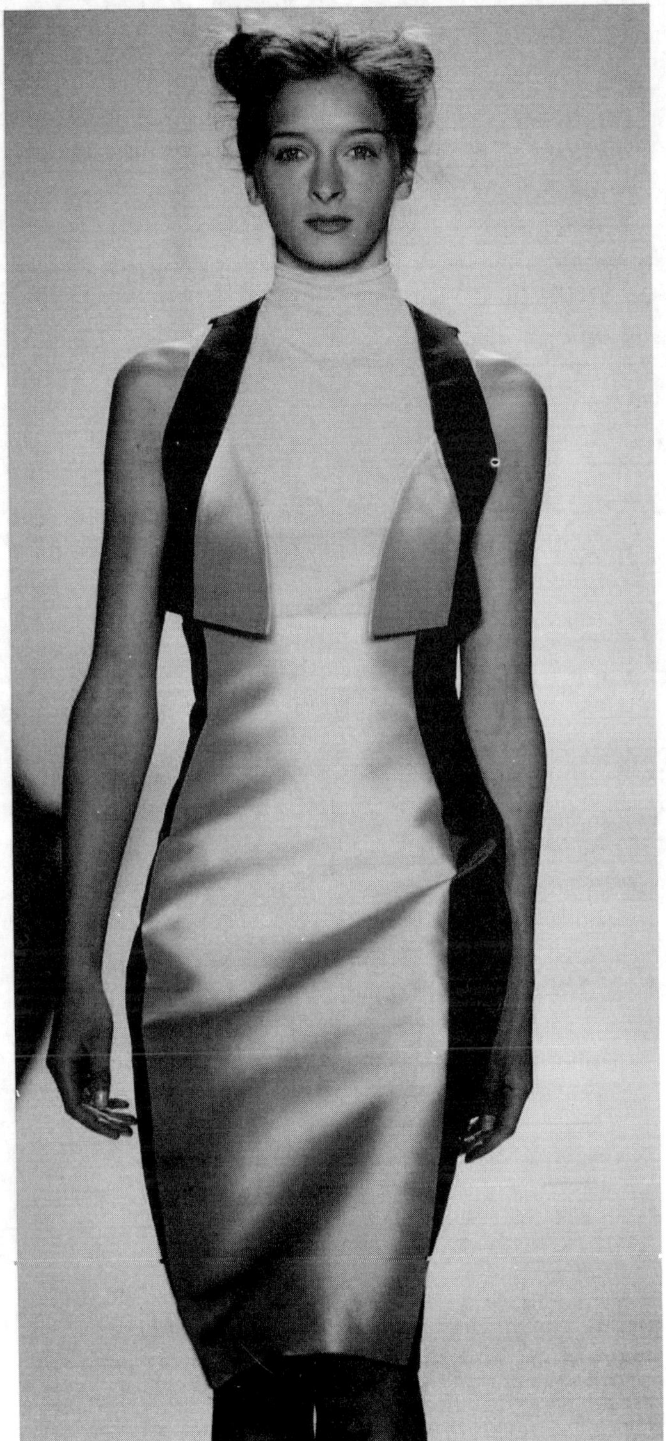

Plate 2. YEOHLEE Spring 2004 Look 16. Roos in spring green/summer green silk zibeline halter vest with spring green turtle halter jersey and spring green/summer green silk zibeline high waist hourglass skirt. Courtesy Yeohlee Teng. Photographer Dan Lecca.

Plate 1. Donna Karan New York: Womenswear Fall 2003. Courtesy Donna Karan New York. Photographer Gerardo Samoza.

Design, Nina at Philip Treacy, Eve Downing at MIT Institute for Soldier Nanotechnologies, Jerry Whitaker and Patty Welsh of the US Army Soldier Systems Centre at Natick, Sarah Warwick and Hannah Campbell of Exposure Ltd (representing Levis), Gerard Furbershaw of Lunar Design, Lisa Burzyck at Cargill Dow, Jennifer Gray at Gibbs and Soell, Valeria Costa at Benetton, Celine Kloetzer at Haberlein & Mauerer (representing Adidas), Andrea Grove at Yeohlee Teng. We also thank the previously mentioned companies and Inditex, Mandarina Duck, Marks & Spencer, Debenhams PLC, Donna Karan and Nike Inc.

Finally both of us recognize that our opinions, achievements and values are built upon those of our parents. Accordingly we dedicate this book to Arthur, Doris, Satpal and Jaswant. We also wish the book to stand in small part as testimony to their quality and character, and our lifelong indebtedness to them.

Colin Gale and Jasbir Kaur

Once agreed upon the topic of this book we set about listing all that might be included. Before long we were overwhelmed by the diversity and complexity of our ever-growing list. Thus in order to make some sense of this project and to provide the reader with a simple 'map' to locate content, *Fashion and Textiles: An Overview* is divided into chapters reflecting some broad themes and subject divisions. The main theme of this book, the relationship between fashion and textiles, threads its way throughout, the contextual theme of individual chapters providing different perspectives on the principal topic. Although we have made efforts to find some natural sequence to the chapters, each is capable of being read independently, thus making the book suitable for specialist and generalist alike. Many of the situations and issues contained in this book rarely conform to simple analyses. For example the political and economic contexts surrounding a garment will not prove simple mirrors of its physical history. Each garment, each fabric, each sector and stage seems to have a story in some sense unique or particular to it. The wise reader should thus be a little wary and initially interpret material on a case-by-case basis. This book is also not a definitive explanation of how and why fashion and textiles interact, it is instead a series of illustrations and explanations that cumulatively build to reveal a complex of relationships between fashion and textiles. There is no straightforward middle ground between fashion and textiles, more a boundary line. Hence the text often moves from fashion to textiles and vice versa.

Much of the content of this book has resulted from our wide research of information that exists in the public domain, whether books, websites or magazines. In this way we hope we have maintained a contemporary and relevant flavour. Our objective has been to try and reflect what is 'out there' rather than what any group or individual deems to be the most important information or issue. Hopefully this book will thus prove to be a useful set of references for the modern professional as well as a snapshot of the fashion and textiles world in the early twenty-first century. Needless to say, given the complexity of the information we have done our best to interpret, contextualize, explain and comment.

Our thanks go to the many authors, journalists, companies and designers whose work has inspired us and the following group who have either made a special contribution to this book or helped us in our search for images and information: Susan Clowes at Corpo Nove, K. Asada at Teijin Fibers Ltd., Ingred Willems at Philips

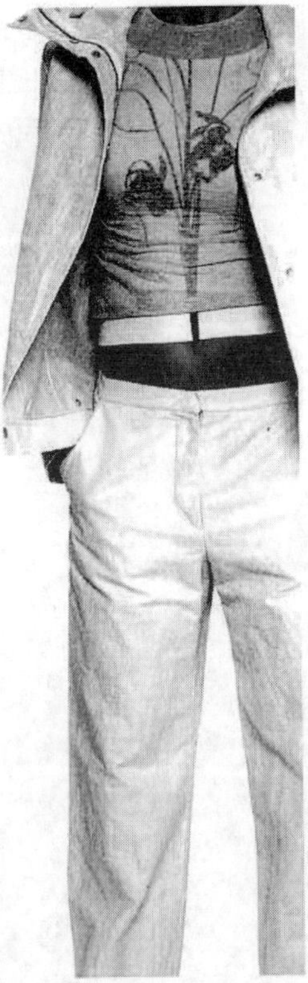

Plate 3. Mandarina Duck: Mens Alinenum SS 2003. Courtesy Mandarina Duck.

Plate 4. A Philip Treacy Occasion Hat. Courtesy Philip Treacy.

Plate 5. Levi Dockers. Courtesy Levi Strauss.

Plate 6. Product Advertising, United Colours of Benetton 2003–04 Fall/Winter. Courtesy United Colours of Benetton. Photographer James Mollison.

Plate 7. Zara Store, Shibuya, Tokyo. Courtesy Inditex.

Plate 8. Corpo Nove's ABSOLUTE FRONTIER jacket especially Commissioned for an Antarctic expedition. Courtesy Corpo Nove (Grado Zero Espace).

Plate 9. 'Future Warrior' project. Concept design for 2025 soldier combat ensemble. Courtesy US Army Natick Soldier Center. Photographer Sarah Underhill.

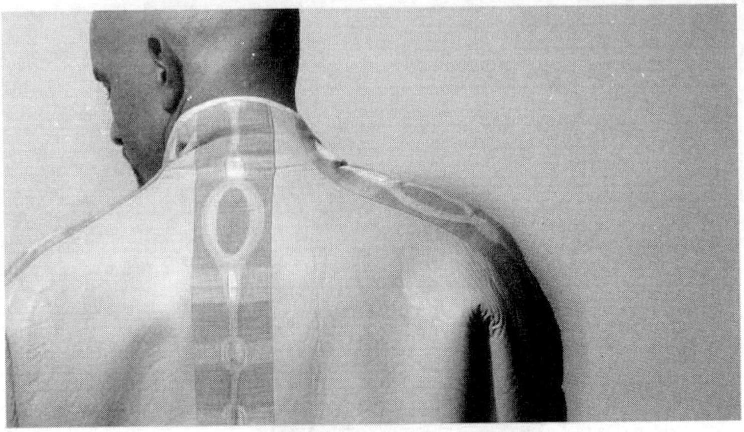

Plate 10. A design investigation into the possibilities of wearable technology, the 'Feels Good' jacket. Concepts developed by Philips Design. Courtesy Philips Design.

Plate 11. The BLU project, undertaken by Lunar Design explored the impact of e-paper and Bluetooth technology from fashion and brand perspectives and resulted in a variety of concept designs, including this interactive shirt for the urban cyclist. Courtesy Lunar Design.

1

The Inter-relationship

Throughout history there have been associations between clothing and textiles. This relationship is not only simply one of being connected, in many ways they are inseparable. When considering one it is very difficult to ignore the other. This intimate bond between the two fields is revealed when changes occurring in one ultimately, if not immediately, have some impact on the other. Perhaps now more than ever, the relationship is at its closest, largely due to technological advances, great changes in lifestyle and the growing sophistication of consumer demands. The current rage for futuristic influences reflected in textiles and fashion goes hand in hand with advances in related technology and scientific research. A phenomenon mirrored, perhaps, in an earlier time when Du Pont's development of Nylon led to the craze for nylon stockings in the 1940s. It is evident that fabrics and fashions are marked with an indelible seal indicating their era and mutual origins.

The complex interrelationship between clothing and textiles was at one time apparent through health issues that led to developments in both spheres. In the late nineteenth century at the International

Health Exhibition of 1884 in London, the dress reformer E. W. Godwin expressed in a lecture:

> As Architecture is the art and science of building, so Dress is the art and science of clothing. To construct and decorate a covering for the human body that shall be beautiful and healthy is as important as to build a shelter for it when so covered that shall be also both beautiful and healthy. (Godwin, 1884: 1)

This philosophy was further reinforced by others who believed health and hygiene were a priority within dress reform in Britain at the time. For example, Dr Gustav Jaeger endorsed the practice encouraged by doctors of protecting the body from the air as well as sealing it against draughts by wearing wool next to the skin. In her book *Health, Art & Reason: Dress Reformers of the 19th Century*, Stella Mary Newton states: 'He liked long tight-fitting sleeves; but if short sleeves were worn then long woollen or undyed leather gloves should be worn with them, and men would do well to draw their gloves over their coat-sleeves so that any draught might be excluded' (Newton, 1974: 101). Individuals like Gustav Jaeger laid the foundations of an interrelationship between health, textiles and clothing. Since then, this affiliation between textiles and fashion has gathered strength and momentum, attracting much research and development from companies involved in advancing technologies in textiles for clothing. Today, it is common to find health-enhancing developments such as antibacterial properties built into fabric and we find companies like Jewel Power Co, in Tokyo developing mineral-loaded fibres, which deliver health benefits to us via clothing (Lennox-Kerr, 2003: 41).

The intricacies of the complex bond between fashion and textiles are steeped in history. The relationship between fashion and textiles involves association between fashion designer, textile designer, fibre industries, colour authorities, global commerce, the consumer and the media industries to mention but a few. As the raw material of fashion, textiles constitute a complex system of primary industries comprising fibre and fabric producers of both natural and artificial materials and including the research, development and finishing industries. The fibre and textile industries have grown and expanded rapidly in recent years, facilitated by technological and mechanical advances in everything from the origination of new fibres through to innovative methods of production. These important and sometimes groundbreaking changes, in turn, continually provide the fashion industry with a vast assortment of materials to choose from.

Fashion Design and Textiles

The textile industries collaborate with a whole host of professionals, all experts within their own fields, from fashion to colour and fibres. These experts play a pivotal role in the textile and fashion interrelationship: they guide the textile companies, designers and technologists, advising them about future ranges and predicting why or how their ranges will appeal to the consumer. Part of the mechanics of the relationship between fashion and textiles is rooted in trends and these influence the preliminary stages of fibre production (which generally operate two years ahead of a season). Trends in fibres and fabrics develop from information gathered from professionals in fashion, textile mills, and other industry experts. From this primary level, colour and fabric trend information is then disseminated throughout the fashion and textile industries. Then initial judgements and choices in textiles focus on colour. At this early stage views and considered opinions are drawn from industry experts such as the International Colour Authority (ICA) and the Color Association of the United States. The fibre and fabric industries also resolve issues of texture, production and construction, which are typically informed by demands within fashion. The textile industry is steered by fabrication requirements that the fashion designer stipulates (Stone, 2000).

The fashion designer's relationship with fabric can be intensely personal. This intensity is very apparent at haute couture level, more so than at any other level, and is largely due to the fact that indulgence and personal expression can be afforded at this level. Designers can develop designs ideas by draping with a fashion fabric, the real material, rather than toiling with a fabric substitute like calico. In the late 1940s and early 1950s Jacques Fath, Parisian couturier to royalty and movie stars, would create designs by moulding fabric directly onto a model, responding to the fabric as he worked, rather than sketching first (Burns and O'Bryant, 2002: 227). Contemporary examples of designers eternally searching for the 'right' fabric and communicating their personal philosophies through their collections are Donna Karan and Helmut Lang. Karan's quest is for that particularly elusive fabric that is precisely the correct colour, texture, weight and handle. One that will fall exactly the way she desires it. This is one of the reasons the fabric producers launch new fabrics; to attract the eye of the influential designer or buyer. Lang, who began combining synthetic and natural fabrics before anyone else did (Davis, 2003) says,

> I have always thought you could use both natural and synthetic, and I have always used both very traditional and very modern fabrics. The way they are put together, the combinations, vary from season to season. It depends on the mood I'm in, on the attitude of the collection. There are still a lot of synthetic fabrics this season, but they have been used in a less apparent way. They were used in a way to highlight the sensitive side of modern fabrics. It all depends on what you want to express. (Lumiere, 1995)

The size of a fashion company, and the type of designer within that company, dictates the attitude they have toward fabrics. For example, a company with a large market share will exercise a safe policy of 'repeat' ordering. Successful fabrics from previous seasons are ordered at a very early stage in the design process. Operating this way, the designers in these larger companies are familiar with the performance characteristics of chosen fabrics and are able to avoid the draping part of the design process. Draping being a normal way to find out how the material behaves on the body. This is in stark contrast to the smaller fashion design company that offers its clientele something original and unique. As a consequence of using a greater variety of fabrics and less repeat fabrics, they need to assess the draping quality of fabrics more than large companies. The designer within a large company is able to sustain good relations with fabric producers facilitating communication about characteristics sought or the nature of emergent trends, this can result in the manufacture of new fabrics in order to update the company's ranges. In contrast smaller companies tend to focus on the individuality their products imply, achieving this through fabric selection as well as silhouette (Sinha, 2001). The fashion designer's fabric selections are relative to the market they are supplying and they will ultimately choose the materials they judge to be most desired and appropriate for their consumer. This is reflected in the individuality, material variety and choice offered by the smaller company, for example Whistles, as opposed to the consistent attributes of fabrics, offered by larger suppliers such as Gap, who have to achieve mass market appeal.

For the larger company, cost factors are crucial when operating to tight profit margins, therefore, these companies will seek cost effective solutions as regards their designing and fabric sourcing. Necessarily larger companies will also benefit from economies of scale. These are key factors if they wish to sustain market share and healthy profits. At the other end of the spectrum, the designer in the smaller fashion company will often create designs either by sketching or draping, rather than selecting material from stocks of fabrics. At this level, the designer may choose to work with a team of textile designers. Experimentation is central to the design process and fabric can become the stimulus for the fashion designer, suggesting new shapes and design ideas (Sinha, 2001). Fabric choice and fashion design, as evidenced by the output of small producers, suggest that fabric cost factors tend to be less important here than for larger companies. Creative extravagance and expensive choices in terms of design and material can sometimes prove to be financially damaging to a company. Over the years this has proved to be the case for both Anne Klein and Donna Karan. Small fashion design companies' attitudes towards the material they employ has much in common with the world of the haute couture designer's studio. Although their market shares may differ greatly, the fashion designers mirror one another's attitudes toward fabric, exhibiting many similarities in taste.

Fashion Designers' Attitudes towards Textiles

Similar to the fashion designer within a small company, at the level of haute couture, the fashion designer's relationship with fabric lies at the core of their creative process. Christian Dior, describing his thoughts about material, stated 'Fabric not only expresses a designer's dream, but also stimulates his own ideas. It can be the beginning of an inspiration. Many a dress of mine is born of the fabric alone.' (Dorner, 1975: 38). When Sigmund Freud posed and left unanswered the million dollar question 'What does a woman want?' it is doubtful he foresaw that his question, along with fabric, would be what now arms designer Emanuel Ungaro. Not only does the fashion industry hunt for the answer to this million dollar question but marketing experts have built empires around this very issue. Hollywood has even made a film 'What Women Want', about the subject. Ungaro's passionate relationship with fashion involves an intimate bond with the raw material, he expresses his attachment to cloth in *Architectural Digest*: 'I caress it, smell it, listen to it. A piece of clothing should speak in so many ways' (Aillaud, 1988). This private relationship that a designer has with material is not uncommon. Donna Karan works with mills to develop fabrics especially for her; she says 'The future of fashion lies in fabrics. Everything comes from fabrics' (Shiro, 1995: 13). Continuing with the almost obsessive and at the same time very respectful attitude that a fashion designer displays towards fabric, in interview, Pamela Golbin, the curator at the Musée de la Mode et du Textile, in Paris, said

> Everything evolves from the fabric, so your relationship with the fabric will change the outcome. If you choose chiffon or wool – two fabrics that have nothing to do with each other – the result of each will be different. Balenciaga and Ungaro let the fabric dictate what will happen, as opposed to using a technician to figure out how to produce a garment from a sketch. (Agins, 2000: 64)

In contrast to how Ungaro 'feels' about fabric, Kim Jones, a new up and coming London designer, has a rather less romantic view of the clothes he makes and therefore a more detached approach to the material. His main concerns are that his clothes should 'wear well, wash well, and sell well' (Rickey, 2003).

Through a clever combination of fabric and fashion design, Armani obscured established boundaries that existed in fashion by first making the business suit informal through relaxed and casual tailoring, then combining this with textured and patterned featherweight wools, cashmeres and linens, in a neutral colour palette. The fabric choices that Armani made set him apart from the rest of the fashion pack. Without fail, he was able to deliver first-rate tailoring in elegant, supple materials, offering comfort. His fabric choices were a contradiction to the typical classic suiting fabrics, and this, alongside his redefined silhouette, provoked the fashion world to reassess how his clothes should be categorized and question what a 'suit' could be. The somewhat sober relationship

Figure 1.1
Donna Karan New York. Womenswear Fall 2003. Courtesy Donna Karan New York. Photographer Gerardo Samoza.

that Armani appeared to have with fabric is not necessarily typical among attitudes fashion designers express. The zealous bond that some fashion designers have had with fabric has landed them in hot water on occasion. A case in point was Anne Klein, who, to the fury of her investors, often spent excessively on copious fabric samples in order to produce her collections. These hand-picked fabrics, accumulated on trips around the world, were the result of a search for the best materials the world had to offer and they came at an astronomical cost to the company. An estimate by the firm's accountant, Dexter Levy, suggests that at a time when the company was making sales of $10 million, 10 per cent of this was actually being squandered on sample fabrics alone (Agins, 2000). This extravagance was purely the consequence of Anne Klein's obsession for both fabric and artistic license. It is difficult to believe that such personal indulgence would be entertained in today's business-oriented fashion world.

Upon the death of Anne Klein in 1974, Donna Karan, her top assistant at the time, continued to carry the gauntlet for the label. However, Donna Karan had also been infected with Anne Klein's fervent passion for fabric. This obsession with fabric was obviously considered as a necessary element of the creative process of the designer. However it was seen as a superfluous and avoidable expense by Frank Mori, who ran Anne Klein on behalf of Taki, investor of Anne Klein. Visits to international fabric fairs such as Premiere Vision (First Look) in Paris were a regular event in Karan's calendar. Together with her design team, she would meet the leading fabric producers from around the world. These trips along with others to Milan and London, for example, would culminate in a hoard of fabric samples and research material sourced from flea markets and auctions. In 1998, when Donna Karan's investors attempted to curb her fabric indulgences within the design studio, she personally compensated them for the discrepancies in her studio budget. Such was the allure of the exquisite fabrics that Karan so desired. It is evident that in her role as a fashion designer, the fabrics Karan sought were a necessary and essential part of the designing process, despite their expense. However, she is not an exception to the rule in fashion design, far from it in fact. This rapport that Karan expresses for material is echoed by other designers such as Yeohlee Teng and Emanuel Ungaro both of whom, in their own way, have a very personal response to the material they work with. The staggering expense that Karan's design studio generated always infuriated the investors, but this wasn't an uncommon scenario in a fashion house, after all, a fashion designer's creative status ultimately lies within their collections.

Apart from being very emotive, the fashion designer's relationship with material can also be subject to their personal philosophy and beliefs, which they choose to express through fashion. Alternatively, their design philosophy may simply be avant-garde or

Figure 1.2
Y-3 Adidas Sport Style designed by Yohji Yamamoto. Spring/Summer 2004 collection. Courtesy Adidas.

culturally alien to a market. This pattern tends to be either generation led, resulting in the emergence of cutting-edge revolutionary fashion designers, or driven by some cultural ethos. These designers have what we might term a radical attitude to cloth in that they challenge preconceived ideas of which materials are 'allowed' to be used in fashion. Yohji Yamamoto's philosophy of beauty is quite unconventional compared to the traditional approach to fashion.

It seems that if a designer undertakes such an evolution in their creative process, it will in some ways affect their material choices or the ways in which they choose to develop a design idea. For example, in collaboration with the sports label Adidas, Yamamoto integrated art with engineering in his Autumn/Winter 2001–2 collection. He professed in the press release accompanying the show: 'It's not about approaching high technology itself . . . It's about approaching a world made of elements opposed to the ones in fashion' (Wilcox, 2001: 2). Another designer firmly in the avant-garde camp is Junya Wattanabe who celebrates a vision ahead of its time by exploring concepts combined with advances in material technology. The fact that a constant stream of young radical designers now explore material innovations raises the question as to whether material innovations themselves actually assist the fashion designer in becoming more adventurous.

Fabric as a Signature

Some fashion designers are as famed for the fabric their collections are made from as they are for the actual fashion collections themselves. In effect, the fabrics act as a transmitter for the fashion label, as is the case with Missoni, Burberry, Pucci, Issey Miyake and St. John Knits. Collaborations between fashion designers and textile companies or textile designers, such as that between Paul Smith and Liberty, have benefits for both fashion and textiles. The use of a limited specific textile design or range of designs can provide an extra edge and element of exclusivity to a fashion designer's collection. A strongly 'identifiable' fabric can 'stand out' over and above any other fabric design and choices that could be made. Through this sort of association, the textile provider is able to reach a greater audience through using an established fashion designer's collection as a vehicle to distribute their fabrics and so spread their name. Fashion designers don't necessarily have to be associated with 'named' textiles; Yeohlee Teng and Zoran Ladicorbic have achieved success through simply being renowned for using particularly exquisite fabrics within their collections. These fabrics aren't necessarily exclusive to these named designers, but, in combination with an implicitly pure design ethos, the outcome is usually outstanding. All of this begs the question as to how we perceive fabric as a component of a garment. For if we view garment and fabric as separate identities we might also sometimes ascertain that the material is as important, if not sometimes more important, than the garment itself.

Missoni, Burberry and Pucci are evidence that it is possible for a fashion company to be as famed for their fabric as they are for their runway collections. They all use very distinctive and globally recognized signature fabrics; Burberry is renowned for its check, Missoni for its multicoloured knitted stripes and Pucci for its printed psychedelic swirls. It could also be said that these companies use fashion as a carrier to deliver the fabric to the consumer; after all, they receive acknowledgements and accolades time and again for their fabric as much as for their fashion. Taking the British luxury fashion brand Burberry as our first example, this is a company that is steeped in history. Established in 1856 by Thomas Burberry, the famous Burberry Check was registered as a trademark in 1920 and originally introduced as a lining material. Thirty years after applying this lining fabric to umbrellas, luggage and scarves, in 1997 The Burberry Check was revamped and in effect re-launched. In simple terms, the signature camel, red, black and white check synonymous with Burberry lifted the company to high fashion status. Following Burberry's first catwalk show for its collections in February 1999, it was chosen as being British Classic Design Collection of the year (www.burberry.com). Overall, the combination of distinct fabric and fashion design was able to reclassify a conservative supplier of trenchcoats into a hot fashion leader.

> Not so long ago, Burberry's management couldn't have imagined getting respect from anyone under, say, 50. The Burberry brand . . . was rediscovered early in 2000 after Burberry started playing it up, even dressing model Kate Moss in a teeny checked bikini in ads. Last year, urban promotion paid off as sales hit $738 million, double the figure of two years ago. An initial public offering of Burberry Group PLC shares in 2002 increased by $440 million. (Lela, 2003)

Pucci, Burberry and Missoni are all brands with an impressive heritage. Unlike Burberry and Missoni, which have an assured spot on the fashion stage, Pucci could be described as a bit of a fashion perennial in that it enjoys a regular revival every few years. However, when it does surface, it declares its presence through its universally recognized strong, swirly graphic print that announces its arrival, on shoes, swimwear and luggage (Craik, 2000). Since Emilio Pucci's death in 1992, the majority of the company has been acquired by LVHM which could mean a more permanent revival for Pucci, especially given that patterns have been re-coloured in quieter blends (Cartner-Morley, 2000). Given this, all is currently quiet on the Pucci front and its last major appearance was in 2000, which coincided with the Austin Powers film (Freeman, 2000). This gave the print the all-important cachet it needs to survive. In the same way that Burberry was revived by the strategic repositioning of the signature fabric in the fashion world, the Pucci print was lifted from the doldrums by Austin Powers.

Missoni, like Burberry is a well-established, luxury brand renowned for its fabrics. The husband and wife duo, Ottavio and Rosita Missoni, originally presented what was described as a strongly coloured striped shirt dress in Italy in 1958 (www.missoni.it/eng/index.html). This, together with the trademark zigzags, went on to become the signature fabric for their fashion company and made them a world leader in fashion knitwear. What has become their signature fabric developed as a consequence of the machinery they were using: stripes were the easiest pattern to produce. They began by experimenting with Rayon-Viscose, which is still a favourite yarn and then broke with all traditions of the knitted form. The results were original, extremely lightweight, and colourful dresses (Lessona, 2003). They now use a huge variety of up to twenty fabrics in an astounding forty colours for each of their collections, reinforcing the importance of the role of the material for them. They have received numerous accolades for their fabrics and their designs, from various bodies around the world, including the 'Neiman Marcus Fashion Award', the equivalent to an Oscar in the fashion world. In May 1972, Bernadine Morris probably best described Missonis: firm position on both the fashion and textile stage, when, writing an article in the New York Times, she said of the Missoni's 'They make the best knitwear in the world, some say the most beautiful fashion in the world' (Missoni, 2003). In 1994, some forty years after they first formed their partnership, Pitti Immagine (the Italian organization staging fairs and events for fashion, lifestyle and culture), together with the town of Florence presented the Missonis with the 'Pitti Immagine Prize' announcing that:

> Forty years ago Ottavio and Rosita began an original and creative research in knitwear: stripes, colours, imagination and invention. A unique style was born giving new fancy and art in the everyday of dress that the public would instantly learn to love. Unique among the most important figures of International Fashion, the Missonis make the magic of colour come alive in knitwear, as well as the substance of the material, the refined and innovative technique of the warp and wool, the deep sense of their culture.
>
> In their work an extraordinary tradition of high handicraft is expressed, a spirit which they claim with pride and which continues to pervade their life and their work harmoniously. (Missoni, 2003)

Most recently, in July 1994, the Missonis were made honorary royal designers for industry by the Royal Society for the encouragement of the Arts (RSA) stating that:

> the Missoni name has been synonymous with the design of knitted textiles for the last forty years. Their distinctive style is recognized – and copied – all over the world and they have established a huge following for their unique use of colour and pattern (Missoni, 2003).

Unfortunately, the fact is that these designers create popular and distinct patterns that lead to cheaper reproductions by other manufacturers and designers. Pucci's and Missoni's signature styles are imitated and the Burberry Check is duplicated. Despite strict trademark policies, it is very difficult to keep up with the counterfeiters. Burberry, have found a way round this problem; while the bootleggers are peddling copies of the Burberry Check, Burberry is promoting a new design: the Burberry Stripe. For Burberry – it was always about the fabric, the check is what has made their name a household one. It seems that the now iconic checked fabric has served its initial purpose in reviving the company and making the name robust enough to carry other Burberry fabrics and fashions. When a fabric speaks louder than the garment it is transformed into, which can be the case with the companies outlined above, the scenario begs the question as to which leads which, does fashion lead textiles or do textiles lead fashion?

Choosing Fabrics

When a fashion designer considers how today's lifestyle makes demands on the modern fashion consumer, fabric choice plays an integral part in the design process. Among those designers who have considered lifestyle, and catered for its demands by incorporating features within their fabrics and clothing, are St. John Knits and Issey Miyake. Although on first impression these designers appear to be worlds apart and, granted they certainly are very different from one another in terms of design philosophy, similarities arise between them in their consideration of the needs of the traveller. Miyake and St. John Knits share a similar viewpoint in that clothes should travel well and take the minimum of care. Both of these companies developed their personal design principles in parallel but in different parts of the world, and they remarkably cultivated a similar approach to fashion in that material research was a priority and became an identifiable trait of each of them.

St. John Knits, over 40 years, has gathered an ever-increasing loyal clientele, largely made up of professional women, for their Chanel-inspired women's knit suits, ranging from about $100 for the sport line to $6000 for couture'. The secret of the success was in the original silk and rayon knit yarn, patented as Santana, which enabled the clothes to sustain their shape and discourage creasing and wrinkles. St. John Knits is distinctive as a fashion company in that it is involved in almost every aspect of its business, from sheep to shop floor (Integrity Publishing, 2003). 'It makes over 90 percent of its products in-house' (GilbertZ, 2000). The benefits of St. John Knits are widely acknowledged.

> The ladies who lunch know the virtues of a flawless St. John ensemble. Let's put it this way, St. John's marvelous knits don't wrinkle (even when packed in a suitcase) and the woman who wears them looks polished, but with the comfort a modern lady demands. (*South Beach Magazine*, 2003)

These properties helped to make a success of the fashion business, as the specific fabric qualities were perfect for roving executives. Miyake has developed his fabric and fashion designs in the same vein; his garments have been engineered so as to enable them to be unrestrictive, easy care and easy wear. Being made from pleated and wrinkled fabrics, they are able to be scrunched up and easily transported by the traveller (Smith, 1999). As Julie Dam explains in an article about Issey Miyake in *Time Asia Magazine*, 'The Miyake design sensibility revolves around change and movement . . . the clothes appear precisely geometric and static. Once worn, though, they take on volume and mobility, as if they are living sculptures' (Dam, 1999).

As indicated earlier, although it is an advantage, it is not a fundamental prerequisite to success, for fashion designers to be associated with fabrics developed exclusively for their use. It can be advantageous simply to have a reputation for incorporating beautiful fabrics into a fashion collection, as do Yeohlee Teng and Zoran Ladicorbic. Zoran's choice of fabric is luxurious to say the least; cashmere, silk lame, taffeta and wool have featured in his collections. Zoran and Yeohlee, like Miyake and St. John, design for the lifestyle of the modern consumer; the jet-set kind of customer, selecting fabrics less prone to creasing that can be thrown in a case and easily transported. Zoran Ladicorbic, a New York based designer, reinforces the strong bond that fashion designers have with fabric. Since establishing himself in 1976, he has been famed for his untailored look rather than for sharp tailoring. His approach towards designing clothes twists the emphasis from cut to fabric, his clothes are so simplistic in shape that some may accuse him of hardly challenging or pushing the boundaries of fashion in terms of design. Yet, it is obvious to see that his clever combination of simplicity in design together with shrewd fabric selection has made his clothes very desirable and him a success. As Cathy Horyn points out in the *New York Times*:

> Zoran doesn't advertise, and even if he did it's doubtful it would do much good, since his clothes are almost indescribably plain, consisting of four or five solid colours, all in the same expensive fabrics, like cashmere and Tasmanian wool, yet minimally cut, without zippers or buttons – a uniform, in effect. The look has been described as 'Gap for the very rich.' (Horyn, 1999)

As Zoran's designs were such simplistic shapes – T-shirts, tunics, pants and skirts – the focus was shifted onto the exquisite fabrics being used, making the clothes alluring. His success was achieved through the simplicity in his approach to design and the clever use of luxurious, expensive fabrics.

> Zoran is one of the last few luxury labels with good reason. He never set out to sell his clothes in as many stores as possible. Available in only about 40 stores throughout the world, Zoran Ladicorbic is the ultimate minimalist. Working with a very focused color palette, his clothes are always of the most gorgeous silk, cashmere, cotton and wool. No synthetic fibers. No prints and no frills. (Enokiworld, 2003)

This didn't put him on a pedestal as a true craftsman of his trade; but, despite this, the fact that his clothes were being made from expensive fabrics combined with simplicity ensured their success. The result of Zoran's clothes being made from the most exclusive fabrics, is that they are placed at the pinnacle of high fashion and demand the highest of couture prices. For example, Zoran could command $600 for a classic slouchy sweater in the richest cotton, and in four-ply cashmere the price would double, while a cardigan in six-ply cashmere would almost double the amount again (Agins, 2000). The considerable price tags applied to these clothes were to a degree justified by the use of the best fabrics available, and this automatically elevated the product to luxury status; we cannot deny that the fabric content of the clothes must have been an influencing factor in the target market and the price point for this product, after all. The design content has been compared to that of Gap. Like Donna Karan, Zoran would seek those mills that could provide the valuable fabrics that were vital to breathe life into his simple shapes. However, economics and the general decrease in demand for precious fabrics has made this task increasingly difficult as the best European mills that supplied Zoran ceased trading in such expensive fabrics. Zoran owes much of his success to his fabric choices, and it wouldn't be far from the truth to say that he sold magnificent materials rather than fashion. His clientele were also aware of this fact, Ann Free said about those attempting to get copies made of their old Zorans, 'But they don't come out the same because you can't get those fabrics' (Agins, 2000: 266).

Yeohlee Teng, like Zoran Ladicorbic, is another New York based fashion designer with expensive tastes in fabric choices, but for her they present a different set of dilemmas in her decisions when designing. In using very expensive fabrics, Yeohlee's most significant concern is to be economical with her fabric, this efficient utilization of fabric, and her interest in the geometry of architecture, encourages her to arrive at ingenious solutions when formulating

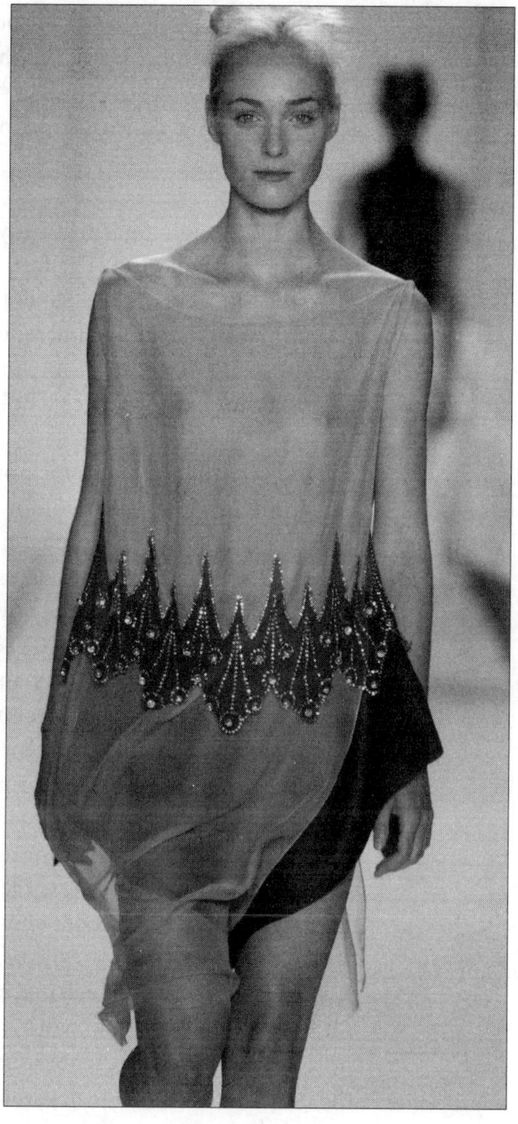

Figure 1.3
YEOHLEE Spring 2004 Look 31. Lisa in celestial crystal tank dress with black silk satin organdy two square skirt. Courtesy Yeohlee Teng. Photographer Dan Lecca.

her designs. For Yeohlee, the fabric is of paramount importance for form and function:

> Her designs are driven by the material, maximizing the use of each fabric by taking into consideration weight, texture, color, and finishing. Through the process Yeohlee 'manages to synthesize style into a poetry about the possibility of

> fabric,' states Richard Flood, curator of the Walker Art Center in Minneapolis. (Yeohlee, 2002)

Reinforcing her cautious use of expensive couture fabric, she reveals

> When I design a garment, my two main considerations are fabric and function. The fabric I use is often directly related to the function of the garment . . . Because I often use luxurious materials like cashmere, wool pique and silk jacquard, I cannot afford to waste any material. I have to be frugal, it's good economic practice. (Bolton, 2002: 107)

When evaluating those fashion designers that are at the cutting edge of material exploration, it is difficult to ignore the work of Hussein Chalayan. In the past he has used Tyvek, the unrippable paper, to create clothes. He has also buried cotton and silk garments along with iron filings to see how they would corrode the fabrics. His interests are similar to Yeohlee in that they continuously explore material possibilities and have a common philosophical interest in architecture and technology, which inspires their work. Yet, they are also quite different, Yeohlee's interest lies in technological treatments applied to materials which are of practical benefit to the wearer, whereas Chalayan's exploration of technology has led him to collaborate with product designers like Paul Topen and textile designers, Eley Kishimoto. Working with Paul Topen culminated in a series of white plastic-coated remote-control aeroplane dresses incorporating motorized panels, while Eley Kishimoto developed pixellated computer-generated prints for him. He says: 'The only new work you can do in fashion is via technology . . . It lets you create something you couldn't have done in the past' (Orecklin, 2000). Chalayan fuels debate with his controversial choice of materials and avant-garde catwalk presentations, which, it must be understood, merely express the concepts behind his collections. He admits 'These pieces might not sell' (Orecklin, 2000), but they definitely draw attention to and spotlight his more wearable collections. The relationship that designers such as Yeohlee and Chalayan have with material and the effect of textile innovation on fashion design will be explored later in this chapter.

In investigating the relationship a designer has with fabric, it is apparent that the degree of involvement that a fashion designer has with material development and selection varies widely. The manner of involvement is largely down to the attitude of the designer. However, it is apparent that the higher the status of the product or the designer – ranging from haute couture to high street – the greater the designer's involvement and the role of material. English designer, Paul Smith, (www.paulsmith.co.uk) has very close involvement with his textiles, even having an interest in yarn choice. Following the initial inspiration or concept behind a collection, fibre and fabric selections are the next item considered on the agenda and can take up quite a large proportion of the fashion designer's time. As mentioned earlier, this could even include fashion designers consulting with yarn manufacturers and mills, attending yarn and fabric trade fairs such as 'Pitti Filati' in Italy, 'Premiere Vision' and 'Expofil' in France, and 'Surtex' in the United States. Some fashion designers, when attending these trade fairs, are already quite clear about the look they are aiming to achieve and so will source specifically the sort of fabrics required. Equally, there are designers who get ideas from fairs. In interview, Paul Smith imparts his comprehensive knowledge of yarn properties and explains his working relationship with textile designers and mills in formulating the fabrics for his collections:

> You start to decide which yarns would be relevant to the look you are building in your head: If it's a chic collection, you're looking at a high-gauge, fine yarn, like a 25 to 30 gauge yarn, which will be very chic and simple . . . Once I've chosen the yarns they are dyed to my specifications . . . After the colour and the yarn selection, you're starting to get a general feeling. You are thinking generally about texture, then you start thinking about if you want prints. If you do . . . you have to think about inspiration . . . For this I work with my textile designer and give her ideas. (Frey, 1998: 124)

There are a number of ways that a designer can gain a degree of exclusivity as regards fabric within fashion. As discussed earlier, it is possible for a fabric to become so closely associated with a particular fashion label that it actually becomes a symbol for the label itself. Alternatively, a fashion designer can collaborate with a textile designer on a one-to-one level or partner a textile company and acquire a bespoke design solely for their use. Frey goes on to discuss this with Paul Smith, exploring the close working relationship he has with a number of hand picked mills in Italy, France and the UK; Paul Smith explains:

> You can do an exclusivity – you can enlarge the scale of a design, or add some colours, or change the fabric in some way so that you get some exclusivity. You have favourite mills that you work with for various reasons, and there is a constant relationship with them. Recently, I was working with a British mill and I spotted a French yarn I liked. I advised the mill to buy the yarn and mix it with British wool. It was very successful. (Fiey, 1988: 124)

Of the various tasks that a fashion designer has to deal with, fabric consideration, selection and delivery take up the bulk of a designer's time. After fabrics have been selected at fairs or through mills for specific designs, the designer goes back to their studio and begins to sample (prototype a garment) rather than toile (develop on a mannequini), in a fabric similar to the real one purchased. This helps the designer to understand how a fabric will behave when used in a particular design. At this stage other issues can dominate the process, sometimes overriding design decisions. For instance, concerns about fabric price, supply, delivery or minimum order quantities may end up compromising a design. There are also lead times to deal with, which again vary according to the mill that supplies the fabric. Delivery is relative to the type of fabric requested, therefore decisions about prints and fibres need to be made prior to material selection as they take longer to process.

Couture to Rag Trade

Up to this point, the focus has been on the higher end of fashion – which includes Parisian haute couture. When a fashion designer designs for haute couture they are at the creative pinnacle of their industry and free of the many financial limitations which would apply to the ready-to-wear sector. They do not follow trends emerging on catwalks for their intention is to be the creators of those very trends. They carry out the enviable task of creating totally original and unique garments/pieces using rare and exquisite materials which would often be an extravagance and too costly to produce in any volume in industry. Of course the haute couture houses are more about selling perfume than garments. Couture houses rarely sell more than 1,500 items per year, only about 3,000 women worldwide can afford their goods and only 1,000 or so buy regularly. Nonetheless in couture design we see the relationship between fashion design and textile design at its most passionate. Traditionally the role of haute couture and high fashion for the wider industry and other designers is to influence and inspire directions in colour, fabric and silhouette. Overall we expect high fashion to inform associated industries, the fashion business world and the consumer, through its extravagant and often theatrical designs. However, sometimes and perhaps increasingly, couture simply 'endorses' trends from the street or wider fashion culture. Colin McDowell points out the intention of the runway in *The Designer Scam*:

> That's where innovations are tried out. The rag trade, which supports many different forecasting agencies working two or more seasons ahead, picks up on couture patterns, prints and weaves and adapts them for the cheaper end of the market . . . This, if anything, is the true purpose of couture for the trade: it tells everyone what is coming next in colours, fabrics and accessories. (McDowell, 1994: 135–6)

In the actual world of fashion today, there is more than one tier of design. An evaluation of the hierarchy that exists among different levels of fashion designers leads us to conclude that fashion designers at various levels of the industry have different sets of priorities and considerations. Elaine Stone in *The Dynamics of Fashion* suggests that there are three types of fashion designer, all of whom strive for creative brilliance. The different levels of fashion designers span the breadth of the fashion industry, from high fashion or 'name' designers at the top end of the market to stylist-designers and freelance designers at the lower end (Stone, 2000). In each of these categories, the designer has to make creative and economic decisions to meet the needs of their particular market sector. Although the cost of fabric is a concern at all levels, it is less of an issue at the higher end of the market, at this level fabric expense, to a certain extent, is allowed for in the price of a garment. The tight economics involved in mass production of simpler apparel at the lower end of the market make fabric price more of a critical feature. A stylist-designer usually takes and modifies designs at the higher end of the market and produces low-cost versions in cheaper fabrics. To draw the mass-market consumer, this requires the stylist-designer to comprehend systems of fabric and garment production. The freelance designer has no real involvement in the selection of fabrics or production decisions; their participation in the design process begins and ends with a sketch. So, fabric costs, together with labour expenses in the construction of a garment, are fundamental considerations for a company in order to maintain required levels of profitability. Costs at the point of sampling can be critical to a company too; if the production cost of a garment does not fall within predetermined wholesale price points, a garment can either be rejected or returned to the design studio in order to be modified in such a way as to reduce the costs incurred. Hence, the financial analysis of materials, time spent in development and production costs are all crucial factors in effective design. For fashion designers these considerations bear directly on their creative role and responsibilities. Considering the variety of tasks that a fashion designer performs, their role ranges from very specialized creative visionaries to all-encompassing workhorse. In relation to material, and largely as a consequence of economic pressures, good fashion designers have to be inventive and quick-witted, seeking the best design outcome within what are often immovable financial constraints.

Textile Technology and Lifestyle Fashion

Over the years many designers have chosen to work with highly functional fabrics, materials that suggest a particularly active and flexible lifestyle choice. These design innovations and trends have formed the foundations of what we now distinguish as active sportswear. These trends in turn have been the motivation behind the appearance of 'designer sportswear' that has, in turn, resulted in developments in textile technologies which serve the needs of this sector. The origins of this movement can be traced back to Parisian designers Gabrielle Chanel and Jean Patou in the 1920s and 1930s who imitated active sportswear through focusing on knits and flexible, unrestricting garments construction, encouraging mobility for the modern woman. The new 'designer sportswear' was swiftly adopted by American women as ideal for their ever more active lifestyles.

> The popularity of swimming and tennis, as well as the need for clothes in which women could move and travel, inspired designers, including Jean Patou and Gabrielle Chanel, to create the simpler, more comfortable garments they called sportswear. (Bradley, 2003)

Subsequent generations of fashion designers such as Bonnie Cashin and Claire McCardell have continued the principles established by Chanel and Patou. More recently designers like Tommy Hilfiger and Donna Karan have played an integral part in the dissemination of sportswear to the masses through their designer ranges. This fashion movement has had consequences in the textile world in that it fuelled innovations and advances in material technologies. The sportswear traditions of comfort, functionality and versatility have become priorities for the modern person's lifestyle. So too the interrelationship between the spheres of textiles and fashion has become more intimate, shifting in the same direction, seeking a shared vocabulary. As remarked, textiles and fashion have always been inextricably linked. However, their increasing collaboration and influence on each other is perhaps a response to the needs of the consumer and a result of creating clothes suitable for a contemporary lifestyle.

The influence of sportswear per se and sportswear fabrics on fashion is very noticeable. It is becoming increasingly common for fashion designers to use high-tech fabrics within apparel. For instance, designer Yeohlee Teng's design aesthetic is greatly swayed by and rooted in the sportswear traditions. It is now common for designers to integrate materials alien to traditional styles, such as rubber, vinyl, metals and plastics, as the designers' high-tech material repertoire gradually grows. This new wave of materials is seen as a great source of inspiration by the fashion designer:

> Helmut Lang adopted the reflecting strips commonly found on backpacks, running shoes, and firefighters' uniforms, into reflective jeans. Fredric Molenac, designing for the Madam Gres collection, used Lycra with neoprene, a rubberlike fabric. Cynthia Rowley incorporated stainless steel organza into some of her designs. (Bolton, 2002: 114)

Not surprisingly, with new high-tech fabrics come a brand new set of construction considerations. Novel coated or non-woven materials such as rubbers and plastics can be assembled with adhesives or by heat-sealing rather than conventional sewing. Of course, the alternative production methods that new materials bring about also present additional design opportunities for the fashion designer.

Over time there have been technological innovations within textiles that have impacted on fashion. Some innovations have shown staying power but it is also possible for specific textile types to develop a negative image. In the 1970s knits manufactured from synthetic fibres flourished. This was the first time that textile technology had had an influence on menswear since the introduction of the sewing machine, and it coincided with the launch of the permanent press finish on cotton. These innovations had varying degrees of influence on the fashion industry; whereas the overexposure of knit in that era left polyester with a tarnished image, the permanent press finish of cotton resulted in non-iron shirts and so revolutionized home laundering. We are in a situation today where technological advances enhance every part of our lives, new fibres, finishes and fabrics with integrated enriching qualities are finding their way to us via fashion and apparel. Bayer Chemicals have created such fabrics to improve our lives:

> Bayscent Aromatherapy. The newly developed fabric contains millions of microcapsules with natural aromatherapeutic essence . . . Bayer Neutralizer, created to eliminate unpleasant odours such as sweat and smoke. (*International Textiles*, 2003a, 832: 12)

To add to this, antibacterial fabric finishes have become commonplace:

> With Hyosung's antibacterial creoraâ the antibacterial material is built into the fibre and therefore garments manufactured from this antibacterial creoraâ will retain their antibacterial characteristics throughout the life of the garment. (*International Textiles*, 2003b, 832: 42)

Companies like Purista (www.purista.co.uk) market the benefits of material treatments to the apparel sector as a means of increasing the worth of their garments:

> Using quality antimicrobial treatments is an effective way of adding genuine value to a textile product. The aspiration for increased hygiene, coupled with improved product performance, provides an opportunity for differentiation in competitive markets. (Cowey, 2002: 63)

These technological innovations are a few among many which aim to make our lives better through the clothing we wear. We are, in fact, in a constant state of wardrobe flux; the only certain thing in textiles and hence fashion is that there is constant change. Given this scenario, it becomes almost a matter of urgency that the companies supplying these fabrics convince the fashion aficionados to adopt their product, in the hope that the populace accept and adopt and, most importantly, seek out the innovation. It is inevitable that innovations in textiles have an effect on fashion, but sometimes, in the extreme, textile technology can subvert the idea that the primary identifier of fashion is the final resolved garment. The material, in some cases, can make silhouette and styling almost secondary considerations; they become the vehicle for a material statement. Mandarina Duck is a case in point, their company concept is built around and essentially defined by their fabric. Established in 1977, by Paolo Trento and Piero Mannato, they started out as a luggage brand, firmly dedicated to technologically cutting-edge fabrics, which now motivate their clothing ranges. Mandarina Duck's apparel range is based around the performance fabric *fibreduck* which is wind-resistant, rain-repellent and breathable (Barbieri, 2002). In addition to the patented *fibreduck*, Mandarina Duck also use combinations of natural and synthetic fabric which are usually treated in some way to enhance their performance, making them

> . . . high-tech and post-modern . . . The attention to design given by Mandarina Duck during product development has gained it the 'Meryl Award' of European Textile Manufacturers for 'innovation and creativity' on two occasions, in 1997 and 1999. (www.mandarinaduck.com)

Obviously, there is much investment in material development within this company, which virtually leaves the apparel as an afterthought. And, yes, it is aware of trends and patterns of consumption but Mandarina Duck is somewhat an exception to

Figure 1.4
Mandarina Duck: Mens Alinenum SS 2003.
Courtesy Mandarina Duck.

the fashion rules in that it isn't a slave to the fashion system; it operates slightly outside of the fashion boundaries:

> . . . instead of chucking out an expensively researched fabric after a season, the company's design philosophy puts fashion firmly on the back burner. New shapes and new fabrics are added to the existing range each season piecemeal, so that the process is one of gradual evolution. (Sullivan, 1998: 183)

Textile Innovation and the Fashion Designer

Designers are aware that the markets react powerfully to innovation, and as fashion is so time sensitive, it makes it all the more important to respond quickly. Recent innovations in textile production have particularly focused on fibres and finishing, in comparison the process of producing woven fabric has seen little change.

Perhaps this is why the pure, noble cloth appeals to designers like Zoran. Innovations in textiles don't necessarily have to mean innovations in the fabric itself, it can be understood to be innovation in the machinery of textiles. Textile chemistry and the n echanization of machinery have bought sweeping changes; the fashion business can be seen to have been a lifeline for textiles – reviving its production and design. Textiles are still seen as underpinning the structure of fashion. The attitudes towards innovation and the generation of new ideas in textiles, and so fashion, differs from nation to nation. The Italians for instance particularly advocate advances in their textile industry and encourage the associations between textiles and fashion. In describing the Italian stance, Nancy Martin explains the collaboration between the designer and the fabric producer:

> Italian companies are highly receptive to unedited fabric proposals. They churn out, at considerable cost in research and development, new collections twice a year. The new designs are prototypes, and many will never go into production. But continual trial and error keeps the eye . . . concentrated on . . . the next big thing emerging in the textile vicinity. The close and confidential relationship between stylist and fabric manufacturer becomes a private language, refining the textile ideology of both. Every stylist has an ideal fabric, and Italian weavers are often enthusiastic to take risks on new ideas . . . if it works, both sides win. (Martin, 1998: 116)

It is apparent that the Japanese, like the Italians, value innovation in textiles and its relationship with fashion to such a degree that they are prepared to invest in it. Successful innovation requires financial support. Also in the future, among the various levels of the fashion and textile world, teamwork may prove crucial in sustaining a satisfactory level of innovation in order to 'stay ahead of the game'. The basic '1:3:9' principle involves a joint effort by a network of designers and researchers, led by an inventor, all of whom are striving toward the same goal. Every inventor would require three assistant designers to build concepts and each of those would in turn require three further supporting colleagues to collate and deliver research information. Harry Beckers points out 'Incidentally, I suspect that in Japan the 1:3:9 approach to invention is much more widely accepted than elsewhere, which perhaps explains Japanese success in the field of technological innovation' (Beckers, 1992). New and improved fibres and fabrics, developed in the ways described above, are initially produced on a trial basis in order to test the market. Only following positive feedback from consumer focus groups would mass production occur. At this point in the process, fashion designers and other potential users of the material would be invited to investigate potential applications and so encourage its use. Given this, it can be concluded that textile manufacture relies heavily on the fashion industries to carry its merchandise to the consumer.

The Fashion and Textile Chain

The coexistence of fashion and textiles is evident through its spread across the globe; wherever we find fashion, textiles for clothing are always in the near vicinity and vice versa. Not only are these industries key employers, but they also contribute significantly to numerous economic systems around the world. Within this complex relationship, the role of fashion is one of supplying a constant flow of new and varied formulations in apparel. Due to the closeness of the relationship of the textile industries to fashion, they are indirectly implicated as a result. Apparel choices made by consumers also signify choices in yarn, fabric and colour; these choices may be seen as trivial when compared to the apparel itself, but they are significant choices in that they affect the textile feeder industries, for instance, the success or failure of a fabric in one season could result in its use either being continued or discarded the following season. Fashion is actually only a relatively small proportion of apparel as a whole. The fashion sub-sector, according to Balestri and Ricetti, is concentrated in a select number of countries, consisting of the UK, Italy, France and Japan (Balestri and Riccetti, 1998). Undoubtedly there will be very different European, Asian, African and American perspectives on where fashion resides and originates! In economic terms, the fashion engine can be seen to boost the value of yarn, fibre and fabric through its use. The fashion and textile chain can be explained by the many transactions and exchanges which link the two fields together. For example the necessary industrial coordination of decision making and commercial actions in fashion and textiles, relating to fibres, fabrics and clothes. Structurally the textiles industry comprises the cultivators of crops through to the chemical industries and the fibre processors and fabric manufacturers. Together they formulate the function, texture and colour that constitutes the fabric. At this stage the fabrics are ready for launch, which typically occurs at international trade fairs or via mills making personal appointments with fashion designers. Fibre and fabric producers, after investing much time and energy into manufacturing new materials, tend to lose their exclusive hold on their goods once they go to market. There are the few exceptions who manage to protect themselves with patents. For the majority, fibres, fabrics and designs, once publicized, can all be easily altered and formulas reinvented.

Premiere Vision, in Paris, promotes itself as 'The world's premier fabric show' (www.premierevision.fr/gb/index.html). The sheer scale of this show – every six months it boasts some tens of thousands of fabrics – suggests that it is not merely to satisfy the dreamy needs of fashion designers, but also to serve the demands of the apparel manufacturers on an industrial level. Economically the fashion engine has the power to add value to yarn, fibre and fabric, but the relationship between the fashion and textile industries is one of mutual interest. Fashion, ultimately is dependent upon and could not exist without textiles; the reverse is not true of the much more broadly focused textile industry, but together the two industries create a cultural phenomenon greater than either of them, an essential aspect of their commercial success and perhaps the impetus for the world of trends. The way in which the fashion world receives the first scent of what is possible tomorrow is usually as a result of what is presented to them by the textile industries. This is a culmination of a vast assortment of information displayed in the form of predicted trends, informing fashion professionals of future colour and taste preferences. This is effectively the trigger for a chain of events to occur in the fashion and textile relationship. In quick succession, the fibre and yarn industries are informed of colour, and they present this palette together with key themes in terms of texture and 'feel' to the fashion world in the form of samples. Fashion designers, will attend a show like Premiere Vision having formed quite a strong overall impression of the collection they are planning, so viewing samples at this point helps to confirm their design decisions. Fashion designers and apparel manufacturers will often request production and prototype samples at this stage, which, despite the huge expense to themselves, mills agree to produce. The textile sampling stage is crucial for the fashion designer in enabling a true realization of a product for presentation to a fashion buyer. Upon a decision being made by the fashion buyer, all the links within the chain are activated: the fashion buyer informs the apparel supplier of the order, the apparel supplier then takes action in alerting their textile manufacturer, who, at the very beginning of the chain informs the yarn or fibre producer that their raw material is required.

Questions about the relative cultural, commercial or creative status of fashion or textiles surface from time to time. Like sibling rivals the fashion and textile communities will also sometimes compete in the arena of style and statement. One thing is clear though, they cannot survive without each other and they benefit one another. On balance, the success of a line of clothing translates into the success of new fabrics and vice versa. The role of a textile trade fair serves the textile provider as much as the fashion world in that it is a platform for the textile industries to exhibit their wares and simultaneously serves as a tool at the disposal of the fashion world. It could be proposed that the textile world directs the fashion world by presenting a specific range of fabrics to choose from, yet the design parameters that are set are open to interpretation and the designer has powers of negotiation with mills to modify fabrics to their personal preferences. Ultimately in the greater scheme of things it also appears that the worlds of retail and the consumer wield a great deal of power over both industries.

Events such as Premiere Vision are instrumental in highlighting advances in textile technology which trigger 'high-tech' fabric trends. Michiko Koshino has used a broad repertoire of materials in her collections, such as polyamide and metallic plastics, synthetic knits and rubbers, reflector tape and bonded fabrics. She

> . . . enjoys using innovative textiles and is deeply influenced by new textile technology . . . The fabrics always determine her collections, and she often takes inspiration from high-performance sportswear fabrics and finishes . . . Every year her textile and design teams visit the trade show Premiere Vision in Paris to source ideas and bring back fabric samples before the designing starts. (Braddock and O'Mahony, 1999: 121–2)

This illustrates a key moment when textiles steered fashion to respond to fabric in a particular way. More recently, Gap's sister company Banana Republic, had a role in generating a desire for suede which snow-balled, strongly stimulating consumers' interest in the material. Gap customers for some reason return over and over for more Gap basics. On analysis, this is not due to Gap's tight hold on fashion as their clothes are designed under the premise of not going out of style year on year. It appears that the underlying cause that stimulates their customers to return, is largely attributable to the availability of new colours and fabrics. This was the case for Gap's Banana Republic stores in 1998. It seems as though the Banana Republic Suede campaign was a 'fashion' originating in a boardroom. Its success for one group of retail stores ensured its dissemination to the greater fashion suppliers who saw and copied the recipe and for once – here was a material-led 'fashion' that did not have its roots on the catwalk. In fact nobody in 'fashion' was using the material, yet, it became a huge fashion statement. Such was the success of suede fabric for Gap, it was only a matter of time before others attempted to mimic the formula:

> After Banana Republic's suede crusade, a number of the sharp-eyed merchants on Seventh Avenue began whispering the unthinkable; they were ready to copy Banana Republic, to come out with their own suede fashions for fall 1999. Banana Republic had effectively turned suede into . . . a 'category killer' by creating such a demand that suede merchandise alone drew thousands of shoppers to the store. (Agins, 2000: 193–4)

For the Gap organization the formula was simple in that their silhouettes remain essentially unchanged, the success came with the combination of material and classic, timeless clothes. The choice of well-known fabrics and materials can help to shift fashion products, this is evident through fibre and yarn producers such as DuPont and the Woolmark Company endorsing fabrics containing their fibre content with Lycra® and Woolmark® swing tags. These reflect the authenticity of the fibre content and assure the consumer that they are getting the quality they seek in their purchase. Via the fashion product, respective fabric producers and trade associations can impart the benefits of their materials. They can also promote themselves in the process, or increase the status of their materials as a result of association with a particular fashion brand. In many ways, using apparel as a vehicle to carry informative messages to the consumer makes the fashion industry the perfect marketing tool for fibre producers. Similar reciprocal benefits are available to the producers of fashion. This is perhaps the last and most substantial synergy between fashion and textiles; in an age dominated by communications, fashion can 'speak' for textiles and textiles 'speak' for fashion. Each industry has the power to stimulate the economic success of the other, because each has a pervasive presence in the life of the ordinary consumer, and each industry is fundamentally associated with the other, at the level of visual and material culture.

2

Materials

Those who work at the final design, assembly or retail stages of fashion and textiles may well imagine that they are involved in a more complex world than their colleagues and counterparts producing the raw stuff of fur, fleece and fibre. It is easy for example to believe that the production of raw materials always takes place in some ordered field or well-oiled factory. Nothing could be further from the truth, the production of fibres takes place in every type of society and every sort of context. It is also possible to overlook that much of the romance of fashion and textiles started with the mystique of cloth wrought from fibres as precious as gold, sought like rare jewels, in dangerous, remote or inhospitable environments. Equally, nowadays, the processes and raw materials within the fabric we wear may represent the absolute frontier of our scientific knowledge of life, nature and the material universe. The tales of fibre production involve everything from the extinction of species to banditry, biotech and world trade. When locked in complex debates about agriculture, economics and science, the stories and issues of fibre production are sometimes inaccessible to the ordinary fashion and textile professional. In this chapter some of these stories are brought centre stage, for it seems now, as never before, fibre production is a driving force in fashion and textiles, establishing new industrial and creative issues.

We also look at some standards, materials and issues that define the common cultural identity of fashion and textiles. Although each industry has pursued joint and independent paths in culture and business, both have raided the same natural resources, and thus shared a common aesthetic language. In the pursuit of quality and sensation, anything that shines, is showy or special has found its way into cloth and garment. Sequin, feather, fur, bone, metal, stone – fashion and textiles have constructed an industrial design philosophy without parallel – anything and everything can be used. Sometimes this has resulted in a relentless exploitation of the animal world. To be so opportunistic tests the ethics of any civilized society. Fashionability will thus always be monitored by politics and social concern, and nowhere is this more evident than in the arena of the primeval textile – the skin of an animal. Once the use of furs, in particular, seemed to be certain to disappear, their synthetic equivalents set to satisfy demand. However the emergence of new consumer groups and changing attitudes may well reinvigorate the battle over fur. The world of materials it seems goes to the heart of fashion and textiles, because material products provide both sensation and identity.

There are so many sorts of material used in fashion and textiles it would be impossible to do them all justice here. For example breaking down each category of material into yarn, fabric finish or trimming produces a dictionary-length list. This chapter therefore approaches the subjects of materials at the level of the 'basic-set' of primary fibre types and a few extras. There are just over one hundred varieties of fibre: Swiss company Swicofil lists them at www.swicofil.com/products.html. A general theme is adopted in the chapter, that of nature and materials of natural origin, particularly plant and animal fibres. During much of the twentieth century, there was a manufacturing focus on a traditional group of natural fibres (for example cotton); some synthetic fibres regenerated from cellulose; and a great number of synthetic polymers predominantly based on oil (the authors' previous *The Textile Book* (Gale and Kaur, 2002) provides substantive coverage and references relating to this group of fibres). The twenty-first century looks set to change the emphasis. New technology is now causing industry to reinvestigate the plant and animal kingdom, and look more widely at them as potential sources of raw material. The recent turn of the century will most likely be seen as a time when the engineering of fibres entered a new era. Initiatives like the European-based BRITE-EURAM SMARTEX project sought methods to create 'functionalised' polymers (Europa, 2002a) and lists of hi-tech performance materials grew ever longer (Conover, 1997). The reasons for this are quite complex, and may not only be due to scientific advance. There are both economic and political pressures on the fibre-producing industry that are causing it to stimulate new markets for its products.

> The average rate of growth of end-use textile fiber consumption has decreased over the last three decades . . . Lower rates of growth of textile fiber consumption are mainly associated with lower growth of world GDP . . . and lower growth of the world population. (Texprocil, 2002)

Now a second phase of engineering seems to have begun. New synthetic fibres are being developed that are either made from natural, renewable sources, or that mimic functions and phenomena found naturally occurring in plant and animal forms. The effects of this recent perspective will be far reaching, and what we might call the 'new naturals' will undoubtedly prove significant for the future of fashion and textiles. As science delves deeper and deeper into the subject of fibre production, many of us will know materials more by what they do, than by what they are.

The scientific theme that starts this chapter is later contextualized by reviews of traditional fashion-related animal products and perhaps a more 'fashion' based discourse. As for the many omissions in this chapter there is already a large extant literature (Internet and book) available on fashion-related fibres and staples. Many publications related to fibres are however oriented to a technical, scientific or economics readership. There are some books that deal with particular iconic fabrics such as denim (Marsh and Trynka, 2002); act as fabric reference (Parker, 1992); or provide social and fashion history on 'innovation' materials like nylon (Handley, 2000). Information about the many contemporary synthetic polymers and engineered fibres is usually readily available through individual manufacturers' websites. Apart from titles and websites listed throughout this chapter, the reader might find the following references useful startpoints. The Internet Centre for Canadian Fashion and Design provides a succinct textile dictionary and fashion glossary at www.ntgi.net/ICCF&D. CyberFiber Online also provide an alphabetical list at www.cyberfiberonline.com/glossary.shtml. There are many more.

New Science, Concepts and Technology

Science has always played a part in the production of materials for fashion and textiles. Whether creating synthetic fibres, re-engineering natural ones, or providing finishes, treatments or colouration. Now 'new sciences' have emerged providing new techniques, philosophies and principles. The new ideas these sciences bring with them also revitalize older scientific and manufacturing methods, and are forcing industry to take stock of what constitute potential sources of fibre and yarn. In part the adoption of these new approaches is due to economic pressures, and the effort to survive in an increasingly competitive global environment. For a decade or more, industrialists and policy-makers have talked about the 'future' in scientific, technical, textiles. Recent evidence suggests this future is beginning to emerge. Of the many current scientific developments taking place, examples given here relate to the pursuit of performance fibres and textiles (particularly through experiments in material composition); the trend in 'engineering' textiles, for example multipurpose yarns; and the 'new wave' of science that is impacting on yarn and fibre production. Many of these developments, taking place at microscopic levels, fundamentally alter the experience and use of fabric. Others, exploiting our knowledge of organic and biochemistry, are creating new 'more natural', synthetic fibres. Together they are making a substantive impact on the destiny of fashion and textiles.

If the last century was the Atomic Age, the twenty-first century may well prove to be the Molecular Age. The new science and methods emerging are built upon the last wave of technological and scientific advances. Now established are a group of disciplines that focus on the world of the very small, not simply the physics of the atom and tiny circuitry, but the infinite permutations of molecules and proteins. Interestingly these disciplines seem to be as driven by the hunt for applications as they are by a quest for new knowledge, and in this simple fact lies the key to their future importance and effect. For fashion and textiles the consequences will include new materials, new processes, new products and new concepts. In this section we look at only one area – raw materials – where the impact of applying new molecular science is already being felt. There are many other areas that it begins to influence, such as the nature and performance of garments, furniture, buildings and even our bodies. Among the 'new disciplines' are genetics, nanotechnology and biomimesis. In fact one discipline is now old (genetics) and another not yet much more than a strategy or technique (biomimesis); but in combination and with a growing facility for being applied, they promise to radically alter our age-old expectations of what is natural 'stuff'. More fundamentally they promise to alter the way we intervene in our own material world. The efforts of our past civilizations to make, build, grow, tend or heal are now either being revisited or made redundant. Practically this is turning the world of raw materials on its head. What cloth will be made from and how fabric will perform, will never be the same again.

Of the disciplines given special mention, genetics needs no explanation here. Nanotechnology is an extension and development of the engineering skills and techniques initially developed for creating microchips and the microcircuitry of modern electronics (more information is provided later in Chapter 6 'Future Wear'). Although biomimetics is not yet a discipline, recent developments within genetics and nanotechnology suggest biomimesis (copying or mimicking things from nature) will become very important. If we suspend the habit of naming all scientific disciplines in ancient Greek, it is perhaps easier to understand why each discipline will 'fuel' the others. Biomimesis translates as 'imitating life', genetics we know is about how life is produced, nanotechnology can be interpreted as 'knowing how to make the small'. Biomimetics and genetics are of course parts of the biotechnology and bioengineering industries – 'knowing how to make life'. All these disciplines converge on the study of life, the living – the small building blocks, and also making the tiniest of things. Together they are an awesome key – unlocking the effects and achievements of nature. They also become a set of precision tools and provide the knowledge to 'remake' nature (Borem et al, 2003).

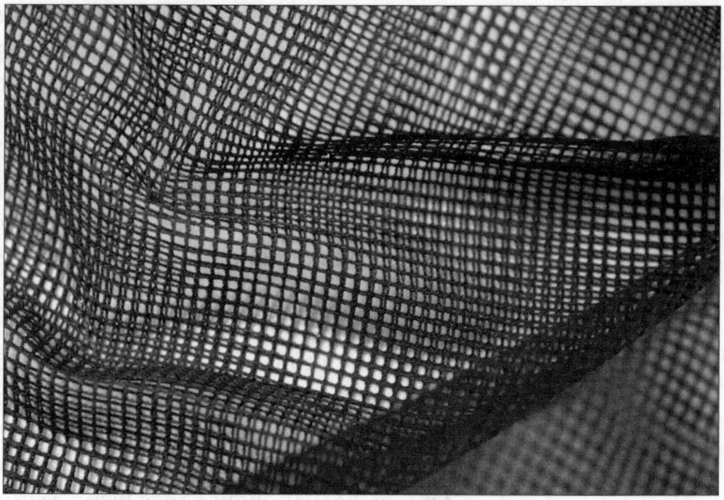

Figure 2.1
Fabric made from the new corn-based fibre Ingeo. Courtesy Cargill Dow.

Natural Polymers and Renewables

The scientific watershed of molecular and biological sciences heralds an era in which not only are new materials invented but older or previously inappropriate materials become potential sources of fibre and yarn. Crops, organic waste materials and livestock not previously supplying fashion textiles are all new sources of cloth. Many of these innovations can be attributed to a growing sophistication in the use of science. This greater facility for applying science is also matched by advances in engineering and manufacturing processes. For example relatively 'conventional' science has recently established corn and soybean as major sources of fibre. Both products required substantial degrees of initial investment. *Ingeo* (the corn-based fibre developed in the United States) took $750 million to be brought to market (www.ingeofibers.com), while soybean protein fibre (SPF) represents ten hard years of research and development, and similar funding, by the Chinese Puyang Huakang Bio-Chemical Engineering Group (www.soybeanfibre.com). Claims are made for both products about being highly eco-friendly – cleaner in manufacture and providing a new use for an existing crop. Another advantage is biodegradability. Ingeo is derived from a resin called *NatureWorks PLA*, this in turn is derived from carbon naturally stored in plants.

> Unlike polyester, Natureworks is biodegradable, which means it will decompose relatively quickly in a landfill. For oil-based products, that process can take hundreds of years. (Heisler, 2001)

In particular Ingeo and SPF, unlike the majority of synthetic fibres, do not depend on petroleum-based fossil resources. They represent a new type of synthetic fibre based on renewable sources. This is a very important development. Fabrics like polyester (compared with Ingeo) are linked to the price and availability of oil. While oil-based products may currently be cheaper than some of the new 'renewables' or natural polymer products, various predictions about oil and the first decade of the millennium are hard to ignore (Deffeyes, 2003). Either the demand for oil is likely to outstrip supply, or we face a collapse of our civilizations as fossil fuels run out!

Ji Guobiao, senior textile researcher from the China Academy of Engineering has drawn some interesting comparisons between the synthetic textiles industry of the twentieth century and what he anticipates will be the features of the twenty-first. Of twentieth-century synthetics he says – they depended on diminishing oil resources; they were polluting; and they didn't have the same texture as natural fibres. Of the current century Ji concluded that

> the new fibre of the new century is the result of comprehensive research that combines both the traditional branches of learning with new branches of learning such as information engineering, material engineering and bio-engineering . . . new fibre should . . . be developed from low cost natural resources (i.e. agriculture, husbandry and forest sectors) . . . its production process should be clean and environmentally friendly . . . it should be comfortable to the skin of human beings. (kuangmei.com, 2002)

Around the world the race is on to develop and market a new generation of eco- or 'natural' textiles. This is in stark opposition to much of the last fifty years when oil-based synthetics outstripped all other fibres in performance for price, and came to dominate the world fibre market. Artificial cellulose products, derived from wood-pulp, were perhaps the first to buck the trend, interestingly stimulated by the aesthetic demands of fashion. With respect to the economic and legislative difficulties surrounding development,

> Courtaulds chose to try to avoid this trap by developing a new environmentally benign cellulose processing-route. The 'Genesis' project of the 80's became the 'Tencel' business of the early 90's, as the new fibre was launched into fashion apparel segment commencing in Japan where sophisticated finishing techniques allowed unusual garment aesthetics to be developed. The Japanese demand for these aesthetics allowed rapid growth, and fashion apparel became an attractive launch segment which has since been replicated in the US and Europe. (Calvin Woodings Consulting, 1996)

Japanese scientists have now used New Zealand milk to develop milk fibre and the American industrial giant DuPont have developed a new polymer from corn called *Sorona* (Farina, 2003). Cargill Dow, manufacturer of Ingeo, has said it plans to expand the process used to other continents, possibly using sugar beet or rice as raw materials. Ingeo now has the backing of more than 85 leading textile and lifestyle partners; production has also recently been licensed to the Taiwanese giant Far Eastern Textiles Ltd. Of course what the optimistic champions of these new fibres may not foresee is that they escape one set of dilemmas for another. The existing economic and political issues of global competition facing the textile industry, primarily concerning cheap labour, may shift to an agricultural agenda. For example SPF is made from the waste residue of soybean after oil extraction, and a very 'green' process is used. These are virtues, but to an industrialist new perceptions arise: plants become multipurpose industrial resources. At this point genetic engineering becomes a factor, the company Monsanto for example has already developed genetically modified versions of soybean. Yet further environmental politics, and the politics of genetics, will start to impinge on the production and consumption of fashion and textiles.

Biomimesis, Transgenics and Nanofibres

The politics of genetics is liable to be even more divisive than that of ecology. Not only can plants have new genes 'inserted' from other species (transgenics) but so too can animals. One example is the use of goats to produce spider-silk proteins in their milk. Research on artificial spider silk first seemed to enter the public sphere around 1996 (Lipkin), and a number of different approaches to its production have been mooted. Genetically modified plants, such as tobacco or potato (Gührs, Grosse and Conrad, 2001), and fungi and bacteria (Zhou and Gary, 2001) have all been considered as ways of 'cropping' spider-silk proteins. Remarkably strong (Henahan, 1996), it is anticipated spider-protein fibres could have widespread applications from very tough or wear-resistant clothing (it is potentially stronger than Kevlar) to architectural uses. Spinning of the protein has remained a central problem. Perhaps the most amazing (or shocking) development in the world of spider silk was Canadian biotech company Nexia's use of the goat to produce the silk protein. Drawing on similarities between goats' mammary glands and spiders' silk glands, Nexia now uses genetically modified goats to produce 'the most authentic, man-made spider silk to date'. Recently in collaboration with the multinational fibre specialist Acordis, they have developed a spinning process and are set to develop applications for the yarn. Nexia is one of the companies that looks to nature as a source of commercial ideas. They use the word biomimicry.

> Nexia's technology harnesses the potential of biomimicry to make innovative, high performance products for medicine and industry. Biomimicry is a concept with two parts: first, discovering and understanding high value, 'rare' biological products; and second, a large scale biotechnology system that mimics the biology. (Nexia Biotechnologies, 2003)

Nexia's approach to product development could be considered as much ideological as it is conceptual. But it most likely represents the shape of things to come. In the last decades of the twentieth century a range of mathematical and scientific ideas, which shared various holistic paradigms and sought underlying connectivities and explanations of the complex natural world became popular. For example, in mathematics – fractals, catastrophe theory, fuzzy logic; in science – genetics, quantum theory, astrophysics. Cumulatively they have encouraged a mechanistic view of nature and living things – nature becomes a toolbox, a game built from myriad similar pieces, repeating shapes and patterns of life. Nature then starts to be seen as, potentially, a series of swappable and interchangeable parts. Finally nature is there to be edited, pieces taken away, parts copied; parts of nature are seen to be useful 'add-ons'.

We are it seems on the verge of what we might call *bio-editing*. This philosophical alignment of a technocratic view of nature, across a range of subjects and disciplines, will shape fibre and textile production throughout the current century. One essential 'tool' in this new era, is the metaphorical equivalent of a data-recorder or scanner/copier – the biochip. Biochips first started to appear in the 1980s and are a microtechnological device for the analysis of biomolecules (Chen and Dan, 2002). As such biochips are likely to play a key role both in analysis of biomolecular forms and in attempts to understand and duplicate biomolecular structures. Until fairly recently, biochips may well have been most likely to be used in the sphere of biochemistry or medical diagnostics. But as our ability to conduct engineering at molecular levels has grown, so the importance of the biochip industry has grown. The consequence has been a recent, rapid expansion in the commercial development of biochips. Biochips and nanotechnology are two of the key technologies that will open the door for a huge expansion in biomimesis. As they grow so biomimesis will become easier and easier to undertake.

As stated fibre engineering has recently made significant advances. The first evidence of this was the growing diversity of performance fabrics; for example, antibacterial, antifungal, antistatic and anti-UV fibres. In the first few years of the new century, these were the fabrics everyone raved about (Marston, 2000 and *Taipei Journal*, 2002). Recent developments in fibre and fabric engineering seem a step beyond this first wave of hi-tech textiles. Swiftly we have moved on from the effects of basic polymer behaviours and the fabric equivalent of the doping found in the microelectronic industry (i.e. the technique of improving performance of the 'main' material by adding further chemicals or materials). More ambitious molecular projects are indicated. Scientists and engineers for example now look at ways to colour without dyes; ways to provide performance without using unpleasant or impermanent chemicals; and ways to construct what are almost 'magic' fabrics that perform any number of functions. With regard to colour, biomimesis will undoubtedly play a part. The animal world is full of remarkable colour effects, from the iridescence of beatles, butterflies and birds to the colour changing abilities of the cuttlefish. An early example of new types of engineered fibre, and in production, is *Morphotex* which 'adopts the color-producing principle of the iridescent wing scales of Morpho butterflies' (Nissan, 2000). A glittering tropical blue, the fibre was developed by Japanese corporations Nissan Motor Co., Teijin Ltd and Tanaka Kikinzoku Kogyo K.K. In collaboration with Kawashima Textile Manufacturers Ltd, the fibre is now utilized to produce *Morphoton* cloth, recently used in Nissan's Silvia Convertible. The iridescence of butterflies is a result of *natural structural colour* a subject within the broader scientific category of thin film photonics (http://newton.ex.ac.uk/research/thinfilms).

The engineering of fibre and fabrics at molecular level now takes place all around the world. China, as the world's largest textile producer, seems to have made rapid development to the point that it now seems, almost contrary to logic, to provide cheap labour costs at one end of its industry and major value-added technical textiles at the other. For example, Chinese molecular scientists developed microscopic surfaces that repel water (hydrophobic surfaces) without using a chemical compound that drives water away.

> Now, aligned carbon nanotubes (ACNTs) film with super-hydrophobic and super-lipophobic properties has been successively prepared . . . In order to enhance the super-hydrophobic properties, different nanotubes patterns are also fabricated. For example, lotus-like ACNTs film and honeycomb-like ACNTs film, which contain both micro-structures and nanostructures together . . . improvement mainly relies on the surface structure, so there is no need to use fluorinated compound furthermore. (Jiang, Shuhong, Feng, Li, Zhai and Zhu, 2002)

In the climate of fierce global competition that surrounds newer fibre technologies, an emerging factor is the relationship of high-tech products and companies to the world of fashion brands. In China, for example, part of the fashion community expressed concerns about the comparative lack of Chinese, internationally known, brand-name fashion labels. Interestingly this may be a problem not only for China's pursuit of global consumer fashion markets, but also for their high-technology fibre industries. The Chinese concern over brands and the growing industrial need for designers, coupled with emergent consumerism, has resulted in an amazing increase in fashion design courses in Chinese universities and colleges (china.org.cn, 2000). In America the nanotechnology

Figure 2.2
Product launch of Ingeo in New York. Courtesy Cargill Dow.

textile company Nano-Tex aims to develop its products to be the fashion and apparel equivalent of 'Intel Inside' in the world of PCs. Apparel manufacturers insert tags and labels advertising Nano-Tex's contribution, and Nano-Tex importantly seek the collaboration of brands like Lee Jeans and Eddie Bauer slacks (Stuart, 2003). An even greater effort in brand synergy was that undertaken by Minnesota-based Cargill Dow for the Ingeo fibre, securing a global network of recognizable 'sponsors'. Du-Pont has kept Lycra 'fresh' by supporting new design 'celebrities' like New York based Design Development Concepts (DDC), who use the product, at the WWDMAGIC Design Gallery.

> The DDC team believes that fiber and fabric technologies are creating new ways of looking at fashion. LYCRA, Kevlar, Nomex and Teflon from DuPont are among the high-performance fibers and treatments that have a prominent place in all of DDC's contemporary offerings. Some of the 'fabrics as gadgets' DDC uses contain metals and minerals such as copper, aluminium and quartz, and a carbon-content fabric sourced from NASA at $80 per yard. DDC is working with DuPont NOVA, a new joint venture division created to market revolutionary non-woven stretch fabrics. (www.lycra.com, 2001)

The benefits, or perceived benefits, of new technology products still need to be conveyed using conventional consumer and marketing channels. This is particularly true for products with which consumers interact directly like clothing, food and so on. As for China, in spite of its programmes of modernization, we can expect yet greater pressures on it to adopt the structures of global consumerism, in order to use brand loyalty and designer celebrity as the platform for marketing its high-technology goods. There are strong indications that the consumers of China are more than ready.

At the 2002 Seventh Asia Pacific Textile & Clothing Industry Forum (ASPAC-TCIF) Mr. Chi-Chung Bai, Vice-President of the China Textile Institute, Taiwan, identified 'four challenges to be faced: the need to develop multifunction composite materials, the need to use nanotechnology applications, the need for testing and certification of functional textiles, and the need for international collaboration and R&D alliances' (ASPAC-TCIF, 2002). These sentiments are currently echoed throughout the world in every national industry and every regional alliance. High-tech textiles and research collaboration are proposed as the lifeline for textile and clothing industries. In this context fibres and textiles that are explicitly oriented to fashion are portrayed as a minority or specialist sub-sector. The implication is that, ultimately, fashion will simply benefit from the trickle-down effect of more demanding polymer, fibre and textile applications. Culture, art and politics it seems are almost relegated to being non-critical economic forces. It remains to be seen whether or not this proves to be true. Consumerism is a powerful force and fashion is at its heart. The more difficult questions concern what fashion wants from advanced textile technology.

Alpaca, Vicuña and Cashmere

It is likely that scientific discoveries and innovations yet to come will make those who work in textiles increasingly aware there is already an ancient textile 'genetic' resource. There is even a textile genetic resource specific to clothing. For centuries, if not millennia, particular animals and plants have been bred and cultivated especially for textile and clothing use. Through selective breeding, our ancestors have already engaged in manipulating nature to achieve fibres that permit the very finest of cloths to be made or alternatively to create the raw stuff of textile production in abundance. At the Eighth Congress of The European Society for Evolutionary Biology one of the symposia addressed the topic of domesticated species and the impact of molecular studies. The question was asked how did we produce the genetic resources we have today, and how with our knowledge of genetics can we conserve them:

> . . . it is now possible to look for common patterns which, in combination with human genetic studies, can tell us much about how humans and their domesticated species colonised different regions of the world. Such data can also inform us about the evolutionary distinctiveness of our types, breeds or species and may be used in conservation and management programs. (ESEB, 2001)

One of the invited speakers, the American archaeozoologist Jane Wheeler, has had first-hand experience of the 'lost treasure' of the Inca – the fleece of the ancient alpaca. In a remarkable story of luck, inspiration and molecular science, the long-forgotten (and lost) achievements of Andean herdsmen are being rediscovered. Starting with the discovery of thousand-year old mummified alpacas, modern science has revealed how the species was once the focus of a rigorous programme of selective breeding. The animal, used today for carrying goods or being eaten, was once the source of fibres possibly the equal, if not better, than cashmere. Alpacas it seemed had once been purebred animals, subject to strict quality and colour controls. The Spanish conquest of the Inca civilization precipitated a serious decline in stock control, alpacas were interbred with llamas; they were bred as pack animals and for meat. Finally Peru's textile industry focused on the abundant production of heavy coarse cloth. Today efforts are being made to retrace history, create a DNA data bank, find the genes for superfine fibres, and recommence selective breeding of the alpaca herds (Pringle, 2001).

One of the most interesting outcomes of Jane Wheeler's efforts is the discovery that the alpaca, first bred some 6,000 years ago, was most likely a domesticated version of the vicuña. The vicuña is the source of the most expensive cloth in the world, so expensive in fact, that sometimes, as a colourway, the name on its own is enough to suggest exclusivity and quality. The reason vicuña and some other animal wools are so expensive is usually based on a combination of:

- the fineness of the fibres they produce;
- the lustre of the fibres;
- the uniformity of their colour;
- the amount of fibre produced;
- the amount left after sorting;
- the availability of fibre, yarn or cloth in the marketplace.

Of these criteria perhaps fineness is the only one needing a little clarification. Fineness is usually measured in microns (short for micrometres), millionths of a metre. Vicuña for example is 13 microns in diameter, cashmere 16, human hair is 40–120 microns. Many synthetic fibres are as fine or finer than the best of natural fibres. The coating on, say, a modern antistatic fibre is as thin as 0.2 of a micron.

Vicuña wool is undoubtedly the 'gold and diamonds' of animal fibres. It is interesting not only because it tells us much about the fashion world's ideas of luxury and exclusivity but also because it tells a very clear story about how precarious some natural fibre resources are. Entirely wild and living in the high Andes, the vicuña is the smallest member of the camelid family. Nearly hunted to extinction by poachers in the late 1970s, it became listed as an endangered species and all trade in vicuña fleece was forbidden. The countries of the Andean region started a concerted programme of conservation and management and now some fleece and vicuña fabric finds its way into the international markets (although as of 2003 it was still illegal to buy it in the United States). Still at risk but somewhat recovered, vicuña products are managed through a combination of specially sanctioned dealers/manufacturers such as Grupo Inca (www.grupoinca.com; facts about the vicuña can also be found at www.bonnydoonalpacas.org/vicunas.htm). In partnership with the communities of the Andes, Grupo Inca strive to protect the species and establish them as an economic resource. Vicuña is now used in exclusive and sophisticated clothing such as that made by the Austrian manufacturer Schneiders (www.schneiders.com).

> Vicuna wool is so highly treasured that a coat made from the material costs an average of $6000. As only one-quarter pound of hair can be sheared from any one vicuna per season, about forty animals are necessary for the production of such a coat. The raw fleece of the vicuna is valued around $225 per pound. (PageWise, 2002)

As vicuña is the golden fleece of the West so cashmere has been the golden fleece of the East. Most sources agree that the very best cashmere fibre comes from the Kashmiri goats on the withering plains of Inner Mongolia. The extremes of heat and cold encouraging the finest material and the all-important underfleece. The goats are combed once a year, each providing a few ounces of treasured fibre. Almost curiously, Scotland, so far from Mongolia, is deemed to produce the finest woven cashmere, providing testimony to the traditionally international character of textile trade. The Scottish cashmere industry is worth about $150 million and is marketed globally; recently, for example, there was a marketing drive on the catwalks of Korea (Singleton, 2002). There was a dramatic blip in the market for cashmere, caused by the Chinese authorities deregulating trade around 1990, damaging quality assurance; however, they swiftly recognized the error of their ways and re-established controls. Today cashmere maintains its value as a prestige product and is also a staple with many a famous designer. Fans include the likes of Ralph Lauren and Donna Karan; in fact, just about every named designer and fashion house, young or old, has used and continues to use cashmere. Lauren in particular identifies with the chic, luxurious yet casual quality of cashmere and was recently seen wearing a slim black cashmere polo neck at the launch of his Menswear Fall 2003 collection in Milan, timed to coincide with the opening of his new flagship store in Italy (Deeny, 2003). The demand for the special qualities of cashmere has led to more countries producing it. Also cashmere is now often mixed with other woollen fibres to reduce the cost and make it more accessible to the ordinary consumer.

Cashmere demonstrates the allure of many animal-based fibre products. Their often exotic and romantic histories, their clear identification with quality and luxury, seem to provide them a mythological strength that no synthetics can ever match. Sometimes if a company maintains a relationship with a 'quality' material, their fortunes and reputation become inextricably linked. Plainly quality, expense and mystique sell. Increasingly, however, good design and marketing savvy are also essential in maintaining market position. This is nowhere better illustrated than in the 'makeover' of Pringle. In a daring strategic move, the Scots knitwear company (www.pringleofscotland.co.uk), has brought in new design, hit the catwalks, opened new retail premises and stopped manufacturing licences for its old ranges around the world (Groom, 2002). Famous for providing the international uniform of the golfer and the classic cashmere twinset redolent of British Empire and country house, they seemed to have reinvented everything but kept the cashmere. Now their revamped label sells to the likes of Julia Roberts, Robbie Williams and David Beckham.

> Sophie Dahl has once again proven her capacity to surprise. The model who once shocked the fashion world by appearing naked in ads for the YSL perfume Opium, is now presented as the epitome of classic casual by sweater company Pringle . . . While the label is more often associated with golf courses than catwalks, Sophie is not the first famous name to reach for a comfy Pringle cardi. David Beckham, Robert Carlyle and Jodie Kidd have all been pictured in the company's timeless sweaters. (*Hello Magazine*, 2003)

Sequins, Feathers and Fluff

Fashion and textiles share an interest in the drama of decoration, embellishment and visual extravagance (Rivers, 2003). Over centuries the reasons why they should do so have varied – displays of wealth, status, exuberance and so on. The decorative materials employed have varied too; they can be expensive but on occasion they are not. Similarly the role of craft skill, in applying them to create surface or silhouette, is not always essential. But one thing is certain, in spite of times when 'plain', for belief or vogue, is in fashion, decoration always makes a comeback. As a section in this chapter it is a little difficult to contrive what decorative materials are 'legitimate', pretty much anything goes. Over the years designers, and the general public, have used everything from junk to jewels. It is obvious that decoration involves raiding the material world for anything that gives effect. It is also the case that sometimes the effect can be enhanced by repetitive or obsessive placement, or the singular highly visible placement, of objects. There are however a few items that have exceptionally long histories and associations with fabric and clothing and two of these – sequins and feathers – are given special mention here. In a way these are as much used to create sensation and emotional charge as they are to create the visually spectacular. To complement or balance such 'seriously' decorative forms, one other dramatic material 'quality' is also given special mention, very much the preserve of the feminine – fluffiness. Somehow quite different in tone to the sexuality, power and luxury of furs (dealt with a little later), the fluffy fur of the Angora rabbit, deserves recognition for its unique qualities.

The sequin, today the symbol of party, glitz and exoticism, has an ancient history and like much body adornment initially held religious or ritualistic meanings. In ancient Egypt for example, gold sequins buried with Pharaohs gave them protection and power in the afterlife and could symbolize rebirth. Believing the flesh of the sun god was made of gold, the sequins established the relationship between god and deceased ruler.

> the Nelson-Atkins sequins were stitched to a linen garment similar to one found in the antechamber of Tutankhamun's tomb, embellished with 47 gold sequins. Sequins made of gold or faience occasionally decorated tunics. Garments, sandals and linen placed in the tomb ensured that the dead

> would be properly clothed in the next world. Nudity symbolized helplessness; bright clothing covered the glorified bodies of the dead. (UMKC, 2000)

The visual power of the sequin, in particular its play with light and colour, has sustained it as an element in clothing and accessories. Interestingly today sequins are to be found in virtually every type of circumstance and in all categories of clothing. They can be bought mass-manufactured and machine-made, already attached to fabric; or they can be made by hand, from precious materials, and lovingly applied. They can be glued, stitched, trapped or bonded to fabric. Perhaps the mixture of desirability, effect, versatility and wide price range contributes to their continued success. At the level of Parisian couture, sheer spectacle has come to increasingly dominate, and the sequin is made good use of by the likes of Christian Lacroix. At his Haute Couture Spring 2003 show 'Intricate brocades of sequins glittered throughout . . .' (Hagy, 2003). The interaction of high fashion, glamour and celebrity also does much to propagate the success of the sequin. Stars of popular film and music – paraded, parading or performing – use sequins relentlessly and create a common language of sequined dress through popular culture. The sequinned and studded jean will undoubtedly be the signature of the early 'noughties' pop diva or rock chick. Nowadays large sequin manufacturers such as Sequins International in the United States or Brody International in the UK feed a public hungry for 'sparkle'.

> Millenium party celebrations in Britain are in serious danger of lacking sparkle – not because the British don't know how to enjoy themselves – but because of an unexpected shortage of sequins . . . Terry Baptist of Brody International . . . said: It's a three-fold thing. It's mainly fashion swinging more in our favour; the Millenium party kick is growing stronger every day, and I feel that people are fed up with grunge and they want some glitz and glamour in their lives. (NetLondon, 1999)

Sequins have also gained renewed popularity due to an increased interest in Indian fashion and Bollywood. The beauty, intricacy or glitter of saris, kurtas, salwaar-kameez and trimmings is of course often made possible by the availability of impoverished craftworkers. Similar workforces throughout the world are often employed by designers and manufacturers of East and West to apply all manner of decorative finishes. Countries like India also offer a myriad of supplies, in stones, jewels, crystals, bone, wood, glass and metals. Motivations behind the use of such workforces vary – patronage, exploitation or even the struggle to improve conditions by the workers themselves are all in evidence. Some types of decoration used in design, and the evidence of luxury, can be as dependent on visibly intensive labour as it is on materials used. In India the Self Employed Women's Association (SEWA) has seen its membership increase from 100 to over 5,000 women. Struggling against all kinds of odds, this group now provides exquisite embroidered Chikanwork to designers such as Tarun Tahiliani, Anita Dongre, Abu Jani and Sandeep Khosala (Fashion India, 2002). On the other side of the world, in South America's largest *favela* or shantytown, Rocinha, close to Rio de Janeiro, local women have started a phenomenon, creating hot items for the catwalks of New York, Milan, Rio and London. Coopa Roca, Rocinha's neighbourhood sewing cooperative, follow the trend that intensity of labour and artistry equals luxury as much as raw materials (Walbran, 2002). Coopa Roca's unique approach to design (and marketing), has allowed them to progress toward using the finest of materials and collaborating with top designers like fellow-Brazilian Carlos Miele on his New York Fashion Week debut collection.

> His collaboration with Coopa Roca, a women's cooperative based in Rio's largest shantytown, that uses patchwork, crochet and macramé in its work, was evident throughout the collection, as everything from shells and feathers to metal mesh and sequins adorned the clothes. (Bailly, 2002)

If the sequin is razzle and money, the feather is *statement*. Timorous, alluring, grand, dashing, wicked, vampy, mysterious, frightening and crazy – think of any adjective – there is a feather to match. Yet today, in mainstream fashion and in ordinary daywear, the feather has all but disappeared. Compare this to the great heyday of the feather when, for hat decoration, many birds were hunted to extinction and the fashion feather market was one of the most competitive in the world.

> By the 1890s, women were wearing whole bodies of birds on hats and clothing. In 1886, noted ornithologist Frank Chapman counted 40 varieties of native birds, or bird parts, decorating three-fourths of the 700 ladies' hats that he had observed in New York City. (Smithsonian, 2003)

The egret, heron and ostrich feathers, so prominent before the First World War, finally succumbed to a crash and the market never recaptured its former grandeur or notoriety. The stock quality of premium feather producers like the South African black ostrich was maintained but only by finding other uses for the bird (http://roostercogburn.com/sablack.htm). In countries like Australia the ostrich is now bred more for meat and leather than for its feather (DNRE, 2002). During the twentieth century, changes in lifestyle, the advent of the automobile, and the growing emphasis on hair fashion, for the most part did away with 'that hat' (Hopkins, 1999). The canvas, so to speak, had gone and so went the feather. But if there is a rule in design or business, it is that *if something worked before it can work again*, the feather may yet make a major comeback. Like the sequin the feather has had (the last century apart) a long and remarkable relationship with our visual and dress cultures, from tribal to decadent, every society has found a role for feathers. Perhaps this is why couturiers still avidly use the feather. For example, for Christian Dior in 1998, Galliano raided the feathered splendour of Native American tradition (White and Griffiths, 2000: 145) and continued a tradition of fantasy and showmanship akin to the film sets of D. W. Griffith or Buffalo Bill's Wild West Show. Designer Jasper Conran also utilized the traditional strength of the feather.

> The designer shone as one of the few in London capable of cutting clothes worthy of being modelled by Erin O'Connor: a cute, demure black cashmere coat trimmed with a powder puff of white ostrich and matching ostrich feather handbag and a scallop-edged ash satin coat and matching knife-pleated skirt being highlights of a highly desirable collection. (Sherwood, 2003)

Today however, for the ordinary consumer, feathers are understated as small decoration or more likely as motifs in print. In the translation from couture to street, the real item gives way to its

Figure 2.3
A Philip Treacy Occasion Hat. Courtesy Philip Treacy.

iconography. For example, the Native American motif used by Japanese designer Hiroaki Ohya in his Fall/Winter 2003–4 ready-to-wear collection. Even then, at the level of image only, for example in the current resurgence of interest in pattern in interiors, the flower is favoured over the feather. The feather however still has definite champions. For example to see where the expressive power and spirit of feathers are maintained, one must turn to the truly exquisite, the Occasion Hats of Philip Treacy (www.philiptreacy.co.uk). Also, in other spheres, the feather still manages to compete at a functional level with some of the very best technical textiles available. Some of feathers' functional qualities explain why they have been a reliable, robust choice as decoration and embellishment. However in the context of high-performance clothing, goose- and duck-down and the rare eiderdown demonstrate the 'ergonomics' and sheer utility of feathers. At altitudes of 8,000 metres, in hurricane winds and with the temperature at –40 °C, mountain climbers require the very best insulation.

Though there are a large number of new synthetic insulators, downy clothes are unsurpassed at present in the complex of

> requirements: little weight, high heat-insulating characteristics, small transportation volume, and long service life. (BASK, 1997)

If the great and serious feather has largely gone, the frivolous feather – the feather boa, or the small trim – remains. As with many decorative items the market for such products involves a staggering number of small and medium-sized suppliers and retailers. Equally the consumer base is as diverse as the supply chain. This kind of marketplace has its problems. For example, while feathers may be artificial or the dyed by-product of edible birds, within such a context the possibility of illicit trade in the feathers of endangered species, or of poaching, continues. Such features – many products and suppliers, wide-ranging variations in quality and price – mark the world of small and special materials that are used as component, accessory, feature or detail. Where animal products are concerned the difference between maverick markets and respectable ones usually depends on the presence of breeding programmes, commercially maintained flocks/herds and/or regulated environments, where quality and quotas are properly controlled. The same issues are applicable across a range of animal materials. Sometimes though, the market for fashion and clothing-oriented materials seems to comprise everything from mass-manufacture to bespoke, and professional user to hobbyist, enthusiast or addict. The hair of the angora rabbit seems to fall into this category of a product fitting many markets. Silky and smooth in texture, the fibre is slippery and does not hold too well in fabric and yarns. Yet angora has been desired for its weight, purity and luxurious fluffiness. It finds use in high fashion, more commercial mixes and also has an avid following of knitters (for example see http://angora.cl). As with some other well-known types of material, angora rabbit hair appears to have no overarching, world, professional or international organizations. This may have led to its declining production. Increasingly products like angora hair need concerted and collaborative global marketing; they need political lobbyists, large companies backing them and brokers of international trade deals. Alternatively angora may just need repackaging, a new fashionable identity or a new process of manufacture that would make it easier to handle.

> China is by far the world's leading producer of angora rabbit hair, contributing about 90 per cent of global production. Chile is the world's second biggest, followed by Argentina. Small amounts of angora are produced in East European countries, including Czechoslovakia and Hungary, and very small amounts in France.
>
> World production figures for angora rabbit are difficult to obtain as there is no group or association specific to the fibre. In 1986 world production of angora rabbit hair raw material was estimated at 7,000 – 8,000 tonnes . . . Production has since declined considerably worldwide. (Petrie, 1995)

The world of odds and ends, buttons and bows, sequins and feathers, and tricky fluffy fibres, holds equal fascination for textile and fashion communities. Such materials provide accent to designs and thus often hold both commercial and aesthetic value beyond their size or cost. They often command affection or attract the obsessive collector. There are, after all, few more engrossing activities than rummaging through a large tin or box of buttons and oddments. Not surprising when modern manufacturers such as Dill (www.dill-buttons.com) offer some 25,000 types of button! Associated literature for the bric-a-brac of fashion and textiles tends to be either scholarly, based in costume history and collectibles, or economic, based in agricultural policy. It would seem there are ample grounds for more contemporary and critical assessments, but then, that might just spoil the fun.

Skin and Fur

Although the use of animals to provide clothing is an ancient practice, it has been increasingly contested by animal rights activists, politicians and ordinary citizens. Many of the examples listed above relating to animal produce raise issues of animal welfare relating to animal husbandry. The aspect of animal use that has provoked particularly acrimonious, and sometimes violent, clashes is the use of skin and fur taken from animals kept in captivity or in the wild. There are undoubtedly absolutist positions – that no use of animals is legitimate; or any use of animals is legitimate. The debates, are perhaps, so well known, there is no need to reiterate them here. It would also be fair to say that the political and media consensus, particularly in much of the affluent West, is against the use of *real* skins and furs for fashion and textile applications. However in a telling article, Janice Breen Burns identifies both the continuing controversy and conflict within fashion and the inconclusive nature of public sentiment.

> Anti-fur groups say that in the US, 80 per cent of 'upscale' or high-income consumers prefer to shop at fur-free stores. Pro-fur groups say that, in the UK, 81 per cent of people say it is 'acceptable to farm animals for any purpose provided there is animal welfare', and 41 per cent 'support fur farming, are ambivalent or have not formed a view'. (Burns, 2002)

Unsettling and brutal tales, are well publicized by animal rights activists (for examples see US-based www.infurmation.com or UK-based www.carn-age.org.uk). Among celebrity designers there is a split between those who work with fur and those who don't. Some like Karl Lagerfeld see no 'issue' about fur and are prepared to say so, drawing the vitriol of anti-fur protesters (Diderich, 2003). It is in the nature of the issue that well-known designers and companies have to be explicit about their policies.

> Top fashion designers such as Oleg Cassini, Calvin Klein, and Bill Blass are refusing to work with fur . . . Yet recently there is clear evidence that fur is coming back into fashion and other top designers as Yves St. Laurent, Dolce and Gabbana, and Versace are all using fur. Fur is described by its wearers variously as warm, sumptuous, voluptuous, soft, and sensuous . . . The wearing of fur garments are an indicator of wealth, status and luxury. (Sones, 2002)

The aesthetic and status connotations of skins and furs, are in a sense, alluring to the fashion community, they are also often part of fashion's cultural heritage. The Fendi family, for example, started a leather and fur business in 1925. In the mid 1960s their collaboration with Lagerfeld – developing a couture fur collection and logo – established their fashion identity and status (*Fashion Bit*, 2002). Fendi's Spring 2003 menswear collections featured leather trench coats, calfskin jerkins, silver snakeskin tuxedo pants and a black-denim jacket with a built-in crocodile back (Deeny, 2002). Leather, skin and fur, by virtue of their historical resonance, can embody elitism, wealth and power, in addition to more generic brand values like craft, quality and exclusivity. Alternatively skins and pelts are the leitmotif of rebellion and superiority: 'Biker woman reigned supreme, too, at Gianfranco Ferre, in stitched, seamed, zipped and buckled croc-skin and leather, while Roberto Cavalli poured her into skintight, hand-painted leathers and jumpsuits, worn with dyed sheepskin and fox' (Alexander, 2003). Also fashion necessarily draws on sexual, music and street cultures, both mainstream and subcultural. The repertoire of materials, identifiable with particular dress codes and social behaviours, are surprisingly invariant over time. Leather for example, together with rubber, plastic and metal, are the de facto, clichéd, iconic materials of choice that resonate with the fashion 'accents' of biker, rocker, goth or sex-worker. So too any number of animal and material products are rich in connotation, association and significance. Faced with this 'material semiotics' it is not surprising that a proportion of the fashion industry and many fashion-conscious consumers find it difficult to abandon controversial materials that readily express identity.

The arguments for and against furs and skins are ultimately not fought on the same ground. For those against their use, the arguments are a priori moral. For those for their use, there is essentially an amorality – there is no moral dillema – and hence pleasure and effect can be pursued. The basic disagreement nonetheless results in arguments for all situations, hence the fur industry has claimed fur production helps communities 'close to the land'. There are also qualified notions of what constitutes the 'acceptable face' of skin and fur use. These range from the unashamed open sale of skin and fur products, for example the snakeskin goods of www.implora.com, to the 'lifestyle-massaged' message of mainstream fashion and journalism. This is particularly applied to the most ubiquitous of all skin products – leather.

> Probably the most unusual development in leather is the varied colors; everything from deep red, burgundy, olive, green, blue, orange, purple, copper, gold and more are available. Leathers textured for a snake skin or crocodile look also are popular. 'I love the versatility of it. Anything that looks quite rich and exclusive is probably what's driving this trend,' said Durand Guion, women's fashion director for Macy's

> West . . . 'We're finding this season is really about lightweight leather made to wear all day long . . . There used to be this thought that leather was too hot to wear all day; that's not the case this year.' (Padgett, 2000)

One of the most interesting features of the skin and fur trades is that there are distinct regional and national attitudes about them. For example, around the globe certain countries and regions seem to favour or are indifferent to skin and fur industries, while others seem to find them abhorrent. This seems somewhat at odds with the markedly international flavour of long-standing debates over animal welfare. Personal and subjective moral responses are, it seems, counterbalanced by community interests, national cultures, social class, employment issues and geographies. For example, within Europe, in Great Britain fur-farming has been driven out, while Finland has the largest fur auction house. The issue of sensitivity is not simply a case of urban versus non-urban sentiment – Hong Kong, a thriving metropolis, is the centre of fur garment manufacture. There are undoubtedly issues of tradition and economics.

> In Finland, for example, the annual value of fur production is greater than that of beef. In Denmark, fur farming is the fourth largest agricultural export after bacon, cheese and canned meat. (FFS, 2003)

In twenty business days the auction house Finnish Fur Sales (FFS) trades $350 million worth of furs a year. Some seven million skins are sold to brokers, manufacturers and skin traders (InfoManager, 2003). Recently the Scandinavian fur industry has been developing links with China; both FFS and Saga Furs have opened offices in Beijing. Although it has a fragmented fur industry, China is nonetheless a major producer, perhaps more significantly it now also promises to be a major consumer market. It is reasonable to assume that the Chinese public has, by and large, not been exposed to the animal welfare debates of the last 40 years. Therefore we do not know whether Chinese consumers will replay the democratic countries' experience of the fashion and politics of fur, or whether they will just stimulate a massive growth in designer fur.

> The 29th China Fur & Leather Products Fair showed that fur, which is synonymous with elegance and sleekness, is retailoring its position to become a true fashion fabric that promises to cater to the needs of increasingly well-off consumers in China. New fur-garment designs were seen everywhere at the fair, such as coats lined with fur, jeans jacket with fur trim and down jackets with fur pockets. The fur exhibition, according to experts, reflected that native materials are no longer confined to pricey full-fur garments. A chic trend is that they are now widely used for trim and accessories, and combined with textile materials. Experts say that a growing number of consumers around the world are seeking a new fur look for modern active lifestyles, which also fits well with China's renewed fashion appreciation and hankering for opulent but affordable clothing. (Renfeng, 2003)

It would seem that probably, in spite of advances in fibre technology or new textile science, nature at its most raw can still remain attractive to designer, industrialist, retailer and consumer. Fashion and textiles have a long history of using nature in its entirety and often without qualm. In this respect, most of us are likely to have some desensitization to where and how our goods originate. Sometimes too, the art and artifice of fashion and textiles make us forget their perpetual relationship with agriculture and the natural world. Whether it is animal rights in fur-farming or transgenic modifications to goats, the ethical dimensions of that relationship are ongoing. In this chapter we have touched upon the idea of what could be called the three 'eras' of fibre production. In the first era, the longest by far, nature was used directly, all species, all materials. The second era was that of what we might call 'dirty fibres'. Oil, heat and chemicals featured large in this phase. The third era, that of the molecular sciences, promises to be cleaner, and to provide greater material quality and diversity. In a sense it also promises to be an era when we return to nature as the defining source of inspiration, comfort and identity. It will be interesting to see whether it ever does away with a taste for fox and mink.

3

Cultural Roles

Over the years, fashion has become a term less associated with haute couture and more appropriate for the high street. This is evident from the considerable presence of fashion and textiles on the high street and in department stores: overall, fashion occupies a substantial proportion of the retail space that exists. Once, fashion was only available in the couturiers' chambers to the few privileged clients that could afford to partake in it. Now fashion it is at the mercy of relentless market competition and consumers who, through the way they live and their product choices, influence trends and design. As is stressed throughout this book, fashion and textiles are inextricably linked; jointly they form a stable relationship, one relying on the other not only for survival but also in order to prosper. Fashion adds value to textiles through the processing of raw materials, and textiles enable fashion to happen. Fashion develops continually and therefore demands new and exciting materials to work with from the textile industry. With technology formulating new recipes to manufacture new fibres and make new fabrics, each concoction boasts that it is better than the one before, which persuades us (the consumers) to reject the old in favour of the new. Giving up the old for the new is easier to do when the new is available to us at moderate 'off-the-rail' prices and does not carry the expense of a hand-sewn couturier's creation. Both fashion and textiles have massive cultural and economic implications; globally they impact on our material world. This *should* detract from the frivolity sometimes attached to them, but the whirlwind of media and journalism surrounding fashion and textiles often makes them seem ephemeral and insubstantial. The subjects encompass creative energy as much as they embrace business and finance and are active at all levels of society and in every community. Both professions vie to produce the 'next big thing' either aiming for international appeal or targeting very specific markets. In order to be successful in an internationally competitive marketplace, fashion and textiles organizations have to track global patterns of consumption and population trends so that they can operate effectively. This constant tracking of changes in cultures not only informs designers of patterns within consumer society, but can also act as a creative feeder and inspiration for design concepts.

Globalization

The way in which materials and labour from around the world are used to produce single fashion items, fibres or fabrics demonstrates that fashion and textiles are deeply involved in the phenomenon of globalization. Fashion and fabrics have also become trans-cultural, they have evolved as a reflection of the migrations within world society. Mobility through travel, in combination with rapid advances in communications technology, has shrunk time and space. The constant change occurring in fashion combined with geographical movement of peoples can confuse and dilute cultural identity as it is carried and spread across the globe. The effect of this is revealed in dress and fabric choice as differences between nations become less defined or obvious, John Quelch emphasizes that 'Surveys point to an increasing convergence of attitudes, values and behaviours among consumers worldwide' (Quelch, 1999). Clothing and fabrics are no longer exclusive to a specific culture or part of the world, nowadays it is not unusual to find a Scottish tartan being worn in Tokyo (Lopriore, 2002); Indian embroidery being worn in London (Kaul, 2000); or African prints being worn in New York (TransAfrica Forum, 2000). Everything goes – everywhere. Having said this, some differences in values and preference do still exist and vary from nation to nation. The older generation in particular forms strong bonds with, and retains traditional dress and fabric; colours, motifs, textiles and styles can all translate as security and reassurance in a dynamic world. In addition to this, the fashion and textile consumer often expresses loyalty to nations and designers, for example, the prestige of being 'Made in a Italy' draws the fashion consumer to Italian merchandise (Malossi 1998). And the 'brand conscious' Japanese feel that 'a well-known fashion or designer brand signifies a history and tradition of quality and superior workmanship' (Japan Information Network, 2003).

The existence of global culture in fashion and textiles directs our attention to transcultural features within the subject. An examination of the mosaic of what constitutes fashion and fabric in a cultural context has now become a social study, embracing anthropological issues and environmental factors, as well as traditions in fabric and dress. It involves a comprehension of the behaviour of people in conjunction with social and cultural influences. An individual's actions are rooted in the environment and informed by the signs and symbols they are surrounded by. For instance, once we have 'experienced' a fibre or fabric that we like, we are encouraged to seek it out again, in order to repeat the feelings of satisfaction. Therefore, it becomes habit for us to consciously look for and be drawn by positive signs and characteristics in fabric performance, usually in the shape of globally recognizable and assuring symbols and brands or traditional pattern, motif and style in apparel. Consumers in general, match their desire for new products with an equal desire for products that they already know. Known products (and brands) provide reassurances about quality, pleasure, or say, value for money. On occasion however, because of political, social or cultural change, consumer groups will radically shift their system of values and become more experimental, conservative or sentimental in apparel or fabric choices. For example recent trends in the USA suggest that loyalty to well-known brands can be seriously undermined when people's fundamental and personal value systems, become more important to them as a result of war and political insecurity. This has proved the case in America. Since the war with Iraq, American consumers have still sought to identify with values embodied in apparel and fabric, but the entire hierarchy of brand superiority or leadership is now informed by an ethos of 'basic American values', resulting in an increased loyalty to brands and types of apparel that are seen as profoundly American such as, for example, Wrangler jeans (logolounge, 2003). In such circumstances the resilience of brands, to maintain or reassert their market position is tested by a 'loosening of the field', and a retail and marketing scramble takes place to secure or re-secure customer loyalty.

The rich and varied world of fashion and textiles is filled with symbols and signs which transport cultural meaning to the consumer, who, as noted, either accepts or rejects it. (McCracken, 1990). Therefore, cultural meaning and communication from nation to nation has to be considered in fashion and textiles as well as in any other business. If neglected, lucrative opportunities may be passed up or disastrous marketing choices made. Of course, fashion and fabrics can be read as no more than symbolic labels, transferring cultural meaning to a consumer via a designer name, rather than through the innate traditional characteristics of a fabric or garment. Global markets have to be thoroughly researched by industry in order to glean local cultural differences which may impact on the success of a fabric or style. Cultural frameworks and fashion are closely tied; and, to facilitate a fashion on a global scale, consideration of local differences in culture in most cases is a critical factor. There are, of course, exceptions; sometimes a standardized approach to marketing does exist on a global scale. Labels in the fashion industry, such as Gucci, Calvin Klein, Gap and Chanel, actually transcend any sort of local cultural differences and are active on a global scale without having to make any modifications culturally or strategically to be accepted by consumers. To be successful in a global environment, these labels typically have a well-defined and strong market image. What enables these 'superbrands' (Moore and Burt, 2001) to operate on a global scale to the extent that they do is the fact that they appeal to all sorts of consumers in spite of variations in culture or ethnicity.

Cultural Differences in Attitudes to Fabric and Design

Although we can draw on a rich diversity of fashion and textile design philosophies and influences from around the world, the focus in this section will be on Eastern attitudes and styles and how these are sometimes adopted by or influence Western fashions. The motive behind the selection is principally due to the fact that a few, mainly Japanese designers hold a prominent position on international runways and their design language, although visually very different from that of the west, at the same time bears a resemblance to it conceptually. Until now, Eastern and Western fashion and textile design philosophies have been treated quite separately. Yet, an analysis of attitudes draws attention to similarities in approach to the design process and attitudes towards fabric and design. For example, Issey Miyake, like Vivienne Westwood, raids traditional historical sources in relation to shape, form and fabric. Whereas Westwood frequently references the corset and crinoline, in Miyake's designs there is reference to the simple geometrics of the kimono (Miyake, 1978). He combines traditional Japanese processes and textiles, for instance, sashiko (cotton quilting) and farmers' checked cloth, while simultaneously adopting modern materials like polyester jersey and so blending the old with the new; trends with traditions. That which was begun with the likes of Issey Miyake, Rei Kawakubo, Yohji Yamamoto and Junya Wattanabe essentially involved innovation in fabric as much as exploration of silhouette, and has been labelled as 'textile-led "artistic" dress' (Wilcox, 2001: 31).

The cultural attitude of designers towards fabric and form in the East, is in marked contrast to Western fashion design ideals. Claire Wilcox, in *Radical Fashion*, explains the developments of cutting-edge technologies in textiles in the East:

> As part of post-war regeneration, Japan built up its industrial base and now leads in the development of 'techno textiles'. Working with specialist technicians and factories, these designers have been central in harnessing and advancing textiles' technologies to replicate commercially the appearance of labour-intensive fabric techniques and develop new fibres, weaving, dyeing and fabric manipulations. (Wilcox, 2001: 32)

For many Japanese fashion designers an intimate relationship with fabric is carried through and expressed in their garment designs and collections. The Western design ethos is generally propelled by, and responds to, the shape of the body, using fabric to sculpt and emphasize form. In Japanese design philosophy, as conveyed by Kawakubo and Yamamoto, an almost spiritual stance is taken in respect of the interaction of fabric with the human form. Drawing on traditional craft sensibilities underpinned by philosophy, aesthetics and reason, 'in time-honoured tradition they exploited the full width of their loosely woven and pre-washed fabrics to create oversize garments that moved sensually with and independent of the wearer' (Wilcox, 2001: 30). Although fashion and fabric are inextricably linked in the West, in the East the bond between these spheres is often marked as being pure; modern silhouettes are thus often simple in their expression, but the fabrics can be complex in their formation. Perhaps though it is worth noting that some of the Japanese traditions of folding, wrapping and tucking cloth, so evident in the kimono (Yamanaka, 1987), are harder to translate into what we might call 'international casual' or more 'convenient' models of couture.

In discussing the steady and perpetual exchange between fashion and fabric, it is impossible to ignore fashion designer Issey Miyake, for thirty years he has worked closely with a team of textile designers and engineers, the most prominent being Makiko Minagawa and Dai Fujiwara. They pool their expertise and together develop fabric and fashion in unison. The culmination of these joint efforts in fabric and fashion have materialized in Miyake's 'Pleats Please' range in 1993, and this was followed by his 'A-POC' (A Piece of Cloth) concept in 1999. Both of these collections generated a fusion of textiles with fashion (www.designboom.com/eng/funclub/apoc.html). The various accolades and acclaim that Miyake has earned throughout his career have encouraged journalists like Julie Dam in *Time Asia* magazine to label him as 'the first Asian designer to have become truly global, not only in renown but also in aesthetic' (Dam, 1999). It is evident from examining the collaborative relationship between the textile and fashion designer that the discovery of a new fabric can revolutionize a fashion design or can create the foundation for the philosophy behind a collection. For instance, the 'Pleats Please' idea was borne out of the realization that a lightweight, stretch polyester could be permanently pleated. Scientific, technological and mechanical input from professionals in the textile industry can fuel a fashion designer's notions about possibilities in clothing. This is a mutually beneficial relationship, in that the fashion designer is equipped with new and exciting materials to work with and the textile industry is provided with an effective promotional tool by fashion.

Not long after a new fabric is launched on the runway by couturiers, it can be found in various formulations seeping into mainstream fashion. This is the case with Miyake's pleats: since their introduction in the early 1990s, wrinkled and pleated fabrics have been and still are widely available in fashion. The same is true of embellished or embroidered fabrics in 2002 the fashion world constructed an 'Indian Summer' fashion story on the runways. This inevitably led to the presence of beading, embroidery and colourful diaphanous fabrics in mainstream fashion, evidence of this was reported in *The Telegraph*:

> . . . the Indian movie industry that has provided the inspiration for the gloriously rich technicolour fashion this summer . . . Asia was a huge influence on the spring/summer 2002 designer catwalks and, as a result, the high street is awash with bright turquoise, fuchsia, brocade and emerald tops, skirts and trousers. (Robson, 2002)

Global influences in fashion and textiles are nothing new. Commenting on Issey Miyake, in *The New York Times* in 1999, Roberta Smith points out 'Like much of the great clothing designs of this century, they combine elements of East and West, which also puts them in step with the multicultural globalism of the moment' (Smith, 1999: 39).

Ever since we have been able to leave our own borders, we have been fascinated with the exotic. As mentioned above, Asian clothing and fabric has been regularly visited as a source of inspiration, resulting in frequent European borrowings from Japanese art and Chinese and Indian culture since the eighteenth century. Fashion designers appear to have been rummaging through sources of ethnicity in clothing and fabric for an eternity. A cursory glance through the archives of *Vogue* and *Elle* reveals fashion designers like Yves Saint Laurent, Zandra Rhodes, Rifat Ozbek and Christian Dior, to name but a few, whose collections have been influenced in varying degrees by ethnicity and global culture. The exploration of the exotic in fabric and couture can occur for a number of reasons. It could simply be that a designer is inspired by the fabric or silhouette of other cultures. Or alternatively, interest in a specific culture could emerge as a consequence of media interest, through, for example, films. The release of the film *Rebel Without a Cause* in 1955 led to blue jeans becoming a symbol of rebellion with the younger generation and they were even banned from being worn in some schools in the USA. The movie *The Last Emperor* in the late 1980s prompted a new interest in Chinese culture, and as recently as summer 2002, the launch of *Bombay Dreams*, the Andrew Lloyd Webber West End musical production, did the same for Indian culture. The opening of the show coincided with an Indian theme within fashion, fabrics and lifestyle in general (Robson, 2002).

Alongside culture, world events also influence fashion and fabric on a global scale. If we make a quick assessment of recent conflicts in the Middle East which led to military action and compare this to the abundance of military styled clothing and fabrics available currently, it is apparent that major incidents can influence changes in fashion and textiles. A similar occurrence was experienced during and after the Second World War. Throughout the period, fashion designers were subjected to fabric rationing which dictated the utilitarian designs of the time (http://fashion-ebooks.com/utility_clothing.htm), although the style and look was perhaps inaugurated by Schiaparelli's crisp, tailored, severely masculine suits of the late 1930s. In comparison, immediately after the war, Christian Dior's extravagant 1947 'New Look', used up to 50 yards of fabric in its skirt (Martin, 1998); a celebration of the end of fabric rationing.

Global Markers, Logos and Labels

The application of signs and symbols on clothing, informing the public about specific characteristics of fibre, cloth and design, helps the consumer make choices and can enhance and elevate the status and value of fabric and apparel. A brand could simply be described as a badge; a trademark; an identifier; or shorthand, conveying information through a myriad of formulas and associations. What logos and labels do achieve is that they distinguish goods from their competitors. In the context of fashion and textiles, fibre brands like Lycra and Tencel and designer labels such as DKNY and Armani, all participate in global competition to cultivate loyalty amongst consumers, guiding us towards specific products or attributes. These are just a few examples of the many fashion and textile signs intended to help consumers choose fashion and textile products. As much as labels and logos communicate fashion savvy and social status through designer branding, they also impart practical information about fabric performance, ecological benefits or quality via fibre company swing tags and symbols which convey fabric and design features.

> All the highly successful brands have prospered because they enable consumers to identify products and services that they can trust; originally, they may have found them through family usage or have been influenced by the consumption habits of friends or colleagues. (Chisnall, 1994: 274)

If we begin at the source of textiles and fashion, we must consider the role of the fibre producers. Regardless of the eminence a fibre may possess with consumers, fibre companies are constantly required to circulate the latest modifications, informing the fashion designer and ultimately the consumer of its applications. This act of constantly relaying innovation to the public is usually carried out by PR companies; an investment in promotion afforded by only the very large fibre and apparel organizations. Such promotion forms and sustains corporate and brand identity in the mind of the consumer. The natural and manufactured fibre companies' approach to marketing their fibres as brands enables them to cleverly carry informative messages via fabric to fashion and the consumer, educating each level about the various benefits of the fabrics they purchase. There are various trade associations and organizations set up specifically to represent a range of fibre producers, amongst them are Cotton Incorporated, The Woolmark Company, and the Cashmere and Camel Hair Manufacturers Institute (Burns and O'Bryant, 2002). Then there are the large chemical companies like DuPont who develop, produce and market a number of branded fibres, such as Lycra. Not only are the fibre companies able to use fashion as a vehicle to promote their wares and so raise public awareness of their brands, but the fashion designers themselves actually endorse particular fabrics and fibres that they use frequently in their collections. Cotton Incorporated promote themselves through associations with designers such as, Bill Blass, Michael Kors and Yeohlee Teng (Burns and O'Bryant, 2002). Similarly, fashion designers endorse Lycra (www.lycra.com), one of the top ten apparel brands in the world, it holds court with the most famous names in fashion 'Consumers around the world recognize the LYCRA® wave logo as a symbol of quality apparel'

(Du Pont, 2001a). Kenzo says, 'When you wear clothes made with LYCRA® fiber, you quickly adapt to them. It changes your way of moving' (Du Pont, 2001b), and Michael Smaldone of leading retailer Banana Republic reinforces the fibre's unparalleled use in apparel, stating, 'We put stretch in everything we can. They're our best-selling items' (Du Pont, 2001c). These sorts of endorsements add some weight to corporate image in a globally competitive marketplace.

We have recognized that fabric can possess specific fibres and technologies which are communicated to the fashion industries and consumers as claiming to be genuinely beneficial to those who purchase them. However, ordinary cloth can also be elevated by the simple attachment of the 'right' label. In a world where most fashion retailers trade in similar merchandise, branding becomes more critical to single products out as being different to others available, and designer brands are at the pinnacle of the branding hierarchy. The attachment of a logo to what is often and essentially pretty ordinary apparel, adds value to it, distinguishes it from others, and automatically drops it into a ranking system of the best to the worst in its field. That fashion is so dominated by branding in this day and age leads us to question what is the status of the actual fabrics themselves when a logo can make an ordinary fabric extraordinary – without the application of any special treatment or process, other than the addition of a label of course. Colin McDowell illustrates this issue in *The Designer Scam*, he says

> [This is] the challenge that sets out to alter our buying habits so radically that we believe that luxuries are, in fact, necessities. For example, on the simplest level, we must be persuaded to be irrational and pay between £50 and £65 for a polo shirt from Ralph Lauren when we can buy a perfectly adequate and remarkably similar one from Marks & Spencer for between £11 and £18. The fact that so many people *are* convinced and *do* buy the expensive item is proof of the enormous success that has attended the designer scam over the last ten years. (McDowell, 1994: 1)

Twitchell forecasts the future of colossal designer brands, such as Ralph Lauren, as a bleak one, suggesting that a generational shift will alter consumer attitudes towards global labels

Figure 3.1
The Nike Swoosh Design logo. NIKE and the Swoosh Design logo are trademarks of Nike, Inc. and its affiliates. Used by permission.

> As young consumers see midcult brands such as Nike, Benetton, and Diesel as hipper than couture labels, as competition increases for finite shelf space within mall boutiques, and as department stores like Saks and Neiman Marcus flood the market with store brands, opuluxe empires may topple. (Twitchell, 2002: 134)

Fabrics and Prestige

Fibres and fabrics alone can contain cachet; we only have to think of cashmere for instance, regardless of what it may be within, to conjure up ideas of affluence. The fashion industry and consumers perceive it to be luxurious and to have 'snob value'. Therefore, these are the values and messages that cashmere is used to deliver. 'The activity of the textiles industry, which is the primary component of the fashion industry at large, is not merely the production of fabrics; it also transfers various messages "into" fabrics' (Malossi, 1998: 156). Perceived values of fabrics and fashions are all-important in the luxury end of the market, it is a prerequisite at this level of the market that prestige transfers from the fabric to the consumer through ownership. The codes that fabrics like cashmere may convey to others about the person in possession of it could perhaps include indications of social class and 'breeding'. Often, when we buy, we enter into building a personality or identity of how we'd like to be seen or perceived by others.

Twitchell explains the psychological factors involved in associating with specific kinds of fashion and textile. Consumption of the right sorts of fabrics and fashions is vitally important in today's market as they are closely tied to personality and status. He cites Hathaway shirts (www.hathaway.com) as having possessed genuine luxury through using only the best fabrics from around the world, rather than the application of insignia. The desire to be linked to objects that possess little real value but high positional status is of great significance to the consumer and useful for the fashion and textiles industries to know too, so that they are able to exploit the situation for their personal financial gains. Twitchell says of Martha Stewart's 'Silver Label' range with Kmart:

> Of her many endorsed products, one is of special interest: her line of matelasse coverlets and shams – really, just bedcovers . . . and come in silk, linen, crushed velvet, Egyptian cotton, cotton sateens, and even . . . cashmere. Remember three things: This is Kmart, a bedspread is something you buy not to show off to others but to please yourself, and cashmere is, well, supposed to be something really special. (Twitchell, 2002: 9)

The notion that our motivation to own products is driven by a consumerist psychology of association and associated value is a standard tenet of marketing, advertising, psychology, sociology and cultural studies. This model of consumption seems commonsensical and obvious; universally we believe it to be deeply embedded in the psyche of the consumer and so the fashion and textile worlds tap into it and apply their business strategies accordingly.

Logos and labels don't necessarily have to be seen, they can be communicated via a 'secret designer code', and those who are truly 'in the know' are able to identify and decipher them. The difference between a fashion novice and a fashion aficionado, is knowing that the single red line signals Prada and red and green points to Gucci. It is particularly apparent now that there are rather more subtle ways to identify a designer through a signature within their fabric, such as a bespoke print or fabric. Of course, this is not a new phenomenon, Burberry and Pucci have been doing this since the outset. However, in an attempt to avoid the stigma of the logo, which has ironically become 'common', fashion designers such as Miuccia Prada, Louis Vuitton and Donna Karan have discovered a quieter means of conspicuous consumption by incorporating identifiers within the cloth. Jess Cartner-Morley points this out: 'Secretly, fashion people still love a logo . . . designers have come up with a polite alternative . . . When Donna and Miuccia – two women known for a love of chic, sensible black – embrace pattern and whimsy, it's clear the trend will be hard to avoid' (Cartner-Morley, 2003). Using fabric and print as a substitute for the logo is certainly a fresh approach to 'marking' clothing as different, but it inevitably leads to remarkably similar prints materializing in mainstream fashion stores.

This new approach to carrying a fashion 'logo' within the print of cloth is a contrast to the traditional reasons for using logos and labels a few years ago when it was au fait to be obviously spotted in them, Cayte Williams stated in the *Independent on Sunday* that 'logos are a gogo' (Williams, 2000). In their original guise, logos had a habit of screaming out to others that you were either a fashion victim, or using them as a visible measure of your wealth.

> 'There's an argument that the big names in fashion have made logos so brash for next season so that it's almost kitsch,' says one industry insider . . . when you consider who'll be wearing that stuff – the ultra-rich who want to visibly spend their money, label-mad celebrities like Posh and Becks, or Puff Daddy who ignited the whole 'ghetto fabulous', label-heavy look in the first place . . . But the return of logos is good news for glossy magazines, who have always had a mutually beneficial relationship with designers. Advertising is the life-blood of the high-fashion publication, and fashion editors filling the front rows of catwalk shows in new logo-mania can only make their advertisers happier. (Williams, 2000)

An overview of the current scene reveals that subtlety is key as far as logos and labels are concerned in couture fashion. However, in attempting to introduce discretion through prints and fabrics, fashion designers may find that using signature textiles as logos backfires despite their efforts to secure exclusivity. Textiles can be tweaked, imitated and disseminated among consumers more easily and less obviously than say a label, this essentially defies the reasons for using silent signals through fabric.

Branding

Branding in haute couture can elevate the most ordinary of fabrics. Despite its origins being deeply rooted in workwear of the eighteenth century, denim has been embraced by haute couture and hit the runways, making it one of the few fabrics that transcends all levels of apparel. It is the name or the brand that separates denim and not necessarily the quality of the denim itself. After all, blue jeans are just machine-made denim at all levels, value is added when it is transformed into a product and it is combined with design, designer or brand. Denim is an iconic fabric, steeped in history, Birgit Lohmann states that in the 1960s and 1970s:

> 'jeans became a symbol of 'western decadence' . . . in the 1980's jeans became high fashion clothing, when famous designers started making their own styles of jeans, with their own labels on them' and then she explains their most recent reinvention at the turn of the millennium, 'something decidedly weird is happening in the world of denim . . . jeans have been back on designers catwalks, at chanel, dior, chloe and versace. The single most potent symbol of fashion, summer '99 . . . torn-knee gucci blue jeans, seen globally, sell out instantaneously at $3715 a pop.' (Lohmann, 2000)

Twitchell reiterates this issue, and says 'What really separates a Calvin Klein swath of denim from one from Donna Karan or from Levi Strauss is the brand. In this sense new luxury is the ultimate branding of branding. The object as object almost evaporates. The luxury brand remains' (Twitchell, 2002: 156).

Companies can only attach so much value to a product and target the market with advertising. After that it is largely up to the consumers and media to deem whether or not a product or a brand is a success. Products are constantly designed and developed to sustain and facilitate brand identity, 'Rather than brands existing to sell more of a product, products are developed as a means of extending and consolidating the brand' (Pavitt, 2000: 39). Branding even stretches into associated industries where further sales can be gained. This is especially true of the couture fashion industry. Today it is common to find a fashion house touting cosmetics, fragrances, interior textiles and products, and accessories. The fashion industry is reliant on the press it receives during seasonal couture shows; this translates into publicity which fuels interest in the fashion house as a brand, and generates sales of brand merchandise down to the cheapest T-shirt or lipstick; it's all in the name. However, this formula isn't exclusively present at the top level of the fashion industry, on the high street stores like NEXT, which began as a mainstream fashion chain, now retails its own range of gadgets, accessories and interior products in many of its stores. As fashion infiltrates other industries, other industries feed off fashion, like cosmetics giant, Estée Lauder who fit into the glamorous fashion world by association. Keeping pace with the cyclical world of the fashion industry, they – like fibre, fabric and accessories suppliers – have to renew merchandise regularly and quickly. Estée Lauder was the first to appropriate and apply the seasonality present in fashion to the cosmetics and fragrance industry, introducing 'seasonal' perfumes and nail varnish colours in smaller measures to fit in with current fashion cycles (Hodson, 2001).

The same system that promotes branding can also damage it. Brands are very vulnerable to any sort of consumer protest or boycott in reaction to an organization's ethics or business conduct. Campaigns or demonstrations against a company can convey powerful and negative messages to consumers. Gap suffered from this just a few years ago when controversy surrounded its use of leather. The organization hit the headlines in March 2000 when Pretenders singer Chrissie Hynde was arrested while protesting with members of PETA (People for the Ethical Treatment of Animals) at a Gap store in Manhattan, New York City (BBC News, 2000). The demonstration was in relation to ethical issues, PETA accused Gap of using leather from inhumanely slaughtered cows in India where cows are considered sacred in the Hindu religion anyway. The strong feelings that the use of specific materials can arouse is quite astonishing. This, combined with Chrissie Hynde's celebrity status was a sure-fire way to get column inches in the press, publicizing PETA's cause, but with detrimental consequences for Gap. Now apparel, fibre, materials and labour are all carefully sourced at companies such as, and including, Gap. In light of its experience, Gap now has a code of conduct which is openly available for public scrutiny (Gap, 2003). Demonstrations like these are not easy to survive or recover from, in the public's eyes the company's reputation may well be tarnished – at least until the incident is forgotten about.

The Media Industries and Celebrity

As we can see from previous examples, the media industries, in reporting on the latest events, play a pivotal role in the success or failure of fashion and textile brands and companies. Whether there is a new film that sparks off interest in particular styles of dress and fabrics, or ethical consumer issues within fashion and textiles

– all have an impact on what we choose to wear. The media industries that deliver fashion and textiles to consumers, do so in a multitude of ways, commonly using magazines, the tabloids and TV, and most recently through the Internet. PR companies supply the media with copy and pictures, filling column inches and helping to sell newspapers and magazines, and in the process informing the consumer about what they should wear every day of the week. The fashion editor has a close relationship with the fashion designer and manufacturer, they are not only invited to view new collections in order to select what they may choose to feature on magazine pages and in the tabloids, but they are seasonally sent press releases and 'look books'. At occasions such as collection viewings, editors have the opportunity to share and discuss their insights on trends and markets in their roles as professional industry experts. Collectively media and industry devise and distribute stories, almost plotting to entice the consumer far in advance of the seasonal release of trends.

As sources of fashion and so textile information, newspapers come only second to the glossy print of magazines (Twitchell, 2002). In, for example, the US and the UK papers such as *The New York Times*, *The International Herald Tribune* and *The Sunday Times*, *Telegraph* and *Guardian* all interpret, style and convey fashion for public consumption, mostly through the 'style' supplements. These newspapers have such prominence with the public at large, for the lead they take in disseminating fashion and fabric news, that the media machine has strangely made fashion celebrities out of the individuals that report on the fashion celebrities. These individuals, such as Suzy Menkes, Hilary Alexander, Alexander Schulman, Anna Wintour and Colin McDowell, have become well known through their critical analysis of whether a fashion or a fashion designer is good or bad. Throughout the world each fashion 'scene' has its own media forum and accompanying style-brokers and pundits.

We cannot underestimate the enormous amount of power that the fashion editor wields over the fashion industry at large, almost shaping it to resemble their own vision of what it should be and so influencing which styles and fabrics ought to be key for a season. In profiling *Vogue*'s editor-in-chief, Anna Wintour, in 1999, Kevin Gray states

> Over the past decade, from her perch at *Vogue,* Wintour has not only dictated fashion tastes to the public but also influenced fashion's course in the back rooms of design shops as well. 'She truly sees the magazine as a bridge between the designer and the consumer,' says Donna Karan. Wintour is often called on by the world's biggest design houses to recommend new blood. She has single-handedly boosted the careers of favoured designers such as Kors and Marc Jacobs, pushing their clothes to department stores and TV audiences.
>
> Another pet was John Galliano, whom she set up with a backer and virtually installed at Dior . . . If she is (a trend herself), the industry knows when to follow. When grunge failed to help advertisers sell beauty products and accessories a few years back, Wintour demanded an immediate return to glamour. 'She went to the designers personally and told them, "This is what we're shooting. If you don't do that, you're not going to be shot,"' says *Times* fashion editor Spindler. 'And they all did it.' (Gray, 2002)

Without the media industries and celebrity system, fashion and textiles would find it difficult to operate effectively; PR companies and the press keep the cogs of these industries turning. It is in the celebrities' interest to be seen by the world's media in the 'right' sort of dress, by the 'right' designer and equally, in the interest of the designer for the 'right' celebrity to be wearing their clothes. It is a mutually beneficial relationship, the designer is provided with promotional tools in the guise of movie stars and pop idols, which gain them valuable exposure in the press and media. The celebrity indicates the level of their fame through associations with specific labels; celebrity status is measured according to patronage from various couture houses. As a general rule, the greater the star, the more superior the couture house that dresses them. The Oscars are an event where on the announcement of nominations, top designers begin to charm the stars to wear their dresses. In 1997 in Los Angeles, CNN reported

> Oscar's red carpet became a fashion runway . . . With more than a billion viewers watching, Hollywood's biggest event has turned into a major marketing moment for fashion's top designers . . . Even the men got into the action, with designer

> Giorgio Armani dressing the likes of Oscars host Billy Crystal and best supporting actor winner Cuba Gooding Jr. (Hillard, 1997)

Since then celebrity and designer tie-ups have become de rigueur for both parties involved, in order to play the game. These liaisons between fashion and celebrity also have repercussions in associated industries; not only does it provide the journalist and the media in general with froth, but it also has consequences for supply industries such as textiles.

The incidental effects of celebrity fashion leading mainstream fashion and affecting associated industries was highlighted again by the Oscars and demonstrated by Gwyneth Paltrow being dressed in a classic Ralph Lauren pink gown. As a result of this incident, pink was suddenly a popular colour and copies of the dress in question were mass-produced, as reported by Cotton Incorporated:

> Suzanne Zarrilli, a co-owner of Wish List, a teen apparel boutique in Westport, Conn. recalls, 'The year before, I wouldn't have even looked at anything pink. It would have reminded my customers of when they were little girls. Paltrow made the color cool.' And Paltrow's Oscar dress turned into the number one prom dress style of the year thanks to ABS by Allen Schwartz, who is famous for making low-priced copies of Oscar dresses. (Cotton Incorporated, 2003)

In their choice of dress celebrities can ignite a new interest in a style of clothing or in specific fabrics. Mainstream fashion invariably duplicates celebrity styles on a mass scale, as a consequence of this, an increase in fabric production is generated and retail industries are stimulated. *The Guardian* reported on Cameron Diaz as having a similar effect on mainstream fashion: 'Diaz's choice of outfits for awards ceremonies has consistently shown originality and willingness to take a risk, such as her stripy Vivienne Westwood outfit at last year's Golden Globes, instantly prompting endless high street copies' (Freeman, 2003). Most recently, in 2003, with the launch of the film version of the musical *Chicago*, fishnets became commonplace in hosiery departments. Trends such as these are encapsulated in promotional images associated with these films and popularized by media coverage and hype.

The star associations in the fashion world were initiated by Armani and followed by Versace (Agins, 2000). Although these designers established new practices of celebrity endorsements, they could not have foreseen the unsurpassed patronage that the late Princess Diana could instil in a product such as the Dior handbag. A massive, sudden public demand for this item, inevitably had immense ramifications on material supply industries:

> Starting around 1994, designer handbags suddenly became the rage in fashion and Dior was lucky enough to ride the wave with its Lady Dior handbag, a quilted box in buttery lambskin, distinguished by the gold-plated letters D-I-O-R dangling from its double handles. At $1,200, the Lady Dior bag was a pricier version of Chanel's $960 quilted bag. But what a difference Princess Diana made! French First Lady Bernadette Chirac gave the Princess of Wales a Dior bag in 1995 and she began carrying it everywhere, within full view of the paparazzi. Before long, retailers had a hard time keeping Lady Dior handbags in stock and more than 100,000 Lady Diors flew off the shelves in 1997. (Agins, 2000: 48)

The idea of stars endorsing products and brands with their names isn't exclusive to the fashion world. Neither is endorsement limited to individuals, companies too can have valuable prestigious names and reputations. For example, in the automotive industry, Pininfarina, the Italian company famed for designing the Ferrari, entered a cooperation agreement with French car giants Peugot in the 1950s which it sustains today (www.pininfarina.it). In 1999 the Peugot 406 coupé was launched, endorsed with the prestigious Pininfarina badge, giving it designer status. Even pop stars like J Lo, and actors and TV personalities like Paul Newman have launched and mass-marketed their own ranges of products. Designers and product purveyors have realized the power of utilizing celebrity as an instrument of marketing and branding and celebrities have realized the potential of themselves as brands and commodities

The public endorsement of products by very well-known individuals, such as actors, is of great appeal to consumers. This is largely due to them being perceived as 'real' personalities, people with depth and with flaws. Fashion designers and labels can benefit from this kind of association too, such was the case with Versace and his famed friendship with Elton John. As Princess Diana had successfully and perhaps innocently and unknowingly endorsed the couture house of Dior, through the Dior handbag, Sharon Stone did the same but on a high street level, with Gap. She appeared onstage at the 1995 Oscars in a $22 Gap turtleneck and a black skirt (Snead, 1997 and Bona, 2002). The result of this was tantamount to the Princess Diana and Dior handbag episode, in that Gap's sales of what was referred to in-house as 'the Sharon Stone shirt' went through the roof in the period immediately following the appearance – such is the celebrity's influence on the level of success achieved in fashion and fabric.

Opinion Leadership

The adoption of style is instigated by the few before being adopted by the masses, and the few are what we refer to as opinion leaders, trendsetters and so on. These early adopters are a necessity for the establishment of new fashions and fabrics which the mass market consumer follows. Mary Lynn Damhorst posits that

> For a culture to have fashion there needs to be some expression of individual uniqueness and some willingness to adopt new ideas that others are wearing. Designers may propose and present new ideas, but without a substantial number of consumers adopting their styles, no fashion process can occur. (Damhorst, 2002a)

Peter Chisnall defines opinion leaders as, 'intermediaries between marketers and the mass markets that they wish to influence' (Chisnall, 1994 163). Over time a number of theories have been presented as to how and why we make specific fashion choices and follow popular trends. Theorists such as Hyman (1960), King (1963, 1964), Nystrom (1928), and Carman (1966) have fuelled debate around the subject of fashion consumption; their theories of opinion leadership are based on 'trickle-down', 'trickle-up', and 'trickle-across' principles (Damhorst, 2002b) that suggest ways in which we are influenced to dress (Chisnall, 1994). Their theories intimate why designers, such as Armani, court celebrities in an attempt to persuade them to wear their clothes, and why sporting icons are lured into lucrative sponsorship contracts with sports apparel companies like Nike. Carmen Galindo-Meyer points out that the candid opinions of certain individuals, seen as opinion leaders, are able to influence the actions of the public. This is illustrated by the earlier example of Anna Wintour, and her single-handed halting of grunge in fashion.

> Researchers now know that when the fashion world uses new innovations such as accessories or new materials, wealthy women tend to adopt the fashion innovations first. By wearing and displaying fashion innovations, they promote adoption. In a way, their behaviour serves as opinion leadership whether they talk to other women or not . . . Opinion leaders can increase the adoption rate of innovations because of their positive comments about the innovation or by using the innovation. Obviously, they could also make negative comments on the innovation, and thus decrease the adoption rate. (Galindo-Meyer, 2003)

Sport, Fibre, Fashion and Celebrity

When examining the relationship between sport, fibre, fashion and celebrity, a generational shift towards the casual and the functional in apparel has played a key part in bringing these elements together, and has given sportswear prominence. We can speculate as to who influenced who. Did sport influence fashion and textiles or did fashion and textiles influence sport? Did fabric development encourage fashion designers to create performance led apparel or did fashion designers demand mills to produce more technically advanced fabrics to make dynamic clothes? And how relevant is all of this anyway? The fact is that the fashion and textiles relationship is simply symbiotic; as stipulated throughout this text, each needs the other to survive and thrive; the promotion of one, by association, assists the other. Due to an evolution in lifestyle since the 1970s, sportswear has grown at a phenomenal rate, the expansion of performance fabric sectors and technological innovation has kept pace with lifestyle changes which have focused on the individual and on well-being. Monika Parrinder, in *'things' magazine*, explains the pull of the sportswear industries.

> Sport has an enduring, indeed escalating appeal, because the further we slope into an Americanised lifestyle . . . the more

> sport and active, outdoor leisure have become an ideal. To confirm this, we only have to look at mainstream advertising and its images of healthy, happy, sporting people. Sports stars have replaced film stars as our popular heroes and preferred product endorsers. (Parrinder, 2000)

Today, fabrics within the sports industries are among the most advanced in the world, being driven by the demands of sports professionals (for example, see www.fabriclink.com/pk/Tactel/home.html), and eventually seeping into mainstream sportswear and fashion markets. Innovations in the field of performance textiles have resulted in the formation of 'star' fibres and fabrics which have, over the years, have had and increasing influence on fashion and made Goretex, Kevlar and Coolmax, recognizable as high-performance brand names (Cailliez, 2003: 70).

The growth of sportswear has encouraged fashion designers to muscle in and profit from what was once purely the territory of the technical boffins in clothing and footwear. Most recently, design collaborations in footwear and apparel have been struck up between Yohji Yamamoto and Adidas, and, Paul Smith and Reebok, making the fashion world as 'at home' on the field as it is on the runway. Sport and fashion are becoming one through partnerships such as these, which prove beneficial for both parties involved, as well as encouraging innovations in textile design to consider aesthetics on a couture level. In 1998 Rebecca Voight reported on the couture crossover into sports, in the *International Herald Tribune*, stating

> Miuccia Prada worked with new technical materials and techniques . . . this year she quietly launched a sports collection. 'For us, this isn't Prada Sport, it is just Prada. The only difference is a new label and a different brand name,' she said . . . 'Our idea is to mix technology with normal dressing,' Miuccia Prada said. 'You don't need to disguise yourself as a champion to practice a sport. In the long term, I see formal dressing for special occasions and an increasing number of people wearing sportswear almost all day long.' (Voight, 1998: 20)

The designer tie-ups with sport take fashion and fabric to another level, in terms of aesthetic and functional material innovation, and as a marketing tool, spreading a brand to untapped audiences. Tommy Hilfiger exemplified this through his 1998 sponsorship agreement with Ferrari in Formula One racing which enabled him to reach a European consumer base through affiliation with sport. Parrinder sums up the fated meeting of sport and fashion:

> If you think about it, the sport/fashion match was inevitable, for the two are essentially about the same thing: the pursuit of physical perfection . . . Until recently, sport and fashion have belonged to strictly different fields: sport has been about inner poise and tone, noble and largely male, while fashion has been about external appearances, superficial and traditionally female. (Parrinder, 2000)

History and Styling

History is a constant source of inspiration for many designers in fashion and textiles, archives are scoured and thrift shops raided to find the key to the next collection. Stylists have become a strategic part of the creative process for fashion designers, the traditional role of the stylist has evolved with the sophistication of the fashion system, the stylist does more than just put a 'look' together for a fashion shoot, their career profiles now tend to encompass creative directorships of leading couture houses. Although the stylist may not necessarily be trained in fashion, they are very individualistic, strongly opinionated and have an innate sense of fashion. Tamsin Blanchard revealed in *The Observer*, in November 2002, that styling is essentially all about the 'stylist's attitude' to what is worn and how it is worn, and 'increasingly, the stylists . . . are becoming the fashion designers' eyes and ears on the world – the secret weapon who pounds the streets in search of interesting reference material' (Blanchard, 2002). On behalf of the designer, the stylist sources or understands current materials, concepts and trends, and perhaps adds a little magic of their own, which the designer can refer to or perhaps even 'discuss' in cut and cloth. Effectively, this process allows the stylist to formulate possible preparatory material for a fashion collection. Blanchard's account suggests that the fashion designer and stylist have a very close, almost intimate working relationship where creative exchanges occur. Indeed, both Venetia Scott, creative director for

Marc Jacobs and Katy England, creative director for Alexander McQueen, compare the relationship with their designers as similar to a marriage. England says

> My job here is to inspire him, and help him achieve what he wants to achieve. I can enable his dreams and fantasies to happen. I try to think instinctively how he feels at the moment. It's Lee's (McQueen's) collection, at the end of the day. The spark has to be his spark; I try to get that out. (Blanchard, 2002)

Designers like Vivienne Westwood and John Galliano, choose to reference history in terms of silhouette and fabric choice, reworking a historical source for a millennial year. In *Radical Fashion*, Claire Wilcox describes Westwood's approach to design as: 'looking to the history of the world for powerful design ideas. By the mid-80's she had revived the corset, introduced underwear-as-outerwear and invented the mini-crini. Westwood increasingly referenced history and high culture rather than street style' (Wilcox, 2001: 47). Wilcox goes on to draw similarities between Westwood and Galliano, referring to Galliano as, 'A romantic fantasist, Galliano has drawn on fashions as disparate as those of eighteenth-century France and Shanghai in the 1930's. Aesthetic influences from East Africa and Burma are applied to a sartorial skeleton deriving from Belle Epoque Paris' (Wilcox, 2001: 49).

The stylist's role often combines historical textiles with a contemporary spin, which mirrors the attitude that is present in textile design. Textiles, like fashion has a huge source of reference in private and national archives and in museum collections throughout the world. Textile designers within long-established companies, like Liberty of London (www.liberty.co.uk) or Brunschwig & Fils (www.brunschwig.com), are most often required to either update or repeat vintage formulas that already exist in their extensive archives. Both Liberty of London and Brunschwig & Fils have similar roles in preserving British and American textile history respectively, which is sometimes drawn on by fashion designers. In addition to this, 'Liberty of London has made a collection of its vast number of textile patterns available to Dan River of Virginia, for use in high quality bed linens' (Stone, 2000: 328). Vintage is valuable currency in both textiles and fashion design terms, Lucia Carpio states in *International Textiles* magazine, 'Designers as well as major brands and retail store product developers often visit flea markets and antique markets searching for inspiration from vintage finds.' (Carpio, 2002b: 111). Textile design studios like UK-based Westcott Design and Helena Gavshon, and Paris based, Simone Design, all trade in vintage textile and fashion finds, supplying all levels of the fashion world with source material and inspiration. Peter Westcott of Westcott Design, says:

> This has been hugely successful so there were often frantic dashes into Steinberg and Tolkien, Butler and Wilson and Sheila Cooke the day before a show to top up the vintage collection . . . Each season we see something different to flavour our collection, such as Ossie Clarke pieces, Water-colour '30s Tea Dresses, vintage Dior and Hermes scarves. (Carpio, 2002b: 111)

Fashion designers like Marc Jacobs with the assistance of his creative director, Venetia Scott, will search for and use these sorts of vintage pieces in his collections.

> In the cavernous, overcrowded basement of Steinberg & Tolkien, Venetia Scott, creative director of Marc Jacobs, is in her element. She has been in the King's Road vintage clothing emporium for three minutes and has already snapped up an 80s suede and knit dress by Yves Saint Laurent and a 60s skirt suit. Both items are part of her ongoing research for the New York designer Marc Jacobs, for whom she is another set of eyes and ears. She is often to be found in one of a whole list of small shops, be it Rellik, Sheila Cook, or the costume-hire company Angels & Bermans, all fertile hunting ground for ideas that might end up in one form or another in the much revered and highly influential Marc Jacobs collection. (Blanchard, 2002)

The Future

Forcing change in fashion is a futile exercise, fashions and fabrics are an expression of the spirit of the times. Fashion designers have to be tuned into 'life' as well as innovation in fabric, and their success is dependent on their abilities to sense, anticipate and even initiate changes. Therefore, taking the pulse of society is an integral part of the textile and fashion industries, and it is the responsibility of textile manufacturers, fashion designers and marketers to act on these findings. This is why prediction within these and many other sectors is growing; social and business forecasters 'braille' the culture to reveal what they feel the next big thing will be (Popcorn and Marigold, 2000). Only time can tell if the prophecies of the 'crystal ball gazers' actually materialize; Faith Popcorn and Asa Briggs have demonstrated that credibility only comes with a proven track record in this arena (Chisnall, 1994).

In assessing the interrelationship between fashion and textiles, ultimately, it is the demand for particular finished products that affects the demand from supply industries, such as textiles in the case of the fashion industry. The demands on the supply industries span a diversity of components from the raw fibre to the capital equipment which enables fabric production.

> The demand for capital equipment is also largely subject to the prospective demand for the goods which the plant is able to produce. Because of the lead times involved in the design development, and production of new capital equipment, problems of assessing likely future demand for the resultant products tend to be particularly marked. (Chisnall, 1994: 218)

Developments in production such as 'quick response' or 'just in time', and signs of changing attitudes towards relentless branding, point to the re-evaluation of fashion and textile supply industries. The reduction of mass production in favour of more variety, together with an emphasis on quality and a return to individuality is perhaps a true representation of the future shape of these industries, keeping pace with and reflecting consumer demands. As consumers have grown more sophisticated, they have become increasingly conscious of ethical behaviour, business practice and ecological policies within industry, expecting management decisions to consider these issues and expecting to be informed by the fashion and textile industries themselves. The cultural role of fashion and textiles therefore has an implicit involvement in the way our society and its interests have changed and will change over time.

4

Business and Industry

In this chapter, a number of different perspectives are introduced that relate to the commercial and manufacturing activities of fashion and textiles. Together they provide an insight into what is often treated as one industrial sector – the clothing and textile industry, of which fashion and fashion textiles are a part. A broad appreciation of context is a prerequisite to understanding the economic and manufacturing relationship between fashion and textiles. The reader should be aware that the examples and issues raised here are a tiny fragment of what takes place every day. A further complication or, for many, point of interest about the fashion and textile industries is that each has their own developed relationships with other industries such as the media or interiors. Also in some instances fashion and textile companies and activities are simply part of much larger industrial concerns such as the petrochemical industry. Given these circumstances it is necessary to be alert to the fact that what may be presented as very straight-forward commercial and manufacturing issues take place against a background of industry trends, policy-making and shifts in contemporary culture. This chapter primarily focuses on two subjects – national industrial policies for the textile and clothing industry, and supply chain management. These topics have been chosen because they provide a broad industrial and commercial backdrop to fashion and textiles. They are applicable to each sector individually but equally are the context in which a wide range of interactions take place *between* fashion and textiles. Necessarily many of the issues and themes are of such a generic nature, that the topic of this book, once again needs to be situated within the broader, more flexible, categories of clothing and apparel. There are also references to general industrial subjects and practices, such as collaborative commerce, which are likely to affect the future of fashion and textile business.

Given the variety of business operations between fashion and textiles and within each separate sector, it almost seems a nonsense to treat the two of them as one industry. Equally, it can be difficult to conceive of either as simply one homogenous industry. However, for purposes of industrial strategy and analysis, it remains a common international practice that the clothing and textile sectors are seen as one sector overall. Most national governments, regional organizations and professional associations produce strategy papers, economic reports and projections bracketing textiles and clothing together. A number of these are used in this chapter. Such documents provide a picture of overall trends, manufacturing outputs, imports and exports and so on. They tend to incorporate *quantitative* overviews of industry; individual case studies and profiles; and consider needed changes in industrial practice. Many major national reports use these forms of reporting and the pattern is followed to some extent in this chapter. Trying to find overviews of the *qualitative* nature of clothing and textile industries seems more difficult. For example why or how particular national or regional characteristics emerge seems to be a recent concern; and one mainly of academics rather than industrialists (Breward, Conekin and Cox, 2002 and Colchester, 2003). So too the social and cultural nature of business interaction between fashion and textiles, seems to have been the preserve of journalistic gossip and media entertainment, rather than organizational study. These and many other factors imply a pluralistic industry we are far from understanding. Many different prefixes are accorded to various parts of the 'industry' – 'creative', 'conservative', 'classic', 'mass', 'niche'. The cumulative effect is of an industry that is quite organic in nature. This complex, often haphazard structure is countered in part by what could be deemed to be consensual self-regulation in the shape of forecasting, seasons and other forms of industrial 'calendars' such as annual trade shows. It is also worth reflecting, when reading the rest of this chapter, that in spite of size or difference, small and specialist companies will find themselves involved in, or affected by, the changing nature of supply chains and industrial policies.

Literature about the topics found in this chapter is often written directly for a specialist business audience. Typically, given the changing nature of industry, books provide information about principles illustrated with case studies. It has to be said that there are not many management and business books that look specifically at the clothing and textile industry and the majority seem to have an American focus. An overview of the fashion business has been written by Gini Frings (Frings, 2001) and a critical assessment of the changing nature of fashion business is provided by Terri Agins (Agins, 2000). There are however more books that deal with specific aspects of the industry such as design, manufacture, production and retail. Professional journals and magazines provide commentary by both journalists and those working in industry these are usually produced for a local market. Finally, Internet sites provide daily updates of industry news or permit organizations to explain their products, services or activities. Much of this chapter is based on the latter. There are books that specifically deal with the global economy and the apparel and textile industry (Dickerson and Hillman, 1998) and there is an interesting account of the globalization of the US industry by Ellen Rosen (Rosen, 2002). With regard to mainstream business titles, many recent books deal with the new challenges facing all businesses and industries, such as marketing (Kotler, Jain and Maesinsce, 2002), supply chain management (Burt, Dobler and Starling, 2002), and retail product management (Varley, 2001).

Companies and Countries

In recent years many large corporations, long associated with apparel and textiles, such as DuPont or Coats (previously Coats Viyella) have sought to entirely or partly withdraw from parts of the clothing and textiles industry, while in the process of restructuring their business. This can often result in smaller companies being formed through management buyout or acquisition by a third party. The industrial, corporate and company landscape is always changing and various reasons underlie this such as

- straightforward losses;
- predicted reductions in profits;
- increasing competition in one area of business activity;
- corporate refocusing in order to enter or develop more profitable business activity.

Problems such as these cause any company large or new, small or old to embark on reviewing their business activities or constructing their business plans.

Companies, whether newly formed or long-standing, often need to respond to one or more adverse situations. They might do this by, for example, developing new products; increasing marketing; changing or increasing the number of their business partners, clients and suppliers. The mindset of the twenty-first century professional is also dogged by a few recurrent thoughts – globalization, technology and branding. Collectively these have become the mantra of competition, spurred by the fear that one day the money and jobs will dry up. Of course, to the wholehearted optimist they are, more positively, keys to success. This modern psyche has a strong influence on business practice in fashion and textiles as it does in other sectors. Explicit themes of competition and survival have resulted in various action plans, initiatives and techniques. Over the past few decades logistics and management have increasingly fused with computing and communications. The result is at least two areas of business activity which are continuously and consciously addressed by politicians, journalists and business people alike:

- supply chain management;
- the formulation of industrial policy.

Also during the 1990s other manufacturing and retail concepts came to the fore as a consequence of a simultaneous increase in market competition and technology innovation. The resultant techniques and practices dealt with efficiency, economy, reducing overheads and meeting customer, or buyer, needs more closely.

- 'just in time' manufacture or supply;
- flexible manufacturing;
- customization.

The activities and practices mentioned above are manifested in different ways depending on how companies evolve, how large a company is, product type, manufacturing process and so on. As broad themes of modern industry they can be considered to be 'in the grain' of many of the more specific or piecemeal examples given in this chapter.

It would be difficult to provide descriptions covering every type of company, product or business situation in fashion and textiles. It is true to say that the larger a company gets, the more likely it is to follow a generic model of business. But within fashion and textiles there are also lots of small, medium-sized and even tiny companies. It is possible for companies that start out as a partnership, or as a single entrepreneur, to become huge multinationals five, ten or twenty years down the line. But it is more commonplace that companies are restricted in size by virtue of serving a niche; having a specialism; issues of supply and demand and so on. Reasons vary and are not always straightforward. In, for example, the creative or cultural lifestyle markets, the nature of smaller companies can be influenced by the tastes, interests or ambitions of their owners rather than by strict business considerations. At the other end of the spectrum, a company may be started as a specialist subsidiary, a breakaway or spin-off from the research and development activities of a giant corporation. Obviously there are also significant differences according to sector and product type – retail or manufacture, sportswear or casualwear and so on. Necessarily infinite permutations of product, company, sector and market result in equally complex permutations of the relationship between fashion and textiles.

Individual companies, in formulating their own business plans, must necessarily take account of local conditions and circumstances. In spite of globalization, countries and regions often have quite distinct business and industry characteristics. Three brief accounts of the industries in Israel, Taiwan and South Africa are provided here for comparison. Israel is an example of a successful textile and apparel industry largely dependent on export activity. Features of its industry include a Free Trade Agreement (FDA) with America; adoption of high technology; and exports sold using the 'private label method' (that is to say companies sell their products under somebody else's brandname). Apparel producer Tefron is an example of a company that has used technology to streamline product development and manufacture.

> The company designs, develops, manufactures and markets high-quality men's and women's lingerie and undergarments for export, mainly to the U.S. Complete apparel production – from thread to completed garment – is a one-step operation replacing traditional finishing and cutting methods, as well as conventional sewing processes. With its high tech edge, Tefron is a world market leader in the production of seamless items, and counts as its customers Victoria's Secret, Donna Karan, Gap and Banana Republic . . . (AICE, 2002)

The evolutionary pattern of some apparel companies is that, through technology, automation and expansion, they gradually develop a 'complete' business operation, undertaking all tasks associated with their products. The same can be true of textile companies that grow to offer clothing or fashion products. This kind of expansion is dependent on a smooth flow of information, materials and process within the company. Myra Lu, reporting on the use of technology in Taiwan's clothing and textiles industry emphasizes the growing importance of both design and automation. Commenting on research undertaken by the China Textile Institute,

> Researchers . . . cited automation as an efficient way to cut costs and respond quickly to fluctuations in the market.
>
> One researcher noted that companies should step-up efforts to build enterprise resource planning – a severe form of computer automation popularly known as ERP. About 30 percent of Taiwan's textile businesses have the mechanism. 'The best scenario is to raise the number to 80 percent by 2010,' he said. The ERP integrates all departments and functions of a company onto a single computer system that can answer to these departments' particular demands. (Lu, 2002)

The potential trophy for Taiwan is quick and easy access to China's growing apparel market, in principal supported by maintaining a technological edge. Tsai Jin-shy of the Taiwan Textile Federation observed that China's consumption of apparel is as yet comparatively low, an indicator of future growth

> In the United States, the average annual consumption of clothes per person stands at 28 kilograms. The figure is 17 kilograms in Taiwan, while in China, the number is only five . . . (Lu, 2002)

Countries that seek to grow their clothing industry are not only dependent on economic advantage, certain industrial and market conditions need to apply. For example in South Africa there is a strong local textile industry and a home market for clothing products, both of these factors can provide stability. However, in 1997 South Africa only exported 10 per cent of its total clothing output which amounted to less than 0.1 per cent of world exports. To significantly increase a percentage of this level is a daunting task. As with much of the clothing industry elsewhere in the world, the manufacturing capability is a little difficult to measure and there is an element of the unknown.

> The clothing sector consists of approximately 1,400 formal clothing manufacturers employing some 139,000 workers, constituting approximately 10% of South Africa's manufacturing workforce. If the informal sector is included, there may be as many as 2,000 manufacturers employing some 200,000 workers which could be substantially more according to consultants. (*South African News*, 2000)

Although the country manufactures synthetic fibres and yarns, the major export categories in 1999 were men's cotton trousers and shirts, men's wool suits and women's cotton blouses.

Industrial Policies and Government Strategies

A ten year strategic plan commissioned by the Australian Textile, Clothing, Footwear and Leather (TCFL) Forum, raises some interesting points about the way the textile and clothing industry is perceived, not only in Australia, but more universally. For example their report points out how the disappearance and decline of large-scale traditional manufacturing, sector job losses and economic downturns generates the impression of an industry in severe decline. In turn this has a negative impact on attracting investment, new ideas and 'new people'. The report points out that new markets are emerging and that the pattern of industry has undergone a global change. What amounts to an optimistic thesis in the report is that the perceived 'decline' of the industry is, essentially, the globalization of the manufacturing supply chain. Consequently and in turn the Australian industry is in transition, taking on a new shape. The transition is hampered by the previously mentioned effects of negative perceptions, but also by a reactive rather than proactive industry. Equally the structural nature of the industry is such that it is difficult to implement forceful or purposeful change across the sector. The plans and visions of the Australian strategy – much the same as in all other countries prey to offshore manufacture – are to develop:

- niche markets;
- consumer-oriented industries;
- innovation;
- design;
- branding;
- internationalization;
- collaboration;
- national coordination.

One interesting feature of the Australian strategy is the suggestion that existing segment definition within the industry does little to identify issues, advance analysis or develop strategy.

> Some sectors of the Australian TCFL industry are highly interdependent, such as footwear and leather, or spinning/knitting and clothing. Some sectors appear to have little in common with others, such as sports equipment and apparel pattern making. Some sectors are very profitable and other sectors not so profitable, and views on the way forward vary widely throughout the industry.

> What the various TCFL sectors have in common is the nature of the changes which they are encountering and to which they must respond. They also have in common some significant perception barriers, some of which have achieved the status of myth. (TCFL, 2002)

There is a proposal to newly conceptualize both the sector and its consumer segments, achieving a new model based on 'channels' or types of supply chain. Supply chain models identified are early stage processing; apparel; textiles, leather and furnishings; and technical and nonwoven textiles. Similarly consumer market segments are reclassified as survival, commodity, performance and image. The question, or of course problem, that the Australian strategy raises is that do ordinary people in industry and companies either respond to or remember new theories? The answer most likely is no. Various factors contribute to the distance between a strategy and its realization. Strategies are developed for industry leaders and politicians. The simpler and more accessible an industry is the easier it is for leaders and politicians to instigate or enforce change. However clothing and textile industries by and large are best described as organic and fragmented. So too, many companies struggle to achieve stability, an inherent stimulus for conservatism. What may ultimately prove the case for the Australian strategy is that it is more a prediction than a strategy, a future that state intervention can accelerate through funding regimes, incentives and financial frameworks.

A general theme of many national strategies is helping the small to medium-sized business. The 'help' is often a matter of encouraging or assisting them to adopt new business practices; paving the way for business partnerships; or assistance in marketing and promotion. The help therefore is usually conditional upon what government interprets as industry weaknesses, which of course may change over time. In the UK, a joint government/industry initiative was established built on previous work undertaken by Cranfield University and the University of Salford. Called Industry Forum its specific remit was to deliver a supply chain development programme. One interesting area of its work focused on the business relationship between designers and manufacturers.

> Sales of UK designer clothing have increased from £185 to £650 million over the past four years. However, a major

> factor inhibiting further growth is the difficulty designers face in finding suitable UK manufacturing capacity. (Industry Forum, 2001)

Slightly reminiscent of the Australian call for 'new people' in the industry, in the UK designers are an emergent entrepreneurial group who want to enter the industry but for various reasons are often frustrated. While there has always been a pattern of designers founding companies, a more traditional route was to seek employment in an existing company. One factor now evident is that significant growth in design education coupled with industrial decline has led to large numbers of creative textile and fashion designers with few obvious local employment opportunities as designers. Vocational choices for this group can become quite stark and a proportion therefore elect the route of establishing design-led or designer-maker businesses. A number of problems were identified that hampered the growth of this sector:

- offshore producers not meeting standards and expectations;
- a reluctance of small to medium-sized manufacturers to:
  - work with designers.
  - see them as sources of future business.
  - market themselves to designers.

It was identified that, in general, designers want manufacturers nearby so they can have more control over what is produced. Also three problems needed resolving:

- connecting designers and small supplier;
- how to convince larger companies to supply the design sector;
- raising the profile of small manufacturers.

An example of the work of Industry Forum was its collaboration with Jensens, a small label run by design duo Judi Sheffield and Steven Dell whose customers include Madonna. Jensens produce outerwear and underwear and made-to-order styles under a subsidiary label Jensens Dainties. The company was able to place business with three manufacturers, one Cortessa, a manufacturer of dresses and light unstructured garments had previously worked with Betty Jackson and Whistles.

> Andrew Fearon of Cortessa says, 'We decided to work with Jensens although it was a small business because we recognised that the designers had potential. Now each season, the orders get bigger and the quality of their patterns has improved. Since we started working with the Jensens team they have become more manufacturer-oriented. Jensens is easy to deal with and we get on well.' (Industry Forum, 2001)

Jensens also had the opportunity to compete for the opportunity to produce a knitwear collection for Pringle of Scotland and was selected from a small group of recommended designers. In the longer term it will be interesting to see what the effect of a growing design-led sector might be. Many of the apparel designer-brands that dealt with Industry Forum used experimental or elaborate fabrics and it seems reasonable to suppose that, for example, growth in designer apparel might stimulate a parallel growth in designer fabric. What is certain is that without established and accepted patterns of business – between fashion and textile designers and small manufacturers – the sector will not grow.

At a fundamental level a more general problem for many national industries is that how and where work is situated; its type and duration; and conventional sector employment are all changing. One example is the problem of recruitment. In the recommendations of a strategy document by the UK Textile and Clothing Strategy Group (TCSG, 2000), companies are exhorted (among many things) to

- seek opportunities for student placements;
- establish relationships with schools and colleges to present a positive image of the industry;
- offer competitive employment packages.

Such activities and commitments cannot be lightly undertaken and similar expectations of industry are, no doubt, made elsewhere. However such actions are often a significant draw on resources. Thus many companies may not be able to commit to such policies. The European Commission in an overview of the textiles and clothing industry (Europa, 2002b) stated that more than two million people, mostly women, are employed in the sector in Europe, accounting for 7.6 per cent of the total manufacturing workforce. This no doubt is likely to increase with the accession of further countries to the European Union. Not only is this a significant recruitment issue but probably exacerbated by the structure of the sector. There are estimated to be some 120,000 textile and clothing companies, many small and medium-sized enterprises.

> The average company is family owned, and employs 20 people. Subcontracting accounts for a considerable part of economic activity, varying from 10 to 60% depending on the Member State. These subcontracting activities are spread between a web of thousands of small businesses, often taking the form of cottage industries, which . . . are often highly concentrated in particular regions. (Europa, 2002b)

Such statistics are far removed from the average consumer's perception of fashion and apparel being largely comprised of giant multinationals and brand name producers. The difficulties of change, recruitment and growth that exist in the apparel/textiles sector might be usefully compared with the area of technical textiles. Most advanced industrial nations see this sector as highly successful and an area of future growth. In a report on the US market for technical textiles (Chang and Kilduff, 2002) various convincing factors are identified:

- the size and cutting-edge nature of local demand;
- the high quality of US textile engineers;
- the technical strengths of supporting educational and research institutions;
- the technical and commercial strengths of suppliers.

Such factors are most likely to lead to a highly collaborative technocracy with significant employment mobility across the sector. There is a good relationship with the educational sector and a continuously renewed and refreshed skilled workforce. The nature of the industry itself would already dictate the need for a high degree of logistical management including advanced process control, project management and efficient supply chain management. In a sense the technical textiles sector has many of the features and attributes that strategy documents suggest the apparel manufacturing sector should have. However even with these advantages there are no guarantees.

> a number of factors could hinder successful development of the industry. Firstly, although the technical textile industry is less vulnerable than apparel-related textile industry to global competition, it nevertheless will face growing competition from companies in developing and other industrialized countries. Secondly, there is a lack of information about market needs that obscures opportunities. Thirdly, there are high investment needs for new product development and/or alteration of production and distribution/ marketing set-ups. Finally, in some instances, there are difficulties of breaking into market segments where there are strong relationships between customers and suppliers. (Chang and Kilduff, 2002)

Overall the US textile industry is declining. For December 2002, textile imports rose 44 per cent compared with the same month in 2001. Foreign fabrics and yarns were increasingly supplied by Korea, Taiwan, Pakistan and China, China leading textile imports overall and Korea leading in fabrics. Similarly in January 2003 apparel imports sharply increased, the main beneficiaries being China and Vietnam (emergingtextiles.com, 2003). In such situations the potential for disruption of national fibre- or fabric-clothing supply chains is enormous. Compare the American situation with the ambitions of the Chinese State Textile Industry Bureau and other official bodies when they sponsored a National Conference on Textile Development in 1999.

> The main purpose of holding such an event is to promote the exchange and cooperation between fabric makers and garment makers, encourage domestic textile enterprises to spend more efforts on developing new products, advertise Chinese famous brands and encourage domestic garment makers to use local-made fabrics, so as to realize the three-year target set by the State Textile Industrial Bureau: substitute 3 billion meters of imported with local-made ones and save 3.5 billion US dollars for fabric imports. (CTEI, 2000)

In a survey of the textile and clothing industry in the EU, Werner Stengg divided the industry into high-, medium- and low-quality segments. The high-quality segment (HQS), in the year 2000, accounted for over 50 per cent of EU exports. This segment was dominated by the trade in technical textiles. Most clothing products fell into the medium-quality segment (some 35 to 40 per cent of exports) and this included items such as tracksuits, brassieres, tights and slips, jerseys, cardigans, and shawls and ties. Fashion and design can however add value and, it seems, provide a further definition of quality beyond technical excellence.

> Although the HQS is mainly dominated by textile products, some selective clothing products also revealed a high degree of quality elasticity, for example babies garments, women's suits, or different types of overcoats. For those clothing products it can be assumed that – alongside quality in the more technical sense of the word – a high 'fashion' content enables European exporters to sell large(r) quantities at high(er) prices. (Stengg, 2001)

It is interesting that industrial policy statements often see technical textiles as the salvation of textiles and clothing industries, but also see them as having little to do with the needs of fashion. Technical textiles are deemed to be mainly focused on performance characteristics suited to other industrial applications. Presumably there is a perception or assumption that fashion textiles:

- are primarily about aesthetic expression and comfort;
- have fairly rudimentary and straightforward function;
- are scientifically and technically 'simple';

and that

- the needs of fashion are already amply met by existing textile types and fabrics;
- any new needs will be met by technology transfer, trickle-down or spin-off.

Certainly much of the technical textiles sector looks for new and emergent markets and the fashion textiles sector, in this respect, may look resolved and oversubscribed while also offering proportionately much lower profit gains. This situation seems unlikely to change unless clothing becomes very hi-tech. In which case consumer demand may drive fashion-technical textiles more than the fashion industry itself. Such a change would be dependent on the ability of the fashion industry to implement technological product innovation as much as stylistic variation. Innovation itself bears some relation to company size – larger companies are more likely to innovate but smaller companies are liable to be more efficient at it (Vossen, 2000). Also smaller companies are less likely to feel the benefit of research and development than larger firms. In the fashion sector there are many small and medium-sized companies liable to be dissuaded from developing product technology or who might expect better returns in activities such as brand development or improving manufacture. Currently the most likely attraction of fashion as an outlet for technical textiles is on the basis of the volume of fabric used. If there is a change to this situation it is as likely to be swift and dramatic as gradual and evolving, it may also involve companies or consortia not normally deemed to be in the fashion sector, producing garments or innovative fabric with a definite fashion application.

The relationship between fashion and textiles is often simply that between manufacturer and supplier. However innovation in one or the other will often pull the relationship into much sharper focus. After all, textiles are an essential aspect of clothing and fashion always expects change, variety, and sometimes even surprise in materials. Thus a change in one often demands change or testing in the other. One such example was a joint UK project to develop holographic fabric. The partnership involved the University of Manchester Institute of Science and Technology (UMIST), a textile converter and a fashion manufacturer. Inspired by existing uses of holographic imagery on flat and rigid surfaces, the project aim was to develop drapeable holographic fabric.

> The proposers have identified a vast potential market if the technique could be applied to drapable fabrics such as those used in the fashion industry. This projects sets out to achieve a woven textile substrate with a very flat and even surface . . . New techniques will be developed for transfer and adhesion of holographic images to the surface of this material and the seconding partner an SME fashion manufacturer will be making up trial garments to test for wearability. The new material will achieve an even greater impact for holographic images as a clothing material than it already has because of the natural movement of garments as they are worn. (ERGO, 1998)

Benefits of such collaborations are usually of a different kind for each partner. Not all projects are about creating new techniques and markets, they might equally be about saving costs or reducing waste or inefficiency. In the situation where such projects are underpinned by national or regional funding, specific aims are usually situated within a broader ambition of either industrial development, industrial regeneration, or increasing competitiveness.

Collaborative Commerce

The ever-growing pressures of competition affect all aspects and types of business. From fibre production to fashion retail there is a need to seek economies, increase efficiency and improve communication. The beneficiaries of the increasingly competitive environment have been those that sell logical solutions, automated systems and communications technology. They promise to reduce costs, use resources better, improve the speed of doing business and so on. IT products used throughout the clothing and textiles industry include the likes of supply chain management systems, CAD/CAM systems, retail systems and e-commerce. The current success and stability of the IT industry has allowed it to develop increasingly complex and sophisticated systems. However the types of systems are profoundly dependent on the way computer science and computer engineering evolve. The evolution of science and technology is less predictable and perhaps less straightforward than the growth in the information society. It is this fact that leads to visible 'phases' in technology. The way this has impacted on fashion and textiles is a growth in the use of management and information systems that far outstrips any other ways in which computer-based technologies are used. The IT community, having somewhat failed in its earlier ambitions to create artificial intelligence (Phillips, 1999), has succumbed to the potential of ever-increasing computer memory, number-crunching power and the ubiquitous network. This has led to substantial efforts developing logistical systems that tackle variously organic, random and geographically dispersed aspects of business activity. The result for users and sellers alike is an increasingly confident and universal view that businesses can control their activities in an almost scientific way. That *success* is available through logical process. This is a primary 'sales pitch' of the IT world. It is as well to bear this in mind and take it with a pinch of salt. For the reality is that any technology can be incorrectly used; the more people that have it the less your competitive advantage; belief alone does not create wealth. Nonetheless complex process control and the coordination of information are two major issues identified in many national strategies for clothing and textiles. In particular the issue of supply chain management is seen as critical. Interestingly companies that sell supply chain management solutions are one of the fastest growing IT/consultancy sectors. The American company Salomon Smith Barney undertook some equity research in the area of application software and 'collaborative commerce'.

> We believe the next stage of growth in the enterprise applications software business will be collaborative commerce. Collaboration can have a broad array of meanings in today's business environment . . . We estimate the size of collaborative markets totalled $5.8 billion in 1999 and forecast it to grow to $36.5 billion in 2004. This represents a CAGR of 44% over five years . . . We believe collaborative applications will begin being adopted in the next 12-18 months . . . we believe collaborative commerce is the next wave in application software. (Salomon Smith Barney, 2001)

The company also identified three areas of application software or collaborative applications as being those that define this 'nascent industry': knowledge management, supplier relationship management and product life-cycle management. Two highly successful companies that fall into the category are San Francisco based Freeborders (www.freeborders.com) and Atlanta-based Manhattan Associates (www.manh.com). Both companies are deeply involved in the increasingly critical use of IT to manage economic performance in the apparel industry. Manhattan Associates is one of the fastest growing companies in America and offers a range of software applications for retailers focused on supply chain and warehouse management and delivering goods to retailers. It is the largest company in the warehouse management systems sector, and has over 870 customers in over 1,300 implementations worldwide. Its expertise is defined as 'retail supply chain collaboration'. Freeborders, in comparison works more broadly across the supply chain management sector but has a more specific focus on the apparel, textiles and soft furnishings sector. As such it provides an interesting window on the use of IT in the sector and trends in both retailing and supply chains.

Freeborders describes itself as a company that delivers software enabling its customers to 'streamline product development processes and collaborate more efficiently'. It promises reductions in product cycle times, and design and development costs, helping customers 'meet the ever-increasing demand to bring products to the market quickly'. The company's Product Lifecycle Management software, and Collaborative Product Management software, are used by over 350 retailers, brands and manufacturers around the world. The company has a prestigious list of customers – Liz Clairborne, Gap, Levi Strauss & Co., Nike, Saks, Burlington Industries, Dillards, J. Crew and many more. Customer interests include both manufacture and retailing and range across the various fashion and textile markets. In a very stimulating article, first published at www.just-style.com, Steve Pearson and David Knudsen of Freeborders provide a concise analysis of recent trends and strategies in the apparel business and suggest where tomorrow's gains and productivity can be sought (Pearson and Knudsen, 2003). Looking at the entire apparel product life cycle from manufacture to retail, they point out that top brands and retailers have squeezed the maximum benefits out of activities like offshore production and retail information systems.

> At top companies per-unit product costs are extraordinarily low, inventory and distribution are managed in a far more efficient manner, and pricing and markdown strategies have dramatically improved net margins. (Penison and Knudsen, 2003)

They then propose that the 'next step' involves improving the front end of the process: planning, product design and product development. Improving and managing the design process is, of itself, not a new idea. Ways to improve and manage design – avoiding expense and error, speeding the process, properly integrating it into a business context – have long been the object of much design research and have recently spawned the discipline of Design Management (Jerrard, Hands and Ingram, 2002). Pearson and Knudsen develop a thesis of future practice that builds on recent trends such as last-minute and flexible manufacturing. They suggest that currently used product data management (PDM) systems might be evolved into systems based on total product life cycle – from design, through manufacture to retail. PDM systems are themselves the consequence of a gradual evolution, therefore a further evolution is, in itself, unlikely to be contentious. Without overly digressing into the history of CAD and IT use in the apparel industry, it has in many respects been markedly different to that in say the graphic design industry. At an early stage, technology providers such as Gerber (www.gerbertechnology.com) and Lectra (www.lectra.com) developed 'branded' PCs and offered increasingly integrated suites of software applications. The result is that the metrics of design, manufacture and production – the data and product history of a garment – has long been methodized. Such data is also often further integrated into publishing, financial and stock control applications and so on.

> With the rise of internet technologies, however, a new class of applications is emerging in product development – enabling greater management of a wider number of product-related activities. Known as Product Lifecycle Management or PLM, these applications better support collaboration both internally and externally with supply chain partners, something PDM systems typically did poorly. PLM is helping enable best-practice processes, while tying line and product creation back to the financial plan and the global supply chain. (Jerrard et al, 2002)

The overall ambitions of collaborative commerce (or c-commerce) are in a sense to move the consumer's deliberative act of buying, as near as possible, into one of commissioning; general retail and point of sale data triggering the supply chain in the process fulfilling all parties' dreams and changing 'they might buy' into 'they want to buy'. This would involve what Pearson and Knudsen call 'post demand product execution'. The authors' cite the way Dell builds computers to order as an example. The UK-based company Stevensons Garment Dyers provide a good example of how collaboration across the apparel supply chain can benefit all participants. Stevensons in conjunction with the UK government and industry sponsored Industry Forum initiative, undertook a research project investigating rapid response techniques.

> The Industry Forum developed a model to demonstrate the benefits of domestic (quick response) processing to give customers superior performance. Research revealed that forecasting errors were extremely high – typically only 70% of orders have forecasting errors of less than 25%. Other research demonstrated that colour is a key determinant of consumer demand and forecasting error for this SKU was even higher.
>
> To obtain accurate data, the Industry Forum project team researched the availability of a knitted, yarn dyed garment, by colourway and geographically in 11 outlets (including 3 flagship stores) across the UK. The results revealed significant forecasting errors and demonstrated the financial and other benefits of local, dyed-to-demand garments. (Industry Forum, 2002)

The logic of rapid response, c-commerce, flexible manufacturing and mass-customization as tools of competition and survival seem the inevitable end-game of information management and automation in the fashion and textile industries. However they are a technocratic set of solutions aimed at meeting and stimulating consumer demand prior to being the means of simply increasing profitability. As we shall discuss, this raises questions about their ultimate effectiveness because consumer demand is driven by many forces.

Technocracy versus Consumerism and Fashion

Some significant questions are raised by the idea of handing over more and more manufacturing and design 'control' to consumers. The structural consequences of this for the textile and clothing industries are unforeseeable, and as a phase of industrial development it is a relatively recent ambition. There are no early signals of the longer-term effects. For example there might be industrial and employment benefits. Quick response, customized and commissioned goods might stop or even reverse the trend of offshore manufacture in some sectors. The path of business would be smoothed, stressful and expensive mistakes in supply, manufacture and retail, done away with and so on. But there may be downsides;

for example, what about creativity? The fashion scene may become no more than a carousel, perpetually recycling old product data, looking for statistical certainties in retail choices. Designers may tire of being no more than managers of data permutations. On the other hand, it is clear that much design activity has always been of a limited type, particularly that which takes place in the mainstream of industry.

> I cannot emphasise enough the kind of creativity that most of us in business deal with. It is most often relatively minor rearrangements of things that have already existed. In the language of science, we are most often dealing within the state of the art, rather than with the basic kind of research that Dr. Shockley refers to when he talks of inventing transistors. (Peterson, 1965)

However even if design is not at odds with the concept of a consumer-driven system of apparel manufacture the 'thesis' of fashion in many ways is. Dependent as fashionability is on social movements, mass- and sub-cultures (essentially collectivism of one kind or another), fashionability thus seems almost the opposite of a personalized and customized retail mechanism. Another issue is that consumers have over the years showed a strong ability to reject the best laid plains of industry. In lifestyle and fashion sectors, many different factors can influence why something is fashionable or unfashionable at a particular time. Fashion 'statements' can also be a reaction to, or rejection of, conformity, tradition or the norm. That garments or styles become unfashionable is a commonsensical observation. Equally consumers are often resistant to being 'manipulated' by retailers and corporations. Also they tire of, or do not believe, brand identities and associations. Geraldine Bedell, commenting on Nike's loss of market position and a plunge in their share values, points out the significant influence of a youth-oriented fashion image.

> On both sides of the Atlantic, however, the story is the same: it's not easy for a global company whose trainers are on every high street and in every suburban mall, to remain fashionable. Young people like brands that are (a bit) rebellious, and Nike is perilously close to being the establishment.

> Levi's faced a similar problem a few years ago, when jeans began to be something your dad, maybe even your granddad, wore. Levi's responded by producing garments that were difficult to wear and distributing them more exclusively. A shop called Cinch, just off Carnaby Street, sell nothing but Levi's; it is in fact a Levi's store. But it's not branded as such, and you won't see the jeans and jackets and denim skirts in there anywhere else. (Bedell, 2003)

Bedell's statement is an interesting one, but perhaps all too easily coloured by our suspicions of business and marketing. Since the 1980s consumers have become increasingly aware, often sceptical and sometimes cynical about the attempts of brands to reinvent themselves through PR and advertising. Consumers and those who defend them are also equally wary of computer technology being used to 'get at' them. However the stakes have changed for many companies, global competition, the general availability of technology solutions and an increasingly sophisticated consumer market, create a new environment where business abruptly clashes with culture on the battlefield of retail. In this environment simplistic marketing responses, data management or the use of technology will do little to maintain the long-term survival of companies. Consumer culture now challenges fashion and textiles companies to provide products that are not simply 'value for money', 'well-made', 'stylish' or 'exclusive'; instead the modern consumer increasingly seeks deeper value in the products they buy, particularly if the product relates closely to their own identity. These values are less one-dimensional than they have been in the past, they revolve around criteria such as our sense of authenticity or genuineness, virtue, affection or indeed their antithesis. Such complex qualitative descriptors of product value are of course hard to incorporate logically within a data-driven model of commerce, whether it is one aimed at customization or at fashion trends. The net effect of this situation is twofold: one outcome is the cultural reaction of companies to this 'advanced consumerism', the other effect is on the ability of companies actually to understand their consumers or predict their behaviour.

Taking the first of these – companies' reactions to advanced consumerism – Levi's, as mentioned, has taken visible steps to move into what we might call 'next-generation retailing', but their stratagem seems far more sophisticated than just buying in technology and opening exclusive and elusive, themed boutiques and concept stores, such as Cinch, Nim or the recently unveiled Rivet. The company's literature about its products has become a hybrid of humanist and liberal philosophy that incorporates complex and interwoven themes concerning an aesthetic of garment construction and material choice, added to this is the heritage of their 'creative medium', denim, this is finally coupled with the heritage of their company. For example Levi's Red collection is described by the company as 'their brand's denim laboratory', its themes are as follows:

> Mirroring the new mindset of the opinion leading consumer and reflecting the streak of self-determination which defines today's youth, Levi's® RED™ creates the future in denim and spurs the next zeitgeist . . . Opinion leading consumers remain optimistic but value integrity and core ethics more than ever, along side careful consideration, responsibility, substance, genuine craftsmanship and products with a story to tell.
>
> Opinion leading consumers desire integrity and authenticity as well as originality and exclusivity, embracing the values of the cultural creative. Merely impressing others and looking good on the outside is no longer enough . . . Combining sex appeal with personality, individuality with freedom and pride in personal identity and belonging to a multi-cultural society, Levi's® RED™ offers integrity, fresh innovation and a unique heritage. (Levi Strauss, 2003)

Given the complexity of much of Levi's product literature it is hard to believe it is 'faking it', it seems more reasonable to assume that Levi believes that loyalty is a two-way contract and that brand viability and longevity is won by reaching out that bit further to the consumer. In essence this is a different sort of customization, one that looks to be about giving the consumer more of what they intellectually or emotionally seek from fashion. The psychology underlying such a brand-consumer relationship doesn't seem entirely compatible with the principles of collaborative commerce or mass-customization because the consumers, in part, become an audience, 'waiting for' and enjoying a performance of design. They don't want to create much of the design choice for themselves. In short they want fashion as cultural entertainment.

Figure 4.1
Rivet, Selfridges, Birmingham. Courtesy Levi Strauss.

With respect to 'knowing your customers' (the second thorn in the side of a totally technocratic solution), the net effect of consumer behaviour is that retail data about consumers' purchases and preferred product characteristics can always, and quickly, become redundant. As for fashion culture, its play with iconic garments and fabrics is not neutral but one laden with value judgements or even political sentiment. The language of fashion is often linked to other social realities that can activate or disrupt retail activity. The consumer shopping for apparel or fashion may thus make decisions not based on formal garment properties. Indeed their decisions may be entirely unlinked to 'retail' descriptors of choice, taste or trend and be rooted in deeper sociocultural currents.

> Meanwhile the chequered keffiyeh – an ordinary, everyday head covering for millions of Arab men – has become the hottest fashion accessory in Japan. In Tokyo, where teenagers wear it around the chin, often with camouflage T-shirts and army-style trousers, it has acquired military connotations. One result, perhaps, of worldwide TV coverage of the Palestinian intifada. (Whitaker, 2001)

Unforeseeable, sometimes swift, consumer interest in a garment or look has implications for the stock on offer and the 'verity' or predictive potential of data held about consumers' choices. Fashionability is certainly a factor that can maintain and stimulate consumer interest in mainstream products and services. The irony is that equally it can do the opposite. The mechanisms and logistics of customization in many ways seem opposite to the idea of fashion and/or the survival of fashion brands. Ultimately we don't know what collaborative commerce (or any other technology solutions), backtracking from retail, will bring. It will undoubtedly be pursued by major corporations and companies operating in the mass market. It may also prove more appropriate for some types of clothing than others. It is also certain that being 'outside' or 'inside' what we might call 'the world of data chains' may come to have a significant meaning for any manufacturer, retailer or consumer.

The Store

In a sense many of the ambitions of coordinating the supply chain to retailing will depend on new retail technology and consumer reactions to it. A technology called radio frequency identification permits data to be stored in clothing tags. The system has been used in Prada's store in Manhattan's SoHo neighbourhood. Sales associates can find out such things as stock levels or the material composition of a garment using handheld computers. The so called 'smart tags' are typically in use in tracking goods in warehouses, so their introduction into the retail environment potentially moves closer to the concept of product life-cycle management. Various criticisms of the use of such technology can be raised, particularly if data about customers' shopping behaviour is held. To some extent these mirror existing general concerns about computer technology, privacy, and intrusive or aggressive selling techniques. The up-side is that sales staff can be more helpful and efficient. In the Prada store, customers can hang up their chosen goods in boxes and then see the clothes and accessories projected onto a plasma screen in the dressing room, by using a touch screen they can then mix and match their chosen items or find out more information about them. There is even talk of one day offering customers virtual wardrobes over the web. Integrating such technology into retail environments raises lots of interesting possibilities for shoppers, staff and company. But like many innovations to do with new technology, sometimes the vision is easier to achieve than the reality. Sales associates at the Prada store had trouble with the wireless tag scanners; shoppers were unaware of the technology or how it worked.

> Eric Wong, 24, of New York, said that although he was impressed with the store's high-tech features he has a 'better shopping experience' at Barney's, which carries Prada and has a more intimate feel.
>
> 'Overall, it seems that the technology wasn't used to enhance the consumer experience, but help the sales people on the floor,' said Mitch Kates, a principal with Kurt Salmon Associates, a retail consulting firm. 'The technology is cool, but it can also be intimidating.' (CNN, 2002)

Prada's commitment to retail innovation is unquestioned (Koolhaas, 2001) but it seems that if the retail environment is to become a high-tech zone, some older and proven criteria need to be retained. The American National Textile Center has funded a project that looks into the role of emotion in the success of global textile product retailing. Run by Jai-Ok Kim and Sandra Forsythe of Auburn University and Qing L. Gu of Dong Hwa University, the project aim is to develop a model that can describe how shoppers' emotions stimulate store loyalty, as well as attract their initial interest. Based on studies in Shanghai and Korea it was found that companies like Carrefour, Wal-Mart and Costco, as well as local discount/hypermarket stores, use textiles and clothing products to differentiate themselves from each other and to create customer excitement and satisfaction. A 'feeling of excitement experienced during shopping was the important emotional response linked to store loyalty' (NTC, 2002). Some of the implications of the study are that the textile and clothing industry may ultimately need to adapt as much to changing global retail opportunities as it has to a global manufacturing market. This will undoubtedly provide further incentives for manufacturers to be proactive in establishing coordinated yet highly flexible relationships with retailers.

> Consumer purchase behaviours in these markets have been greatly altered since the economic and financial market turmoil in 1990s, with more consumers patronizing discount

> stores than upscale department stores or specialty stores. As a result, it has provided unprecedented opportunities for the entry of multinational discount stores or formats. Hence, it is critical for US apparel/textile manufacturers to capitalize on such inroads of multinationals or US discount/hypermarket stores by identifying the most appropriate US products to be distributed through these channels in international markets. (NTC, 2002)

Information and Technology

Identifying 'channels' and products and putting one with the other is, of course, the ancient premise of any market. In the global business environment, not only is such information key, it is in itself a new type of commodity. Sometimes information is sold, sometimes it is free. Information is variously broadcast, narrowcast and packaged in all kinds of ways in all kind of media. Information can swiftly move from being secret and valuable to being public and given away free. The value of business information is often tied to time, and the business opportunity the information represents. However, in general, significantly more business information is free. This latter has resulted in the construction of substantial industry websites offering views of virtual economies and business communities mirroring the real world they represent, such as the Hong Kong Trade Development Council's TDC Business Infocentre (http://infocentre.tdc.org.hk). Also there are business-to-business sites that support journalistic or quasi-journalistic content such as Global Source's e-commerce site www.globalsources.com. As mentioned in the previous paragraphs collaborative business activity conducted using IT is liable to be a major growth area. But there is possibly a more general trend of collaboration in business that is also evident in other sectors. Such collaborations often involve not only legal arrangements but a degree of ordinary trust based on the prospect of mutual benefit. The trust however is not always easily come by when money is involved. However the Internet and global competition have, it seems, jointly created an impetus for a kind of collectivism, possibly even a kind of corporate tribalism. The benefits include the opportunity to indulge in varieties of protectionism. Also to create closed information communities. For many large companies there is no simple vertical supply chain. In these circumstances a 'quiet pond' with a limited number of trusted business partners, sharing information resources, possibly doing business 'as and when', looks very attractive. These new types of consortia will use a variety of c-commerce and supply chain management software to coordinate their activities. The history of e-commerce during the time of this shift in business culture underscores the move to consortia. Prior attempts to offer supply chain management through e-commerce sites has moved to providing intranet/network based equivalents.

> Sources indicate that approximately 1,500 e-marketplaces were set up during the late 1990s and that about 90 percent have since gone out of business. Vendors have resisted e-marketplaces, not wanting to add middlemen to already complex customer relationships . . . most e-marketplaces have had difficulty in developing successful supply chain management systems and in persuading clients to adopt those systems. Many companies such as Verticalnet Inc., which operate industry specific e-marketplaces, have largely transitioned into e-marketplace software as a means to providing solutions for supply chain management. (Global Sources, 2002)

While e-marketplaces have found it difficult to prosper, overall companies that sell IT reliant solutions to the clothing and textiles sector can benefit from a fractured and disparate industry as much as from a cohesive industry with fewer companies in it. Although individual sectors or national industries may boom or bust the overall number of actions and activities within the textiles and clothing sector must have increased. This is of course impossible to verify, but the general expansion of the global economy, coupled with the consumer's demand for increasing choice, has presumably led to an exponential increase in information 'transactions'. Thus if one company breaks into ten, there is more rather than less information activity. If a nation's business moves from manufacturing to retail, once again, there is more rather than less, information processing to be done and so on. Thus the IT sector benefits from all our socio-economic behaviour. While generally individual IT companies may be very competitive, as a global industry it is more buffered than most. However the bursting of the dot com bubble did much to sharpen the industry's responses. The demand for better control of the supply chain, industrial collaboration, and the closing of the gap between retail and manufacturing have met with various reactions from traditional suppliers of manufacturing technology and software. The actions and announcements of companies that supply the clothing and textile industry, in many ways, directly reflect the concerns and preoccupations of the industry itself. Lectra Systèmes, the French supplier of CAD/CAM systems upgraded its software offerings and systems to include:

- prototyping;
- management of fashion collections and product development cycles;
- data exchange through the supply chain;
- cutting room management;
- customized apparel production;
- sell before producing;
- colour management and communication.

These align or bear similarities with some of the project descriptions of the American Textile (AMTEX) Partnership, a government/industry consortium; overall reflecting what are increasingly the research norms of industrial development, focusing on customization related to retail.

- demand activated manufacturing architecture;
- rapid cutting;
- sensors for agile manufacturing;
- electronic embedded fingerprints.

Lectra identifies seven strategic challenges facing its customers including reducing time to market; dealing with globalization; securely communicating across the supply chain; and mass customization. Interestingly Lectra states that it has considerably revamped its technology and services to provide 'new technological answers' for its customers. In 2000 Lectra entered into a strategic partnership with Tecmath a German-based software company specializing in body-scanning, human modelling and e-commerce. The two companies seeking to develop integrated body measurement solutions for mass customization based on the premise that 'mass customization defines a paradigm shift for the apparel and fashion related industries, from design through retail'. They identify mass customization as a key factor of the 'new economy', where the Internet and a total systems model are applied to the life of a manufactured item. In this situation:

- retailers are seen to minimize costs and improve customer relations;
- manufacturers reduce the risk of investment and inventory;
- designers offer more styles and combinations;
- information on customer preferences are vertically available in the entire textile chain.

It seems almost ironic that at a time when the complexity of the global economy gives rise to industrial confusion and business hazard, there is an almost universal consensus on 'the way forward' for mainstream clothing and textile industries. Everyone it seems – from retailers to policy-makers, from manufacturers to the suppliers of equipment and software – agree that remarkable control of an individual product will solve 'the problem'. Currently it seems there are few voices of scepticism countering this view. If the nature of 'the problem' were simply about locally saving losses in manufacture, investment, etc. the proposed solution might well work. However, for the majority of nations and companies, 'the problem' is also about gaining or securing advantage in the marketplace. And ultimately if everyone in the marketplace uses the same 'solutions', market advantage will be difficult to gain other than by conventional means, such as capital investment and good management.

From the point of view of aesthetics and style it is interesting to conjecture what 'the way forward might bring'. Customization and supply chain management are themes driven by business, managerial and technological culture. The product life-cycle management approach suggests that designers will be able to offer more variations of product, using what might be called a 'recombinant' approach to design by adapting and recycling product data. It may prove that certain formal properties are 'cheaper' to offer as factors leading to design variation than others, for example colour. This in a sense is a restrictive model of customization, but the opposite is also possible. Customization may prove to do for apparel what fully automated factory production did for other sectors, not only did it reduce factory workforces and labour costs, it permitted a technological evolution of manufacturing processes. In the automobile industry this seems to have introduced (or at least reintroduced) the possibility of quite fanciful design. To believe that technology produces 'greyness', mediocrity or the sub-standard proved to be a nineteenth-century fear. However that technology produced the same cultural menu everywhere was a twentieth-century observation. Whether customization and c-commerce prove to be the antithesis of fashion or spur it on, only time will tell.

5 Consumers

The role of the fashion and textile consumer is a complex one. Consumers are influenced by a number of factors, some of which do not necessarily fit what we might call rational decision-making. Patterns of consumption are all influenced by the interrelationships between opinion and behaviour; the interactions of group and personal behaviour; and the slight or intense effects of culture on consumption. Personal consumption largely takes place in a social and cultural environment. The social and cultural norms which influence personal textile and fashion consumption will be explored in this chapter. Each of us, through our buying choices, affects in some small way the expansion or decline of fashion and textile providers, such as raw material producers, assemblers and retailers. The ramifications of understanding consumer preferences and buying patterns is therefore important to the whole fashion and textile industry. 'Consumer behaviour', as defined by Stephen Sutton in *The Social Psychology of Consumer Behaviour*, 'consists of the psychological and social processes people undergo in the acquisition, use and disposal of products . . . services . . . ideas . . .

and practices' (Sutton, 2002). A number of groups, originating in the 1970s, have shaped the advance of consumer research, from a social psychological perspective. These organizations were the Association for Consumer Research, ACR (www.acrweb.org), founded in 1970, promptly followed in 1974 by the rather more academic *Journal of Consumer Research*, JCR (www.journals.uchicago.edu/JCR/journal/available.html), which has more recently been joined by the *Journal of Consumer Psychology* (www.journalofconsumerpsychology.com).

How and why consumers behave and consume is investigated in a multitude of ways and the extensive information gathered is then collated and analysed (Zaltman, 2003). This task is usually carried out by large specialist consumer profiling organizations like, for example, Teenage Research Unlimited (www.teenresearch.com), a marketing research company whose expertise lies specifically in tracking teenage trends. Large companies also conduct and analyse their own consumer research in-house, especially when they are considering expansion into new areas. Consumer research usually encompasses anthropological, psychological and sociological perspectives in explaining the whys and hows of consumption, as culture and social interactions play a fundamental role in the process. These companies track consumer behaviour according to various criteria expressed by a client, and forecast future trends which both industry and consumer become aware of. Typically, they conduct meticulous interviews or use focus groups. Some carry out tests, trials and surveys in an attempt to glean information about the consumer. This consumer profiling identifies patterns of interactions amongst groups and subgroups within the general structure of society. Issues such as cultural ideals and values, social desires and inhibitions are bound to affect consumer decisions. Both public and private sector organizations are increasingly dependent on specific knowledge about the pattern of the individual's consumption of fashion and textiles. In turn this can have a significant impact on the economic and social life that these organizations influence.

Marketers realize that we buy fashion and textile products on more than the merely functional basis of providing physical protection against the elements. It is on this basic foundation that a complex network of motivations exists for consuming specific fashion in specific colours and fabrics, which appeal on a tactile and visual level. Also consumers seek fashion which fits in with current styling trends. Any one of these elements is inextricably linked to the others. For instance, the 'right' fashion design but in the 'wrong' fabric will not sell, and vice versa, the combination has to be just right and match current market conditions for the consumer to buy. Hence the need for the analysis of fashion and textiles in relation to the consumer. Thus far, overall, the study of fashion and so textiles, relative to consumption, has been far too simplified, largely focusing on either women being victims of developments in silhouette or more recently as a display of empowerment through identity. In reality, things are rather more complex and the consumption of fashion and textiles is very much ingrained in the social structure of the world (Entwistle, 2003). Generally, consumption in fashion and textiles can be aligned with social events. Entwistle, in her assessment of fashion and its relation to associated systems says

> The analysis of fashion is therefore calling for an integrated approach, which deals with it as a cultural industry. Such an approach would overcome . . . division between production and consumption and in doing so give a more complex account of how 'fashion' as an aesthetic discourse on dress is produced and disseminated through the practices of a whole number of agents in a complex chain of relations . . . Thus, when we speak of fashion, we speak simultaneously of a number of over-lapping and interconnecting bodies involved in the production and promotion of dress. (Entwistle, 2003)

These 'interconnecting bodies' between fashion and the consumer, of course, include the textile business and intermediary organizations in media, trends and prediction, production and distribution. So, although the fashion and textile industries operate independently from one another, they are at the same time very closely linked via these industries, in addition to the wider economic and cultural forces they share. Fashion designers and the textile industries cannot ignore consumers; after all, fashion and fabrics on the catwalk only become popular once they have been disseminated and consumed, which is where the consumer's role takes effect. Consumer activity is very important to all sorts of organizations, for textiles and fashion it signals changes in lifestyle and attitudes which, when analysed and applied to the fashion and textiles industries, provide indicators which can influence the direction an organization takes and helps businesses make the right decisions. Fashion combines fibres and meanings, fabrics and signs – none can exist without the others and together they create prosperity. The textile industry is the primary component of the fashion industry and both are at the whim of the consumer. In general, fashion companies and by implication fabric producers adapt to cultural shifts and changing preferences in consumer tastes at least every six months in order to satisfy consumer demands. While some companies may be more directional or be known for a particular, relatively unchanging product, the majority have to respect the typical consumer.

Value for Money

Consumer research, in tracking and profiling the consumer, serves its purpose in that it spots where consumer trends occur, analyses and reports on them. This equips the appropriate subsector of industry to react accordingly and in the long term, benefit. One such change, traced in consumer attitudes has been the growth of casual dress in the workplace. This change has had ramifications on fashion and textiles which has included 'value for money' issues in apparel for the consumer. Principally due to the dress-down or 'casual Friday' culture in corporate America during the mid 1990s, casual trousers soon became a key element of the office wardrobe in companies like Hewlett Packard and IBM. It wasn't long before the trend crossed the Atlantic to be adopted by British corporations like Arthur Andersen (although the casual Friday culture is showing some signs of reversal (Bartlett, 2002)). The same era saw a general shift in dress towards jeans, T-shirt and trainers culture, which coincided with developments in comfortable and functional fabrics. This attitudinal shift away from 'high fashion' was a result of the consumer becoming sharper and more alert to particulars such as quality of fabric and value for money. Consumer groups and magazines now realize that the public not only demand performance and value for money from their electrical appliances but they also demand style and durability from their clothes.

The demand for value for money is evident from the numerous wear and tear tests that consumer magazines like the American *Consumer Reports Magazine* have carried out in recent years on everything from khakis (a common term for casual cotton twill trousers) to blue jeans to hosiery to polo knit shirts. In addition consumer magazines reveal the properties and performance of fibre and fabric constituents of clothing, such as Spandex 'Lycra), Cashmere and Pashmina. The results of such tests culminate in rating specific brands according to their value for money, in August 2002 *Consumer Reports Magazine* judged the best fit in blue jeans. The criteria used included not only the way they were made and deviations in size from one pair to another, but also the quality and characteristics of the denim, such as shrinkage and handle (*Consumer Reports*, 2002). The results of these sorts of evaluations can be quite revealing; for example, in March 1999 the magazine put khakis to the test. In response to the dress-down culture in the workplace, a number of retail analysts had forecast that over the next ten years khakis would become as popular as jeans. In view of this khakis were assessed and the headline revealed trial findings, '$19 Farahs held up better than $55 Ralph Laurens and looked as good after laundering'. *Consumer Reports* goes on to say, 'our tests prove that you don't have to spend top dollar for top quality. In fact, two inexpensive pairs – men's and women's versions of the J.C. Penney Authentic St. John's Bay, each $24, are CR (*Consumer Reports*) Best Buys' (*Consumer Reports*, 1999). Earlier still, during a 1997 value for money trial, the magazine gave its highest ranking for men's polo knit shirts to Honors, a store brand that sold for only $7 at Target, but whose quality scored well above those versions by Polo Ralph Lauren at $49, Tommy Hilfiger at $44, Nautica at $42, and Gap at $24 (Agins, 2000: 12).

Revelations like these educate and inform the consumer who becomes aware of the various nuances of quality and performance of a garment; their response to fabric quality and performance within a fashion garment is as relevant as their response to fashion itself. As consumers become wise to issues of worth and function, they subsequently grow to be clever shoppers, perhaps driven by value for money rather than labels. Fashion's origins lie in Parisian couture; now, however, fashion represents a world of commerce gratifying the whims of the consumer in the marketplace. The fashion gauntlet has passed from couturier to the consumer and business world and it seems the only route to survival is to join the party. Those who have succeeded in this arena have become iconic figures in the fashion world, they are flexible and reinvent themselves, keeping pace with changes in lifestyles and attitudes, diversifying and integrating vertically and horizontally. Their ranges span mass market to exclusive high fashion and labels such as Ralph Lauren, Tommy Hilfiger, Armani and Calvin Klein venture into related markets like interiors. This diversification is not a new phenomenon; it has existed for many years in the cosmetics and perfumes industry, Coco Chanel's launch of perfume being a classic and much cited example (Newman and Kendrick, 1998). Since then, fashion has permeated many other industries as listed above.

The Designer and the Consumer

Consumers, markets and lifestyles are all influencing factors on fabric choices for fashion designers. However, the fashion industry has a more obvious relationship with the consumer than the textile industry; it is through this liaison that the textile designer and industry acquires information about the consumers preference in fabric. It is clear that those high fashion designers interested in what the consumer wants will have a better chance of survival in the financially driven fashion world, and it appears, as we will see, that fabric selection within this framework has as much importance as silhouette. During an interview, Bernard Arnault, chairman of the luxury goods empire LVMH (www.lvmh.com), highlights the metamorphosis of fashion changing from a creatively driven business to a financially lucrative one. He says of Michael Kors, 'He goes to the Celine shop to talk to the customers. The reason to be a designer is to sell. Fashion is not pure art. It is creativity with the goal of having as many customers as possible wearing the product' (Newman and Kendrick, 1998: 52). This reaffirms the importance of the consumer to the fashion and associated industries. In addition, Arnault's comments also reflect the reality that commerce has overtaken fashion; in today's fashion world profit margins are as important as the length of hemlines.

As established, the fashion designer's interaction with textiles is fundamental to their practice. It is in the designer's interest to find out whether their customer prefers silk to rayon or cotton to polyester. In their quest to get to know their customer, designers like Donna Karan for instance, perform their own type of market research by maintaining contact with their clientele through regular appearances at trunk shows. Attending trunk shows and being aware of the customers' preferred tastes helps when selecting fabrics for future designs. Trunk shows are by and large an American phenomenon (see Maneker, 2000 and *Taipei Times*, 2002), and for the most part they have remained so, although they have begun to attract new British designers such as Ashley Isham. As James Sherwood reported, 'Isham is hitting New York and Palm Beach with a series of trunk shows that get his made-to-order pieces from runway to reality' (Sherwood, 2003). Once established, trunk shows are useful in that they give the designer a chance to view their designs on the women who actually buy and wear their clothes in different parts of the country, and this assists the designer in discovering what is successful and what isn't within their collections.

The way in which a fashion designer, through a successful line, can raise the demand for a specific fabric literally overnight is quite remarkable. This was exemplified by Donna Karan in the 1980s. Her biggest accolade during that era was the invention of the 'body'. *Vogue* called it 'one of the most practical items of clothing to come out of the Eighties, Donna Karan is now one of the most recognisable names in American fashion' (www.vogue.co.uk/whos_who/Donna_Karan/default.html). The 'body' comprised a combination of fibre, fabric and design philosophy, and something that was created as a 'basic' became a 'permanent' and a staple wardrobe addition. Karan's personal balance of quality fabrics incorporating the Lycra fibre became a feature of her 'user friendly' designs. Indeed, she could be marked as the pioneer of using Lycra in clothing, which is commonplace today. Her designer stockings were reinforced with the Lycra fibre and nowadays it is difficult to find hosiery without Lycra content. Karan's design philosophy of creating lavish, comfortable clothes was aimed at flattering real women, women like herself, big-boned, healthy size 12 women with active lifestyles, which meant that fabric choices allowing for comfort, movement and function were an integral part of her design process. These issues are recognized by Martha Nelson, the editor of *In Style* magazine (www.instyle.com), she says 'women are interested in clothes, but the average consumer isn't interested in the "fashion world"' (Agins, 2000: 14). It seems as though fashion designers at all levels are driven by consumer preferences and the same philosophy is echoed by another American-based haute couture designer Yeohlee Teng, Yeohlee, designers fabric selections and the influence of consumer lifestyles will be explored later in this chapter.

Consumer Choice

The textile industries today produce diversified fabric finishes and manufacture a vast array of fibres, more than at any other time before. Mills simply cannot afford to specialize in the way they did in the past, a time when dealing with a specific fibre type was the norm. The nature of textile manufacturing has changed and adaptability is the name of the game now. To meet the desires of today's consumer, mills are constantly challenged to adapt procedures when new blends and mixes of fibres and yarns are required. New combinations of fibres and yarns are not the only innovation the textile industry has had to become accustomed to. Fabric finishing is an area that is of great interest to fashion designers and is useful in delivering novel ideas to the consumer. Retailers like Marks & Spencer have, for some time, been using fabrics coated with an application of Teflon (www.dupont.com/teflon/fabric protector/news/uniforms.html), an industrial protective coating. This has been especially successful on children's clothing, which need to be rather more resilient to spills and stains than regular clothing. Fashion designers are always searching for new fabrics, as they can spur the designer's creativity or refresh mainstream design. In their pursuit of new and exciting materials to keep the consumer satisfied, they have ventured into 'industrial' products and finishes.

The constant requirement of companies and designers to generate collections, fill stores and gratify catalogue shoppers begs the question about who *really* controls fashion, the consumer or the providers. Also, are designs primarily formulated on the basis of what will attract the consumer? It is logical that it is the consumer alone, not the fashion designer, who establishes a fashion and this simply happens as a result of the adoption or rejection of what the fashion world offers. Given this, it is a fallacy that designers are able to successfully design creative and artistic expressions, without considering their potential customer. In order to succeed, fashion needs the customer's endorsement and approval. This question of customer acceptance applies throughout the chain; they make the crucial decisions, be they customers of fashion designers or fashion designers as customers of textile manufacturers.

As business generators, consumers are or should be of paramount importance to the fashion and textile industries; fashion businesses need to know who their customers are in order to profit from them. Hence, it is crucially important to precisely interpret and profile the customer; this enables manufacturers, retailers and designers to make informed decisions, and so creates confidence in successfully supplying the market. Conversely, the misinterpretation of information can be detrimental to a business. A variety of sources supply information about consumers, ranging from analysed and measured data collected from national censuses through to consumer profiling organizations that collate data and statistics specific to a market sector. Consumer profiling organizations, like Claritas Inc (www.claritas.com), MORI and ACNielsen (www.acnielsen.com), and companies such as BrainReserve (www.faithpopcorn.com/consulting/consulting.htm), who specialize in lifestyle prediction, identify general cultural trends affecting consumer choices.

Certain products can be perceived by the consumer as having significant properties which are transferred to the consumer upon purchase and use. These properties may be purely symbolic and bestow on the consumer a sense of belonging to a particular group, like a pair of Gucci sunglasses or a Hermes scarf for instance, or the product may impart a very personal enhancement like 'Fastskin', as worn by Ian Thorpe in the Sydney 2000 Olympics (Gale and Kaur, 2002: 30). In consumer societies individuals tend to align themselves with specific groups according to the products they own, 'markers' such as those Gucci sunglasses for instance. It is the media and journalism machines that keep the consumer happy with fashion, and deliver to them news about cutting-edge innovations, the most recent 'must haves' and where they might be bought at the best price. In order to keep the fashion machine well oiled, the consumer has to desire to replenish their wardrobe, and to facilitate this, the fashion industry diligently promotes new styles and colours which tend to make consumers feel inadequate and unsatisfied with their earlier purchases. This works particularly well in the fashion world, as it is a segment of industry that is strongly driven by trends, which call for speedy and regular renewal, even if it is simply in terms of colour and fabric. The fast pace of fashion and fabric technology is a reflection of being part of a dynamic consumerist society. This can give rise to the consumer feeling agitated or rebellious, tired or cynical about being constantly presented with, and consuming, a huge range of objects. Consequently, personal attitudes and emotions about consuming change all the time and become entwined with other anxieties and

Figure 5.1
Levi Dockers. Courtesy Levi Strauss.

aspirations relating to the self. It appears that the principal function of consumption is not simply to consume the object itself; it is, in fact, rather more intricate, involving signals and meanings in fabrics and labels that objects transmit in relation to the status they display (Desmond, 2003). The messages that clothing and fabric convey are further elaborated by Bender:

> It was once easy to judge, by the quality and amount of fabric or the amount of labour-intensive lace and embroidery, the social status of a person, which only knew the dimensions of 'up' or 'down'. But nowadays there are many more dimensions to consider . . . They all seek expression through consumer goods, not the least of all clothing. (Bender, 2003)

Fabric and fashion have generated a history of meanings; the consumer, in wearing specific types of textiles and apparel transfers messages of sophistication, wealth and status to others around them either consciously or subconsciously.

The trends which affect clothing will inevitably have enormous consequences on the fabric supply markets. For example, recent years have seen a universal shift in cultural opinion and social conduct, which have resulted in the reduction in sale of formal suits for men. Due to a change in attitude from formal to informal dress in the workplace, both fashion and textile designers, manufacturers and suppliers have to reassess their position as they are tied into a textile and fashion chain of events which is impossible to ignore or escape. The increase in smart but casual dress in the workplace led to Levi Strauss & Co. introducing *Dockers* which are their brand of khakis. Since being launched in 1986, they have sold 150 million pairs, Gap has also done a roaring trade in khakis, and they have grown to become a staple Gap item. In fact, 1998 was the year in which Gap opened a new store every day. This was an indicator of a pivotal change in the definition of 'fashion' which led to the sophistication in demand for quality and performance fabrics by the general population who wanted something different and new but weren't prepared to pay a penalty for the pleasure. The editor of *Women's Wear Daily*, Patrick McCarthy, talking about changing consumer attitudes to fashion remarked 'The big shift started about 18 years ago, but didn't reach fruition until the last 5 to 7 years' (Agins, 2000:185), he goes on to say 'People now consider moderate, inexpensive clothes as chic' (Agins, 2000: 187). This development in fashion retail wasn't exclusively an American phenomenon. In 1982, NEXT was launched in the UK 'with an exclusive co-ordinated collection of stylish clothes, shoes and accessories for women. Collections for men, children and everything for the well dressed home followed' (http://orders02.next.co.uk/AboutNext/history.asp), NEXT now trades from 300 stores in 16 countries worldwide satisfying consumer demand for quality, stylish clothing without the fashion propaganda.

Market Research

The role of consumer profiling and study of demographics is crucial in fashion and textiles in that they are industries shaped by changes in the population and consumer demands. Philip Kowalcyzk, director of retail services at Kurt Salmon Associates, said of the fast pace of change in trends in 2001 'Trends now have an average lifespan of just eight to 12 weeks instead of five months two years ago' (Kowalcyzk, 2001). In order that industries are prepared for what is to come, they need to be aware of indicators that inform them of upcoming lifestyle and consumer trends. So much of what applies to fashion also applies to textiles; whatever changes occur in fashion have some effect on textiles and vice versa. Demographics, geographics and psychographics are all fundamental to market research and the analysis of the fashion consumer. Age, occupation, responsibilities and disposable income are all factors influencing consumers' buying habits in clothing and all other consumables. Therefore it is imperative that all industries are aware of changes – however subtle. Demographics and geographics both trace changes in the populace, such as age, sex, race, education, religion, occupation, income, family size, nationality or ethnicity. Broadly categorizing the population according to these criteria and organizing the data collected can begin to help industry profile consumers and target specific market sectors from country to country. Psychographics are rather more complex, they scrutinize consumer habits in more depth, considering social status, personality, lifestyle and cultural values. In doing so, they formulate an extensive representation of the potential client, predicting patterns of product consumption. This process can also work inversely, in that occasionally, desired benefits of a product are sought from consumers by researchers, enabling them to match the product profile to that of their consumer. For example, it is not uncommon for consumers to seek specific characteristics in their purchase of clothing and textiles; consumers essentially have buying expertise, Elaine Stone states in *The Dynamics of Fashion,* 'consumers (are) requesting to know the performance qualities of a fabric before purchase . . . i.e. non-iron, crease resistant, easy-care, waterproof, stain repellent' (Stone, 2000: 25). She explains that

> The market researchers conduct consumer studies relating to the demand for or acceptance of finishes, blends, and other desired characteristics. Such studies also help fabric and garment producers to determine what consumers will want in the future, where and when they will want it, and in what quantities. (Stone, 2000: 111)

In order for textile and fashion industries to glean this type of information about consumers they use a range of market research companies to profile consumers and maximise sales. By definition, a profile is a representation of the various characteristics and tendencies of a subject. Thus, in the textile and fashion world, the success of a company is down to determining the needs, requirements and interests of the consumer through implementing market research. In turn this helps them to target potential users of particular products. As mentioned, there are a variety of market research companies, most of which have been established for many years, have proven track records of success and some of which are globally recognized names, such as, Kurt Salmon Associates (KSA), MORI, Claritas Inc, Daniel Yankelovich, The Gallup Organization, Miller-Williams Inc, Montgomery Research Inc and Stanford Research Institute (SRI). The time it takes to perform, evaluate and interpret research depends on the size and type of market research undertaken. In the fashion and textile industries, research is required on a constant basis; this is predominantly due to the cycle of change occurring within these industries. The speed of change is perhaps more apparent in the fashion rather than the textile industries because the silhouette is quicker to transform. Textile research and development in contrast spend longer in gestation and, once established, remain for more than a season. Fashions tend to change, sometimes quite dramatically every season, whereas once a fibre is introduced that has particular benefits for the consumer, such as its comfort, performance or appearance, for example Lycra or Tencel, it remains a strong component within the fashion industry for the long term, occasionally being reformulated.

We might term the companies listed above as the traditional established players in the general market research field. As well as these, some fashion and textile companies actually conduct their own consumer profiling; for example, VF Corporation, which was established over a century ago and is the world's largest apparel company (http://www.vfc.com/pages/profile.asp). Returning to the established key players in broad market research for a moment, most of these organizations originate in America and boast common aims and objectives in their company mission statements. The Gallup Organization, having studied human nature and behaviour for over seventy years, now has a thorough comprehension of consumer behaviour to draw on for clients, such as identifying the factors that drive purchases. They say that their intention with clients is to: 'seek to improve their business performance by developing better leaders (and) more profitable customers . . . with one single purpose in mind: to help organizations and individuals maximize their performance' (Gallup, 2003). Similarly, Claritas Inc, a marketing information resources company state they, 'are dedicated to maximizing our clients' profitability', their vision is 'To have every business in the U.S. rely on Claritas information to define and target their customers and markets.' (Claritas, 2003). Created in 1961, Claritas, like Gallup, is also built on the premise of consumer behaviour. Its founder, Jonathan Robbins developed the PRIZM segmentation system, which organized the population into small groups according to actions and attributes so that companies could react to information they had, such as whether consumers are loyal to specific types of fabrics. MORI (www.mori.com) and Daniel Yankelovich, both focus on consumer or public opinion research, which survey and track values and trends. Daniel Yankelovich is considered to be a pioneer of public opinion research (www.danyankelovich.com) and annually publishes the famed Yankelovich MONITOR, a survey of American opinion.

Market research can be viewed as too broad and general unless it is customized specifically to apply to textile and fashion issues. It is difficult to comprehend and profile customers and their segments when purchase and transaction information alone is available. Therefore – successful market research needs to combine the above with impartial consumer interviewing, so as to identify the logical and emotive reasons behind purchases. As an insight into consumer activity at Nordstrom's department store, Jeanne G. Harris and Thomas H. Davenport discovered:

> Though Nordstrom knows that when it comes to fashion, a human can extrapolate from a client's past choices to current styles much more reliably than a computer . . . Clearly, companies investing in customer knowledge management must focus on particular customer types and objectives, employ both transaction-derived and human-based knowledge, and manage the broader customer knowledge context . . . Customers, first and foremost, are people – and building a relationship with them entails more than just tabulating their transactions. (Harris and Davenport, 2001)

This more focused and specific type of consumer analysis is echoed by organizations such as ACNielsen and Kurt Salmon Associates. ACNielsen, a VNU company (a major international media and information organization), boasts on its website that it 'is the world's leading marketing information company'. As such, it has gathered 126,000 households in 18 countries to participate in its consumer panel services. Through the detailed analysis of consumption in these households, it is possible to reveal existing and future patterns of consumer activity. In order to glean consumer attitudes to specific products like materials and apparel, ACNielsen customize research, 'services include quantitative and qualitative studies that deliver information and insights into consumer attitudes and purchasing behaviour' (www.acnielsen.com/site/about/).

Kurt Salmon Associates (KSA) highlight the importance of a directed and controlled approach to research into consumer goods and retail practice, especially in the fashion and textile industries. In an age when companies form longer supply chains, from yarn manufacture, through design idea, to their final destination, it is an advantage to have some notion of what is required by the consumer. The pace of change in the fashion and textile industries needs emphasizing; these features make it unlike any other manufacturing and supply industry. By its very nature, fashion, and so textiles, needs to constantly feed the consumer with the 'new' and the 'innovative' in order to stay ahead of the game and survive, this is especially true of sportswear or stylish athletic apparel. KSA point out that the aggressive pace and competition in fashion increases the demands made by investor groups, business managers and board directors to top previous sales figures, which puts pressure on those controlling the design and production of the textiles and apparel. In this process, questions and issues arise like:

> What new and innovative product have you developed? How do your inventories look? Can you speed up the R&D effort to get that new high-performance fabric ready? . . . Leaving competitors in their wake, the winners are focusing on finding quicker routes by which to speed new products to the marketplace. By reducing their time-to-market, branded manufacturers, marketers, and retailers can improve their ability to capitalize on R&D breakthroughs, service the unique needs and requests of their customers more effectively, and decrease the risk that their inventories are going to slip into obsole-

> scence. All the players have equally challenging roles in this race. Manufacturers and marketers must bring innovative product to market quickly, and must have the agility to service the dynamic patterns of consumer demand. (KSA, 2002)

With concerns such as these from various levels of industry, it is easy to see the reasoning behind the need for a focused approach to consumer and market research within the textiles, fashion and all other industries.

Innovation

Innovation, as applied to fashion and textile firms, is not only a means of generating design output and ideas, it is also relevant to developments in marketing, manufacture and supply. 'All businesses have opportunities for innovation in their markets; for some, such as fashion clothing manufacturers and distributors, it is the vital life blood of their organizations' (Chisnall, 1994: 248). Economic history is peppered with examples of practical inventions which achieved varying degrees of success, amongst them are the textile innovations that define the industrial revolution, such as John Kay's flying shuttle in 1733 and James Hargreaves's spinning jenny in 1765. This was followed a few years later in 1769 by Richard Arkwright's water frame, his mechanization of the spinning process has made him one of the greatest pioneers of the Industrial Revolution. Since this time, the textile and fashion industries have come to rely greatly on innovation in an industrial sense as well as in terms of business activity. More recent milestones in textile and fashion innovation have included fibre developments like nylon, lycra and microfibres; CAD and CAM as aids for design and manufacture; and the emergence of Quick Response (QR) to connect the various components of the textile and fashion industries, from concept to consumer, with the aim of maximizing profits. Much of the innovation summarized above, be it practice- or business-based, is very much tied into technological advancement of one kind or another. Peter Chisnall, in *Consumer Behaviour*, analyses Carter and Williams's 'The characteristics of technically progressive firms' in the *Journal of Industrial Economics*, March 1959, and also Ansoff's, *Corporate Strategy*, Penguin, London, 1968. He surmises that in innovative strategy, firms either lead or follow, and it is the entrepreneurial leaders who continually adopt and apply technological innovation in their own and adjacent fields that succeed in delivering new products to the consumer in time with changing seasons (Chisnall, 1994).

For market leaders like DuPont and VF Corporation, innovation is an essential part of business development and strategy. Being aware of market needs and opportunities, as well as new scientific advancements is key. Manufacturers and designers in fashion and textiles know that consumers strongly react to innovation, be it in shape or fabric. The innovation of seamless technology for use in fashion is a case in point, being applied by designers such as Calvin Klein and Emilio Cavallini in America and Hanro in Switzerland. Seamless technology, as developed by Cavallini, bears some formal similarity to Issey Miyake's 'A-POC' (a piece of cloth) concept, in that an item of clothing is fully fashioned on machinery alone, Lucia Carpio quotes Cavallini as saying: '(the collection) was designed without the use of scissors, or fabrics, mannequins or conventional sewing machines' (Carpio, 2002a: 97). Rather than being driven by a designer's fashion concept, Cavallini's design philosophy appears to be rooted in technological innovation within the creative process, which occurs on the computer. The technology is further fuelled by consumer demand, if research indicates that consumers accept a modernization, advancement or innovation in respect of a technique or process. Designers and industry are thus further encouraged to use technological innovation and this is the case with seamless technology. Innovation within fibre production and fabric manufacture is largely informed by assessing consumer research and taking action

> Dupont's market research in Europe established that the superior comfort and seamlessly smooth fit of these garments hold great appeal for today's consumers . . . Consumer research confirmed an unusually high repeat-purchase rate for seamless intimate apparel, where there is the largest selection of garments presently available. (Carpio, 2002a: 98)

Fashion and fabric design is very sensitive to time as styles and colours change from season to season. Economic success in industry today involves a combination of style plus promotion, manufacture and consumer knowledge. However, with innovation comes risk; it is both unavoidable and inseparable. Failure, as a result of innovation can occur for a number of reasons, not least of which is the fact that the launch of a business strategy, fabric or apparel onto a market might be premature. Radical moves made within manufacture and retail need to be calculated and could be misinterpreted, this would call for investment in re-educating both industry and consumers of various advancements. Market research knowledge has an integral part to play in the analysis of industry and consumers; this reduces risks and can identify potential areas of profitability through strategy or product launch. Thus, through continually monitoring and evaluating markets, it becomes easier to recognize trends and fill gaps when opportunities arise. Given the effort industry makes in order to track consumer activity, preference, lifestyle and values, it is still a fact that the assumptions made about future consumer activity are not infallible.

> Experienced marketers know that what people say they want and what they will actually buy often fail to coincide. But skilful researchers do not expect to obtain guarantees of future behaviour; they will aim for insight into patterns of consumption and levels of satisfaction and aspiration related to particular kinds of products and services. (Chisnall, 1994: 270)

Quick Response

Success in the fashion and textile industries requires that the fabric producers supply the fashion industry, the fashion industry supplies the fashion retailers and the fashion retailers supply the consumer with what they want, when they want it. The demands of the consumer, the ultimate beneficiary at the end of this chain of events, along with the requirements of competition, have instigated a 'speeding up' of the production and supply cycles in order to deliver goods even faster. This acceleration of response times to satisfy consumer demand involves the fibre and fabric industries, apparel manufacturers and fashion retailers all working as a team to efficiently speed up the delivery of fashion goods to the consumer. This innovation in the fashion and textile industries has been labelled 'Quick Response' or 'QR'. The QR concept was adopted in America from the 1970s onwards in an attempt to increase competition with imports. The Quick Response Leadership

Committee was established in 1994 by The American Apparel Manufacturers Association to stress the importance of QR. Grace Kunz, author of *Merchandising: Theory, Principles, and Practice* (Kunz, 1998), generally defines QR as, 'a comprehensive business strategy incorporating time-based competition, agility, and partnering to optimise the supply system, the distribution system, and service to customers' (Stone and Farr, 1997). Since its introduction, QR has been accompanied by JIT (Just-in-Time), which is more applicable to the textile side of the process rather than the fashion or retail side. JIT is a form of inventory management; in effect, it prevents the unnecessary storing of materials used in manufacturing products. The upshot is that suppliers only deliver the required materials at the moment the manufacturer needs to make the product. Therefore, the on-costs involved with holding stock are kept to a minimum.

A more accurate definition of QR in relation to textiles and fashion is suggested by Lesley Davis Burns and Nancy O'Bryant in *The Business of Fashion*. They say:

> Specific definitions of QR vary, depending on the industry division. For textile producers, QR focuses on connections among fibre producers, fabric producers, and apparel manufacturers; for apparel manufacturers, QR focuses on increased use of technology and connections among fabric producers, apparel producers, and retailers. (Burns and O'Bryant, 2002: 23)

Quick response is a true reflection of the way in which the fashion and textile consumer has transformed the structure of the fashion and textile industries from a 'push system' to a 'pull system'. Whereas originally fashion erred on the side of supply, pushing products on to the consumer, now it has shifted the emphasis to customer demand, using precise data to supply what the consumer needs. The role of technology, in supplying exact statistics to the appropriate links in the chain of supply to the consumer, is an integral part of the Quick Response methodology. At its conception in 1985, QR was the outcome of an amalgamation of a number of major American retailers, their suppliers and IBM. This alliance consulted with Kurt Salmon Associates before embarking on their ambition to reduce the amount of time between the apparel ultimately reaching the consumer. The Quick Response process was actualized using computer-to-computer transmission of sales data (EDI or Electronic Data Interchange), which systematized the exchange of information between groups. Manufacturers, retailers and distributors were all kept informed of what was selling, where it was selling and what needed to be replenished. The results of this modification within the textile and fashion supply industries had a phenomenal effect on trade:

> In 1985 the Top 10 retailers in the U.S. (Wal*Mart, K Mart, Sears, Penney, Dayton Hudson/TARGET, Federated, GAP, Limited, Dillards, May) sold about 46% of all the apparel we buy. Now, they sell 80%. This consolidation by retailers allows them to dictate the logistics strategy to their suppliers. (AAPN, 1998a)

VF Corporation also reported extraordinary reductions in restocking times

> VF launches its Market Response System (MRS), spearheading the industry's move to EDI and flow replenishment. Through MRS, VF gains the ability to quickly and efficiently replace inventory on retailers' shelves as products are bought by consumers. Turnaround times for restocking many of the Company's products are cut to one week from 90 days. (VF, 2001)

The American Apparel Producers' Network have suggested that 'Quick Response' is really another term for a logistics strategy which has remodelled fashion, steering it away from its traditional emphasis on design. Quick response has its obvious consequences, although retailers are content with higher margins, less markdowns, more sales, and less stock, it seems as though distributive industries are left with a rather more complex set of supply issues. As buying cycles speed up, fabric and garment producers need to work at a faster pace in order to deal with the streamlining in retail and keep up with consumer demand. Renata Echtermeyer, head of design at Olsen, in explaining the consequences of consumer research and the increase in company design output, says:

> Now that we have six collections a year instead of four . . . we are becoming more independent of the show dates. We

Figure 5.2
Inditex Headquarters.
Courtesy Inditex.

> have more regular contact with the mills and work with them strategically . . . Pastels and colours are good sellers and colour will go through to spring 04. (Collins, 2003: 88)

Although Quick Response is firmly rooted in and widely implemented by American textile and fashion industries, it has been adopted in other parts of the world too. The Spanish company, Zara, owned by Inditex, declares it is able to get products to the shop floor within five weeks of it merely being a concept. The reason this is even possible has everything to do with localized design and manufacture in Spain and neighbouring Portugal. If the production of its apparel was to take place in the more common centres of apparel manufacture, like Asia, lead times could be six to nine months on average. The fairly standard industrial production decision to 'make or buy in' applies to fashion and textiles; in Zara's case they retain control over everything themselves, rather than using outside contractors, specialist producers or allowing their goods to be manufactured under licence. Stores like Zara and Hennes & Mauritz, are setting their sights on cutting lead times from concept to consumer to only two weeks; a fashion cycle of two weeks is a stark contrast to the traditional four per year. In discussing the length of fashion cycles, Robin Anson, Editorial Director of *Textile Outlook International* says

> Fashion cycles are getting shorter for a number of reasons. To some extent the trend is consumer-led, and is affected by shorter attention spans and fast-changing cultural influences, which are picked up by designers. Retailers are happy to capitalise on such trends on the grounds that shorter cycles encourage impulse spending. (Anson, 2002: 66)

Li & Fung, a Hong Kong based specialist sourcing company, has a philosophy similar to that of Zara, its strategies point towards flexibility, speed and efficiency in manufacture and supply. Li & Fung state that the elasticity in their approach is largely down to modern technology which enables clearer communications. Similarly, Zara uses the same flexible approach to initiate colour, fabric or style changes at factory level if items are not selling well in store. The advantages of a flexible approach for Li & Fung clients are clear.

> Best of all, they can make last-minute changes electronically. Until the fabric is woven, customers can cancel their orders online. Until the fabric is dyed, they can change the colour. And until the fabric is cut, clients can change the design or size of the garments. (Anson, 2002: 66)

In contrast to old models of the 'push system' of supplying fashion consumers, the new framework of the 'pull system' relies on the consumer activating demand through personal choice.

Infectious Trends

The world of branding and producing trends sometimes leads the consumers to develop an inexplicable and irrepressible 'must have' desire for specific products. This need for product ownership can be an irresistible urge or persistent desire. Martin Raymond likes to refer to it, as 'a plague, a virus, a hyper-infectious contagion' (Raymond, 2001: 227). The desire for a product spreads on account of its associations and this phenomenon usually takes place as a result of being labelled as 'the next big thing'. Consumers are ultimately responsible for turning a trend into a 'virus'. Being trend driven, the fashion and textile industries occasionally create and witness viruses occurring within their boundaries. From time to time, the combination of a brand, an object plus its relative scarcity, is able to stir an inexplicable desire that grabs the attention of the consumer.

> in a world in which so many different brands compete for our attention, the prestige of one seemingly overnight luxury soon cancels out another, and 'the best' is simply the latest, the hottest, the most talked about. The world of new luxury is the world of 'butterfly economics,' a world in which every Christmas must have a sold-out toy, every summer a movie

> too crowded to see, each year a car with a six-month backlog, a baguette handbag almost impossible to own. (Twitchell, 2002: 25)

Indeed, the result of the heat of a virus on the Fendi Baguette alone, revitalized the fortunes of the ailing Fendi company and had a beneficial knock-on effect on all of the associated fabric production, manufacturing and distribution industries. Twitchell's analysis of the works of Seabrook *Nobrow* (Seabrook, 2001) and Brooks *Bobos in Paradise: The New Upper Class and How They Got There* (Brooks, 2001), points toward an evolution in consumer groupings. He suggests that we have moved on from being grouped according to the traditional social classes of higher, middle and lower, and this system has been replaced by new-fangled categories of consumers like bobos (short for bourgeois bohemians), nobrows and yuppies. This new classification of consumers brings with it different sets of values and aspirations as far as goods are concerned. With the great variety of fashion goods on offer, fashion consumers can afford to be individual about their choices and not necessarily follow dictated trends. The innovators among fashion consumers initially adopt a style; then the rate at which it is copied is in line with its popularity; ultimately it reaches the mass market, where, due to its abundant availability, it loses its appeal for consumers and is replaced by the 'next big thing'. The one thing that is clear is that, within the practice of fashion consumption, the old needs to be discarded and the new needs to be adopted: this is a constant in the fashion world and relies exclusively on the consumer to make the fashion system function. It is as a consequence of this regular renewal combined with human nature that 'big things' happen periodically

> The clear conclusion is that while organisms may possess the skills to act rationally, they often don't. Individuals are not calculating machines with fixed tastes but rather social animals that interact with and are influenced by the flock, the tribe, the in crowd. As they say in advertising, you drink the advertising, not the beer; smoke the commercial, not the cigarette; drive the nameplate, not the car. So too in consuming the new luxury, you buy the trend, not the object. And how do you know the trend? You check what the other ants are doing. (Brooks, 2001: 95)

Affiliation, Consumption and Identity

British sociologist Robert Bocock points out the relation between consumers' identities and products.

> The construction of a sense of identity can be seen as a process which may make use of items of consumption such as clothing, footwear, popular music or sporting activities, including being a supporter of particular music groups, singers or soccer clubs. Such consumption patterns could be used as a central means of defining who was a member and who was outside a specific group. (Bocock, 1993: 28)

At its most basic, the consumer views function as a necessary element of fashion and fabric. However, once this is fulfilled, we have or seek alternative reasons when making choices in clothing and fabric. This is where affiliation with groups in society plays a part in consumer activity. Coco Chanel purported that if we do not consume out of necessity, we consume for the pleasure of possessing something luxurious; she stated, 'luxury is the necessity that begins where necessity ends'. Therefore, although it is unnecessary for the consumption of fashion and fabric, affiliation with specific fashion and textile brands and items is important to many consumers. Labels, apparel and fabric act as markers, enabling people to portray a model image of themselves, conveying that they belong to a certain group within society. These indicators or signs in the form of fashion and textiles begin with a single individual acquiring something new and unique that appears on the market. Through its use, the new item is introduced to companions within an individual's 'group', therefore spreading the word about the new 'big thing', until it is gradually obtained by the whole group. Twitchell suggests that once the latest 'must-have' item has been adopted by the majority of the 'group', those that do not possess it are left with feelings of inadequacy. Being seen in, and wearing, the 'latest thing', in the right fabric, colour, style and, crucially, with the right label, shows conformity with and acceptance of 'group' norms. The possession of the right outfit or accessory satisfies basic primal needs for individual reassurance and approval. This is not to say that everyone fits into 'groups'; just as valid, are those individual personalities that elect to use clothing and fabric as an expressive tool. This sort of statement, due to its novelty is significant; the deviation from 'group norms' makes an individual

Figure 5.3
Anthony Symonds – Chiffon Print Tie-Neck Dress, Autograph 2003. Courtesy Marks & Spencer.

noticeable in a crowd. Typical strategies of the modern fashion 'expressive' are personally customizing garments; the use of vintage, unfashionable or clashing garments and fabrics; anti-fashion statements; or the incorporation of the unexpected and atypical. Through deviating from consensus fashion these personal expressions can be highly visible, particularly in urban or social venues. Sometimes these differences encourage curiosity and others to copy, resulting in the generation of trends, feeding back into the fashion and textile industries.

Figure 5.4
Sonja Nuttall – Grey Nehru Jacket, Autograph 2003. Courtesy Marks & Spencer.

Individual affiliation, or association with specific fabrics and fashions form membership for particular clubs or 'groups'; for example, the 'Burberry' check on various items, the 'Hermes' scarf and the 'Barbour' jacket, can all be tacit declarations of consumer status. Consumption of these objects, through their distinctive design and historical nuances, represents a conscious affiliation, equipping a consumer with entry to an affluent section of society where the likes of Gucci, Chanel, Versace and Prada reside. Obviously, affiliations such as these come at a price, and so sit at the luxury end of the fashion and fabric market. The luxury market is quite small and specialized in comparison to say the mass market supplied by Gap or Marks & Spencer. Nonetheless, the larger mass-market fashion and fabric suppliers also have a loyal customer base that associates itself with quality, volume producers. Segmenting consumer groups according to the market, be that luxury or mass market, allows the marketing industry to formulate various strategies which relate to the needs of these groups. These strategies in turn can be modified by the way advertising, styling and distribution of goods are configured for different market levels.

The consumer demand for affiliation with 'name' designers has led high street chains and department stores such as Marks & Spencer, Top Shop and Debenhams to collaborate with couture designers. Reporting on the Marks & Spencer Autograph range that includes Julien Macdonald and Betty Jackson, Hilary Alexander says:

> Such designer/high street marriages are not new, although they are a uniquely British phenomenon. The closest overseas equivalent would be the "diffusion" ranges of many American and European designers, or the capsule pieces that the French mail order catalogue La Redoute secures from Emanuel Ungaro or Jean Paul Gaultier. (Alexander, 2001)

Working together, the fashion designers create diffusion ranges exclusively for stores, attaching their name to their designs, and in the process blurring the line between high street and designer fashion. The alliance between fashion designer and high street began with Debenhams and Jasper Conran in 1995, and has since been joined by designers like John Rocha, Lulu Guiness and Matthew Williamson. The winning formula has turned out to be an astounding success for Debenhams. 'Designers at Debenhams' accounted for £140 million in company sales for 2002, which was a rise from £35 million three years before and has expectations of reaching £200 million in 2003 (Foster, 2003). Association with fashion designers has not only satisfied consumer demand for designer clothes at high street prices, but has also elevated the fashion status of these stores, and led to Marks & Spencer advertising in *Vogue* for the first time in 2002.

Ventures such as these not only bring designer names to a wider audience, but the clothes are also available in a greater range of

Figure 5.5
John Rocha menswear. Autumn/Winter 2003, available at Debenhams. Courtesy Debenhams PLC.

sizes, something which would not have been readily available under the designer's mainline collection, but is possible through the scale and volume of manufacture and distribution handled by high street stores. In creating something exclusive for the fashion consumer, Belinda Earl, Chief Executive for Debenhams says: 'Consumers these days have everything they need and we're selling desires. This is about promoting the emotion that goes with the fact that it is something different, it is exclusive, and it's exclusive to Debenhams' (Foster, 2003: 85). Professional opinion on the potential long-term effects that this sort of affiliation will have on the fashion designer are split, Vanessa Denza of Denza International, a designer recruitment specialist, says: 'Four or five years ago it was perceived that association with a high street store undermined a designer brand. Now there is an understanding that a designer can be a designer at all different levels of the market' (Foster, 2003: 86). Conversely, Jess Cartner-Morley, in *The Guardian*, September 2002, reported on the damaging effects that growing designer ranges in stores were actually having on the designers themselves during London fashion week:

> while high-street stores are delivering manna to shoppers, they are bankrupting British designers. If they are in trouble – and a quick peek at the balance sheets of most of the names on this week's schedule would confirm that they are – then part of the blame must be laid at the door of the overachieving British high street . . . Paradoxically, designers have become dependent on the very high-street stores who have brought them to their knees. They can only hope that designer diffusion lines stay in fashion longer than most hot new trends (Cartner-Morley, 2002).

It seems as though this other level of fashion or, as Twitchell refers to it 'second-stream luxury' because 'it flows below the upper crust to the common consumer', could possibly have detrimental consequences for the designers who have contributed to its phenomenal success.

Although we can buy many goods that attempt to describe our personalities and status to our peers and society at large, few are as obvious or as portable as the clothes we wear. In *Consuming Behaviour*, John Desmond explains how the theories of Jacques Lacan, the French psychoanalyst, are the basis for many who critique consumer society, advertising and media organizations. He says of Lacan:

> The basis of the argument is that the media bombard consumers with idealized and unattainable images of control, mastery, beauty, perfection and youth, which are snatched at eagerly by those who consume them and who use them to

> shore up their fragile and battered 'egos' . . . The quest for wholeness and identity is thus to be illusory and a sham, with modern-day 'Don Quixotes' armouring themselves with brand-names such as Ralph Lauren, Paco Rabanne, Chanel, Matanique, Lacoste, Ferrari, Adidas, Martini, Rolex and Calvin Klein in a futile bid to be 'themselves'. (Desmond, 2003: 264–5)

This reinforces the idea that the consumption and use of fashion and fabric as symbols pertaining to a perfect self-image and lifestyle are an important driving force behind fashion and textile purchase. 'Fashionability' for the consumer is clarified as

> the desire for images of novelty and fashion springs directly from the desire of consumers. On the other hand, those firms, which collectively make up the fashion system actively promote the ideal of fashionability. This involves the ability to trade in one identity or lifestyle for another, which has more novelty, or seems more appealing to the person who 'wears it'. (Desmond, 2003: 270)

The constant trading-up of styles within fashion and the recurrent cycle of rejection and acceptance of old and new fashion, in line with the seasonal changes, led Oscar Wilde to ponder over the fickleness that is fashion, referring to it as 'a form of ugliness so intolerable that we have to change it every six months' and leads Desmond to question the effect that this continuous change has on the consumers. He suggests, and perhaps in the extreme case, that the relentless change which occurs for the fashion consumer could potentially threaten to destabilize their self-identity. However, this viewpoint appears to be rather harsh. Realistically, old and new fashions tend to coexist; very rarely will a consumer routinely reject a whole wardrobe and image in favour of a totally new one.

Lifestyle

As much as the consumer swings the pendulum of change in fashion, lifestyles too, obviously have some influence on fashion and fabric choices. The influence of the consumer could be accused of being the culprit that led to the demise of haute couture. Led by couturiers like Yves Saint Laurent in the 1960s, haute couture, diversified and descended into the ready-to-wear market. This encouraged the traditional haute couture consumers to opt for shopping experiences in young trendy boutiques where ready-to-wear collections were available. This move to ready-to-wear ultimately meant that haute couture was being ostracized, which cleared the path for the likes of Anne Klein, America's most acclaimed sportswear brand of the 1970s. This sportswear brand continued under Donna Karan, and the focus continued to be on comfort and manoeuvrability to fit an active lifestyle, akin to current 'supermodern' designers like Yeohlee Teng. The notion of lifestyle points to the distinguishing characteristics, attitudes and behaviour which describe the way in which we choose to live, in different segments and at various levels of society. In modern society, lifestyles do not remain unchanged; in fact, occasionally they undergo significant alterations which are evidenced in the fabric and fashion of the time. Fibre and fabric manufacturers need to be aware of changes in lifestyle trends in order to develop and produce suitable fabrics that fit modern consumer needs. The presence of relaxed and informal styling in the American wardrobe is self-evident.

> A look into the closets of the American population of the 1990s would probably reveal one aspect that is much the same from coast to coast, in large cities and in small towns: Most would contain an unusually large selection of casual clothes and sportswear. The market for casual apparel developed with the growth of the suburbs in the 1950s, and has had a continuous series of boosts in the years since. (Stone, 2000: 33)

This casual, untailored approach to clothing can be interpreted as a reflection of lifestyle or vice versa. Whichever way round we wish to see it, the impact of sportswear on lifestyle and its influence on fabric is inescapable. Over time, sportswear merchandise has vastly improved with the use of technologically advanced fabrics, treatments and finishes, which find their way into mainstream casual fashion.

Lifestyle has had a profound effect on fabric choice and design decisions for fashion designers such as Yeohlee Teng. She is somewhat of a pioneer in blending a lifestyle-friendly fashion concept with cutting edge, functional, beautiful and practical fabric choice. She combines the luxury of exquisite fabrics with technologically advanced finishing techniques which make them windproof and rainproof yet still breathable. Although some of the fabrics are treated in order to enhance their performance and function, Yeohlee endeavours to retain the innate nature and characteristics of the luxurious fabrics she uses. Yeohlee's couture has been described as 'supermodern'; she explains her approach to her practice, 'I aim to make clothes that enhance movement, clothes that allow you to run for a cab, train or plane without ripping or tripping you up' (Bolton, 2002: 108). For Yeohlee, mobility and functionality in clothing for a modern lifestyle are paramount considerations in the design process and they define her approach, but she is careful that they are not at the cost of aesthetics. Yeohlee's design philosophy, in relation to both fabric and design is conveyed to Ruth La Ferla in *The New York Times*

> Meandering seams and exposed selvages are often a garment's only decorative elements. 'I believe in using the selvage rather than cutting it off, in allowing the fabrics to be what they are,' Ms. Teng said, though she is not averse to giving her materials a boost from technology.
>
> Not long ago Ms. Teng created a white wool coat that seemed at a glance both gorgeous and hopelessly impractical. 'I thought when I saw it, "How can you ask a New Yorker to wear that?"' Ms. [Valerie] Steele [Chief Curator, The Museum at the Fashion Institute of Technology] recalled. '"It's going to get filthy instantly."'
>
> But she coveted it just the same, all the more when she realized that Ms. Teng had coated it with an imperceptible layer of Teflon. '"Whoa," I said at the time. "This is what I've been waiting for" – someone to invent an immaculate white coat that I could wear everywhere, forever. (La Ferla, 2001)

In summary the new fashion system is streamlined and is reducing risk and surplus stocks through closely observing consumer trends. All components of the supply chain involved with fashion and textile production from raw material to the consumer are beginning to manufacture to order rather than stockpiling unnecessarily. The adoption of this new practice of working has been initiated, largely through the application of rapid technological advancements and speed of communication. This makes for a fast-moving environment and a continually evolving lifestyle, encouraging suppliers at all levels to give the consumer what they want in a variety of configurations. It has been implied that logistics have more to do with Quick Response than being driven by customer interests. However, the power of the consumer cannot be underestimated, Fred Schneider of Arthur Anderson wrote, 'We are moving from a world of consumer choice to consumer control' (Schneider, 1997). Bill Webb, in his concluding remarks on futures in retail brands and marketing, stresses the importance of the consumer to business:

> Only truly customer-oriented businesses will achieve long-term success. The top executives, company culture, and all operational management and staff will truly champion the needs of their customers . . . These organizations will be open and . . . enjoy the automatic confidence and trust of their customers. (Webb, 2001: 86)

It appears that in this day and age, the consumer holds the trump card. As the American Apparel Producers' Network (www.usawear.org) sees it:

> The consumer has gone from 'hunting and gathering' to 'demanding and getting'. They will buy from anyone. They are loyal to no-one . . . The retailers who win are those who can give the consumer what they want, where they want it, when they want it at the price they want to pay – period. Retailers use QR to do what has always been the fundamental mission of any retailer – to get the right product to the right place at the right time at the right price. (AAPN, 1998b)

6 Future Wear

This chapter considers the future relationship between fashion and textiles. In so doing, almost incidentally, it provides a window on an as yet unrealized future, where our relationship with what we wear will be markedly changed from what it is now. In particular the chapter provides an account of a new industrial context for fashion and textiles: how different industries now express an interest in clothing; how textiles act as a feeder for technology transfer; and how the once direct relationship between fashion and textiles is being complicated by these industrial changes. Attention is paid to a growing and important conceptual distinction between clothing and fashion. Many types of textile and clothing research and innovation are categorized and clarified; and an attempt is made to identify what is genuine and what speculation. New products and markets are discussed and significant attention is paid to the startling redefinition of the roles of fabric and garment – the new uses – that redefine and perturb the traditional tenets of fashion and textiles. Finally the future nature of fashion is considered. Although predicting this future may seem highly speculative, the most unpredictable aspect of fashion and textiles – tomorrow's looks, style and taste – the arena of forecasting, are not dwelt on here. Instead this chapter looks to more logical and evolutionary trends based on advanced technology; the use of clothes; and the social nature and purpose of fashion.

At the very heart of any debate about the future of fashion and textiles is the matter of what constitutes genuine innovation in a market driven by seasonal and stylistic change; a market in which innovation is, in and of itself, unremarkable and continuously expected. Currently the answer depends on the realization that new 'players' are entering the industrial world of clothing and fabric: corporations and industries who are finding new 'smart' applications for fashion, clothing and textiles and consequently will introduce truly significant changes across the sector. The strategic motivations of these new players are quite different from the traditional economic and market interests associated with the fashion and clothing sectors. The resulting political and strategic interplay between the differing business cultures while interesting is largely unavailable to us, and as yet relatively benign. What we might call the 'smarts sector' shows a high degree of overlap in research objectives, outcomes and applications. The increasing number of organizations now involved in the technological development of fabric and clothing is matched by the complexity of interactions between them. Overall, and around the world, the sector is notable for the high degree of collaboration between different (often previously unconnected) industries, government agencies and universities. Evidenced for example by the almost byzantine collaborative organization the International Centre of Excellence for Wearable Electronics and Smart Fashion Products (www.icewes.net). In addition many research projects and centres are creating new spin-off companies or are transferring advanced technology to the fashion-clothing-textile supply chain. The result is an extremely broad-based technological push to develop new types of clothing and fabric. When considered as a totality, it is as if we are creating a quite radical, fundamental, evolution of textiles and clothing; a genuine quantum leap without historical parallel. To understand the magnitude of this change or to predict its ramifications is very difficult. On the ground, it just looks like an awful lot of projects and products, many seemingly unrelated or natural developments within their own sectors. But from a distance the change is reminiscent of other great transformations in our material culture, like the Industrial Revolution. Consequently we see innovations that are:

- singular – say a 'smart jacket';
- fundamental – for example a fabric technology as important to clothing as the internal combustion engine is to transport; a core technology;
- accumulative – as in the history of the clock, a series of inventions and improvements great and small.

It is important to understand that there is no single set of questions or a technological project on which all researchers and industries are engaged. When we look at fabric and clothing innovations we can see there are lots of different interest groups, companies and agencies involved in pursuing their own specific agendas. The wealth of investigation and creativity creates a rich climate for technological synergy and further inventions. Throughout the world the race is now on to lay claim and be a stakeholder in this new technological goldrush. Resultantly there is also much journalistic spin and hyperbole, and many corporations invest in giving the *impression* of success, preparing the ground for claiming patent or copyright.

The subject of technological innovation in fashion and textiles receives increasing attention from scientists, designers, manufacturers and politicians but its nature and definitions remain somewhat scattered and elusive. Sometimes the general bracketing of technological innovation within the fashion and textiles industry gives the impression there is a single goal or collective and consensual basis to research and development. There has been for example the wide use of the futuristic prefix 'techno' as in *Techno Textiles* (Braddock and O'Mahoney, 1999), *Techno Fashion* (Quinn, 2002) and *Techno Style* (Pesch, 1996) and the derivative *Sportstech* (Braddock and O'Mahoney, 2002). These implying a 'new frontier' redolent of the populist belief in science and the future in the 1950s and 1960s. The current 'frontier' is a little less satisfying: complex, often difficult to understand, spread across a wide range of research fronts and frequently clouded in hype. It lacks the type of simple visionary coherence that was afforded by Frigidaire's 'Kitchen of the Future' seen in the 1956 movie *Design for Dreaming* (viewable in the Prelinger Archives at www.archive.org) or 'space travel'.

There seem to be many varieties of innovation and varying degrees of technological advance. For example there are many new special coatings or cores for yarns and new performance fabrics (Horrocks and Anand, 2000). In textiles, there have been new approaches to practice (Gale and Kaur, 2002: 21-33); and the consumer electronics industry has researched new concepts in clothing (Verbucken, 2000). There have also been inclinations to see the modern urban environment as a new landscape, demanding a revised, radical, concept of fashion (Bolton, 2002). Given that industry is often involved in innovation and designers are often involved in creative invention the question arises as to what is our yardstick, do recent developments really constitute substantive innovation? Or was there just an era 'techno' which was simply the design zeitgeist of millennial change? Does innovation equate with the use of metals, fibre optics and the 'just landed look' or are we on the brink of something more remarkable? The answer to all three questions is most likely yes, but explaining why requires some fairly subjective assessments. For example it appears that, in the relative advance of technology, textiles, in particular yarn technology, has progressed more quickly and changed more radically than fashion. What is also evident is that textiles has found it easier to bring its new technology to the marketplace. In comparison, fashion, as we shall see, is on the brink of some profound changes but in general the promise of what is to come is currently far greater than the reality. We are still primarily in an era of research and development. There are a large number of reasons for this, ranging from economic disincentives to manufacturing difficulties and a different industrial research culture to textiles. At the moment therefore high-tech fashion is often conventional fashion that uses high-tech fabric. Perhaps it is the latter that stops us from wholeheartedly believing a revolution is underway.

The Redefinition of Clothing

Future business opportunities and hazards in the 'smarts sector' are equally substantial. Success will depend on having a clear conceptual grasp of market, culture and technology. One aspect of this will be understanding the difference between what clothing is, and was, and what it might become. To understand the technological and social direction of fashion and the fashion industry we need to perceive it as part of something much greater and the concept of clothing is key to gaining that perception. Many of the changes that are beginning to influence fashion start elsewhere within the broader industrial landscape and bring with them unexpected and new agendas. Clothing in general, rather than fashion, is in many cases proving to be the stimulus for technological innovation and new business opportunities. In some cases, such as the growing interest from the computer and communications industries, fashion is potentially a marketing platform for their own products and services; but *clothing* is understood as the system of delivery. These technological and business ventures into the world of fashion bear some similarity to the 'use' of Paris couture for brand-based merchandising (White and Griffiths, 2000: 128-30). The range of new markets, products and services which are potentially 'seen' within clothing (and often hence fashion) is extremely varied and quite often disconnected. What is evident is that the concept that clothing can be used to deliver a secondary product is becoming increasingly understood across a wide range of industries.

Drawing a distinction between clothing and fashion is perhaps easier said than done as the terminology available to us is not scientific or exact, there is a broad range of synonyms for what we wear, and their meanings frequently overlap. In the English language the term *clothing* sounds fundamentally utilitarian, its semantic emphasis or typical usage invoking thoughts of body coverage. In comparison *fashion* or *apparel* add more explicit meanings of style, identity and appearance. As a descriptor *clothing* is more often than not a generic, bland or neutral term, broadly applicable to all garments. The inclusivity which the term *clothing* represents is quickly lost when style, function or fitness for purpose are added to the mix, giving rise to other categorizations like workwear, sportswear, fashion, menswear, evening wear and so on. Consequently in ordinary usage and conventionally for the fashion and textile industries, the concept represented by the term *clothing* lacks specificity and is of limited use. However recent changes and innovations in technology and social habits indicate that the broader generic concept that *clothing* represents is an important one, and in many cases, important to industries we would not normally associate with fashion such as the computer industry. At the same time the narrower definitions of clothing-types are becoming increasingly blurred. Why the broader concept of clothing is becoming more important is dependent on three factors:

- the homologous relationship between the distribution of new technologies and clothing, i.e. personal mobile technology and clothing are both either worn or 'accompany' us wherever we go;
- the increasing trend of fabric-technology transfer between sectors;
- the blurring of clothing sectors, e.g. smart casualwear or fashion sportswear.

Coupled with the recent research into conductive yarns and fabrics, and fabric switches, clothing and computing grow ever closer. In turn this alignment coincides with the incorporation of mobile leisure and communication technologies into garments. Of course these leisure and communication technologies are themselves increasingly 'computerized'. In many ways since the late 1990s the scene has been set for a massive convergence of a wide range of technologies with fabric, and hence clothing, and hence fashion. As a result the business and design community became very aware of a new market which was potentially full of 'converged' products. The dilemma (or challenge) facing these communities is that the product archetypes for this new market do not exist. The result has been a period of design speculation and corporate efforts to stake intellectual claims on new products. Many of these products have universal potential. Their basic technology need not be tied to any particular category of clothing, but clothing, at a generic level, is part of the 'design mix'. Hence the indication is that *clothing* is being reborn as a paradigmatic concept, not within the world of fashion per se but within the worlds of information technology, textiles and lifestyle marketing. The consequences of this for traditional *fashion* are dealt with toward the end of this chapter.

Categorization

As stated the technological and marketing objectives will be to identify and create new fusion products. This will involve identifying the synergy between different types of clothing, fabrics, consumer products and services. Currently there are some well-identified areas of product research and a number of emergent, technological 'clusters'. These clusters may be broadly categorised as follows:

- body-centred;
- social;
- performance and work related.

We might add to these categories of research, other researches which concern technical underpinning. This fundamental level of technical research is generally directed at fibre, yarn or fabric and includes research into various types of *control* and *delivery* systems, which might themselves be broken up into further categories of *physical*, *biological*, *chemical*, *electrical* and *electronic*. All of these technical categories in turn permit us to distinguish between clothing products we might describe as

- naturally autonomous in their performance (due to inbuilt physical or chemical properties etc.);
- autonomous but incorporating monitoring and/or control systems;
- under our own intentional control.

It is worth noting that individual product ideas, whether clothing, fabric or yarn, often belong to more than one category. This may be because a function that a product incorporates is generic across a range of markets and applications (e.g. monitoring our bodies); or it may be because of the high degree of industrial or sector convergence implicit within the product (e.g. a sports garment might combine the results of materials research in space projects and deep-sea diving). Also new technology products are often named or classified according to prevailing market and cultural conventions, rather than some broadly generic schema. Hence phrases such as 'smart fabrics' or 'intelligent clothing' or 'wearable technology' are employed now, but they may not stand the test of time. The categories provided above, however, are probably sufficient to comprehend the pattern and nature of current innovation. More detailed definitions of product research and various examples are provided in the sections below.

There are a number of key, readily identifiable technological steps/goals to achieving truly 'smart' clothes. However at the moment the imaginative concept garment is often more prevalent than tried and tested solutions. There are a number of recurrent themes that either facilitate product development or are in themselves research goals. These are listed and categorized below, each with a brief explanation of typical use or a general explanation. Three categories are given (in italics, heading each list) that together comprise the overall thrust of current technological advances:

The merger of clothing and technology.

- Pocketing
  which permits the incorporation of small devices within a garment.
- Embedding technology in fabric/sandwiching
  for incorporating smaller devices or wiring.
- Fabric with integral technology
  permitting the fabric equivalent of electronic circuitry and components
  or
  incorporating materials that bring special properties as follows:

The advance of fabric technology

- Thermal
  fabric that reacts to, resists or controls heat and temperature.
- Chemical
  fabric that filters or releases chemical substances including gases.
- Microbiological
  most commonly fabric which is anti-bacterial or anti-fungal.
- Light
  fabrics which block or emit light or create light displays.

New functions of fashion and textiles

- Active
  products that can take actions on their own or under our control.
- Reactive
  products that react to environmental circumstances e.g. body-heat.
- Sensing
  products incorporating sensor technology.
- Dispensing
  products that release medical, healthcare or cosmetic substances.
- Communicating
  products that have communication and remote control technologies.

- Protecting
  products which protect us from, or help us avoid, hazards and injury.
- Empowering
  products that enhance or sustain our physical and sensory abilities.

Underlying Technologies

The range of technical research is so great it cannot be properly covered here. Innovations concerning the natural performance characteristics of textiles would generally fall within the definition of *technical textiles* and are discussed throughout this book. But smart clothing and new technology fashion, in general will require a range of core devices and performance properties. These will ultimately result in textiles and clothing that exhibit startling properties. These properties will range from fabrics that 'feel' or 'hear' to garments that 'know'. The majority of the ways that we access entertainment and communication through our senses – televisions, phones, music systems – will find technological equivalents in our clothes. But they will have new formal properties like flexibility, softness and even greater miniaturization to the point that some are almost imperceptible. Two examples of these underlying technologies are provided here. The first, 'sensing' fabric, already has a number of solutions to it, and simply awaits greater and greater refinement. The other example, nanotechnology, is an awesome new scientific 'project' for this and future centuries. We begin with the switching and sensing skin-like fabric technology developed by Tactex Controls Inc.

> The Tactex smart fabric technology is based upon a patented fiber-optic based pressure sensing technique. These fabrics consist of thin cellular elastomers, typically of urethrane or silicon. Within the fabric a large number of overlapping pressure sensing zones, or taxels, are constructed. An outer skin protects the fabric, and serves as a wear surface.
>
> Pressure being exerted on the outer skin, for example by a finger or stylus, is detected by several taxels in the vicinity of the finger. The exerted pressure changes the pore size distribution in the elastomer, which in turn changes the optical

> scattering properties in that area – this change in scattering properties is detected by the fiber optics, and interpreted as a pressure . . . detection and processing involve simple photonic devices and traditional digital electronics. (Tactex, 1998)

Tactex have a well-developed product but not one specifically aimed at fashion applications. However what is demonstrated by their product is that the integration of computing, communications, fabric and clothing is not a fanciful goal. Another example of a switching and sensing fabric, one that uses conductive fibres, is ElekTex made by Eleksen (eleksen.com)

During the twentieth century one of the great themes of technology was miniaturization. This theme was applied not only to the ubiquitious microchip but also to what are called micromechanical devices (Angell and Barth, 1983). The world of very small objects and machines, capable of being constructed at molecular level, like genetic engineering, will prove one of the great scientific quests of the twenty-first century (for a sample of the world of nanotechnology visit www.sciam.com/nanotech). This nanotechnology is now one that promises fundamental changes to the nature and properties of yarns and fabric, hence suggesting or permitting radically new applications for clothing. The simplest way we might think of it is as if somebody had invented a finishing process that allowed yarn or fabric to be coated with invisible microscopic robots. While it is still very early days, ultimately nanotechnology implies things like robotic fabric or clothing that could monitor its own or its wearer's condition and undertake various actions. The American National Textile Center has investigated the relevance and potential textile uses of what are called MEMS:

> a new type of machine tooling has been developed called microelectromechanical systems (MEMS). MEMS are characterized by being less than a square millimetre in size and include both mechanical and electronic components . . . Using technology similar to that for electronics manufacturing, actuators, sensors, and motors can now be developed. It is now possible to design equipment with mechanisms that are smaller than the diameter of fibers. (National Textile Center, 2002)

MEMS are perhaps one of the most futuristic of developments and likely to change all our goods and technologies, not just fashion and textiles. But they demonstrate that the future of technology holds much to surprise us. In the sections that follow the reader will need to be patient with some of the examples. They open up perspectives on new types of fabric and clothing. Some almost stand as symbols of what is to come, they are innovations yet to be transferred or find a role in what we ordinarily wear. Some are still at an early stage of research. The reader must therefore exercise his or her imagination to see their design potential and implications.

Performance- and Work-related Products

These may be defined as those

- that enhance physical performance or add functionality;
- that modify appearance;
- that extend the environment and circumstances of human–computer interaction.

Clothing has always been developed to help us endure, perform or enjoy our physical interaction with the world. The category of task- and performance-related clothing best known to the modern consumer is sportswear, but many individual items – denim, the blue jean, the overall or even the boot – resonate instead with the history of daily work. These two categories of performance- and work-related clothing products often share design criteria and research goals. Mobility, strength, weight, and the control of temperature and moisture are typical goals of fabric and garment research. Today these physical goals are joined with garment technologies that alert us to danger, prevent us from damaging ourselves or prosthetically exaggerate and enhance our natural abilities. One of the more interesting aspects of these types of clothes, is that while the research goals are often similar, the economic and legislative framework surrounding their manufacture and production vary widely. For example the economic and production criteria for military and space garments bear little equivalence to those for ordinary sportswear.

Although fashion has demonstrated quite forcibly that there is a continuum between what we wear for work and what we wear for leisure or special occasions, there are some particular categories of work-related clothing where the appearance or comfort of clothes are secondary to functional purposes. Uniforms, protective clothing and various suits for extreme environments have, until recently, been the mainstay of workwear. They are now joined by a range of new clothing products which extend the field of potential definitions and classifications of workwear. Infused with 'smartness' and employing an array of new fabric and constructional technologies, these new types of clothes begin to have qualities we associate with comic-book heroes and the adventurers and beasts of science fiction. This new workwear pushes the limits of where the body can go and what it can do much further. The goals range from the pursuit of invisibility to the impenetrability of a superhero.

The economic might of America and in particular of its various nationally funded organizations, such as NASA or the United States Army, does much to fuel research into smart- and high-performance fabrics and clothing. While some projects take place within the research confines of these institutions themselves, more often than not projects are commissioned or put out for tender. One example is the US Army's decision to select MIT (Massachusetts Institute of Technology) as the winner of a competition to create lightweight molecular materials for incorporation into soldiers' clothing. The Institute for Soldier Nanotechnologies (ISN), a $90 million project, will focus on the development and use of nanoscience and nanotechnologies to enhance key areas of soldiers' abilities – threat detection; threat neutralization; concealment; enhanced human performance; automated medical treatment; and logistical goals. It is intended that microscopic devices and materials incorporated into the materials employed in soldiers' uniforms, will allow the uniforms to be instantly transformed into armour, weapons and even medical casts. Other goals include creating clothing materials that will enhance soldiers' physical abilities, for example allowing them to jump over 20-foot walls (MIT News, 2002).

One obvious beneficiary of the research undertaken by the ISN will be US Army's Natick Soldier Center (NSC). Apart from the military objectives of the NSC's research programmes, it is, in and of itself, a real crucible for up-to-the-minute clothing research and many of the NSC's projects will undoubtedly influence and benefit the civilian clothing sector. Research projects at Natick include stitchless fabrication and seamless garment production; the integration of electronics into clothing; in fact, many of the essential goals

Figure 6.1
'Future Warrior' project. Concept design for 2025 soldier combat ensemble. Courtesy US Army Natick Soldier Center. Photographer Sarah Underhill.

of future clothing. Few civilian organizations could match the NSC's 'ordinary' clothing research. However the NSC's purpose also takes its research into other spheres altogether. In this chapter we have already introduced various categories of future clothing, the requirements for tomorrow's combat uniforms add many more. Future Warrior (FW) is described as a visionary concept of how the warrior might be equipped some time around 2025. Embodied

Figure 6.2
'Objective Force Warrior' project. Concept design for 2010 soldier combat ensemble. Courtesy US Army Natick Soldier Center. Photographer Sarah Underhill.

within the FW concept there is a model of multifunctionalism, not really seen in non-military visions of future clothing. For example the FW combat uniform specification comprises three functional layers – a protective outer layer, a power centric Layer and an inner life critical layer – each layer integrating a range of sophisticated and practical technologies. The majority of technologies to be incorporated, by and large, either exist already or are not hugely fanciful. The FW project is essentially about how advanced garment engineering can be aimed at delivering exceptional and highly flexible functionality. Part of a staged and evolutionary approach to design, FW represents the step that follows another of the projects at Natick, the Objective Force Warrior, scheduled for realization by an altogether more tangible 2010. The clothing and equipment requirements of the modern infantryman or woman has spawned a range of research programmes around the world. For example alongside the United States, the United Kingdom, Australia and Canada all support programmes with overlapping or similar objectives, including resistance to chemical and biological weapons; body armour; lighter loads; and integrated communications, command and control systems (Erwin, 2002).

Now researchers are also investigating artificial, extra, 'muscle power' and seeing how it can be incorporated into clothing. Research currently aimed at military and medical applications might one day be aimed at the tired hiker, the weary cyclist or rockclimber. Perhaps our clothes might even teach us new dance moves! So far though, it is very early days. But the economic potential and the correlation between clothing and muscles may one day change the way we experience tiredness, incapacity or movement itself. Typically research of this kind, when at an early stage, is often to be found where moral or academic agendas apply. For example the robotic creation of Dr Hiroshi Kobayashi currently being developed at the Tokyo University of Science:

> Elderly people could one day be relying on a bodysuit, rather than a Zimmer frame, for support. Scientists in Japan are developing the 'Michelin gran' lycra suit, which is covered in pairs of inflatable "muscles" which assist the wearer's real muscles. When they inflate, they help the wearer move their limbs with more strength and stability. (BBC News, 2002a)

The way in which military and medical research connect with fashion is through the mutual world of textiles. Fabric performance characteristics, perhaps initially sought for hazardous or very practical situations, are translated into their consumer or lifestyle equivalents. Such technology transfer is not only limited to the world of electronic and mechanical devices, new science and new manufacturing processes are also providing innovative yarns and fabrics. For example, space research is one sector readily known for the way in which it seeks new materials. NASA's requirements for products offering very high thermal insulation properties have already found their way into clothing.

Figure 6.3
A jacket designed by Corpo Nove incorporating aerogel. Courtesy Corpo Nove (Grado Zero Espace).

> The New England company Aspen Systems, who helped NASA design new flexible aerogel insulation for cryogenic applications, has expanded into specialty clothing, especially useful if you are planning an Antarctic expedition.
>
> The Italian apparel manufacturer Corpo Nove started manufacturing the *Extreme Weather Jacket* using Spaceloft in 1999. This specialty jacket was designed for harsh weather conditions like Antarctica and will be sold by Hugo Boss. (NASA, 2001)

First discovered in the 1930s, aerogel is the lightest solid known, 90–99 per cent air, and a phenomenal insulator. Aerogel was of limited use until in 1999 Aspen invented a high-speed, low-cost

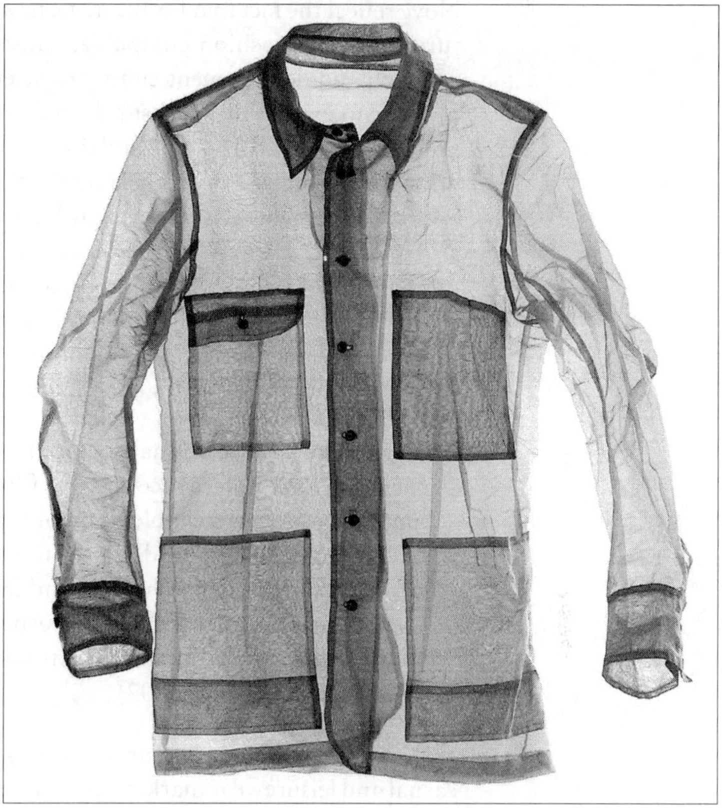

Figure 6.4
The 'Oricalco' shirt designed by Corpo Nove using shape memory metal alloy. Courtesy Corpo Nove (Grado Zero Espace).

manufacturing process. Starting with a contract from NASA's Small Business Innovation Research programme, Massachusetts-based Aspen Systems developed a range of flexible aerogel products for cryogenic applications. With over 800 applications identified for it, it is set to become a revolutionary new material.

The manufacturer of the Extreme Weather Jacket, Corpo Nove (www.corponove.it), has an exciting track record when it comes to innovation, experimentation and conceptualization. Their use of areogel arose from the company's previous research efforts in developing a cooling jacket. Apart from being the first company to develop commercial garments exploiting aerogel, they are also the first to have experimented with garment applications for shape memory alloys. In collaboration with Becagli and Texteam, Corpo Nove developed a special fabric using shape memory alloy. They subsequently developed the concept Oricalco Shirt, which will always resume its original shape as a result of gentle heating. Corpo

Nove reflect the fact that for future fashion and garment manufacture to evolve, fashion companies must themselves mirror the research and development culture of scientists and technologists in order to exploit the newest materials and manufacturing technology. In the field of fashion and textiles, the most obvious application for a product like aerogel is in the field of winter sportswear. Sportswear in general is increasingly high-tech and, given potential revenues, increasingly in pursuit of the culture and marketing mechanisms of fashion. The sports market, clothing and equipment combined, is some €37 billion in Europe and $46 billion in America. In comparison with many other clothing sectors the introduction of new performance fabrics can significantly open new markets

> The market for performance apparel fabrics is also being fuelled by the emergence of new fibres, new fabrics and innovative process technologies. Synthetic fibres and coatings have largely replaced traditional fabrics such as cotton. The development of high-tech fibres and fabrics have also led to greatly improved comfort levels, especially in high-energy sports and activities pursued in extreme weather conditions. (*Textiles Intelligence*, 2002)

Overall the sportswear market has begun to blur with lifestyle, casual and leisurewear markets; consequently for some time it has played with its own versions of haute couture. A good example would be the limited edition Cocoon Coat manufactured by the Japanese-owned company Descente and created for the Canadian ski team. It was designed by Oscar-winning costume designer, Eiko Ishioka.

> The coat looks like a sleek, pea shaped high-tech Teletubbie with bell-shaped arms. With it, Descente claims to have broken new ground by making garments designed for their psychological effects such as helping athletes to relax, to concentrate and even heighten awareness.
>
> They are shaped to 'wrap the athlete in tranquillity.' The bonded material from which they are made includes minerals that contain negative ions – apparently negative ions have a powerful positive effect on both body and mind. The minerals are powdered and impregnated into fibres, 'wrapping the athlete in a cocoon of natural energy.' (McAuley, 2002)

Figure 6.5
Example of the *ECOSYS* range of officewear. Courtesy Teijin Fibers Ltd.

Technologies that permit us to perform better or enter extreme environments are, in a sense, a particular case of body-centred products. Performance wear has to be designed with the body in mind, it increases our abilities by removing obstacles, hazards and distractions. But the extent or nature of assistance afforded by new fabrics and clothing technologies varies dramatically. Some allow us to endure where we would normally perish, while others provide us the mildest assistance and contribute to general comfort levels. Two products which amply illustrate this difference are the Smartcoat System for firefighters (www.smartcoat.com) and the *ECOSYS* clothing range for office workers. In combination they also allow us to draw subtle distinctions between the world of pure performance-wear, and performance-wear that can be 'situated' within fashion. That is to say some performance-wear is clearly designed without fashion in mind, while others implicitly or explicitly relate to fashion.

The Smartcoat System is an example of non-fashion performance-wear. In pursuit of better performance we tend to think that technology, as it progresses, continuously improves products, but sometimes new problems are created. Clothing developed to insulate and protect us, from sea, vacuum or fire can also detach us from potential warning signs. One example is the modern firefighter's outfit; high-tech thermal insulation is now so efficient it jeopardizes the safety of the wearer. The Smartcoat System has been developed to counter this problem and alert a firefighter to dangerous heat conditions that might lead to flashover, roof collapse or personal danger from burns. Employing a range of sensors strategically placed around the coat, heat conditions are evaluated every five seconds. An alarm is sounded if conditions become dangerous and life-threatening. The Smartcoat System represents a type of performance clothing designed to counter specific work-related hazards. Many design issues are therefore quite stark and functionality takes precedence over fashion. If there are fashion outcomes from the research represented by Smartcoat, they are most likely achieved through technology transfer.

The *ECOSYS* clothing range is, however, altogether more subtle in conception. In a joint research programme the Japanese companies Nisshinbo, Teijin and Nippon Keori Kaisha have developed a new range of textile materials for use in officewear. Originally with different interests in synthetics, wool and cotton, their combined expertise has resulted in officewear that simply keeps you a few degrees warmer or a few degrees cooler. While this may seem unremarkable, when translated into global corporate energy savings from reduced heating or air-conditioning bills, the importance is obvious.

> *ECOSYS28°C* was created under the concept of providing comfort in an office environment where air-conditioning is set to a moderate 28°C for energy-saving purposes . . . Similarly, we have commercialised *ECOSYS20°C*, a combination of materials for warm winter shirts that provides excellent heat-retention capability in a mildly heated office. . .we have begun to commercialise suits and slacks in order to increase our presence as a total office wear manufacturer. (Nisshinbo Co., 2000)

The *ECOSYS* range demonstrates how the advance of technology can 'find' performance issues that did not previously exist. It exemplifies how one sector – officewear – through innovation, has also become performance-wear. But unlike the Smartcoat System, officewear can never be purely functional. Status, identity and style will always concern the office employee and their employer. The *ECOSYS* range also demonstrates how many advances in performance-wear are still based within the world of 'conventional' textile technology. Also the idea that new performance issues can be 'found' can be attributed to the degree of control that new textile technology affords. After all, clothes have always kept us warm and kept us cool, but the precise way in which this can now be done allows us to create fabrics and clothes for specific uses. Often the motivations to create such fabrics and clothing arise outside the world of fashion and textiles. One example would be the increased concern about exposure to the sun and its linkage to skin cancers. Special fabrics have now been developed to block the sun's rays.

> Solarveil Sun Protection Apparel . . . blocks almost all of the UVA and UVB rays. This is possible because of the complex yarn structure, which reflects, refracts and blocks the UVA and UVB rays. The fabric is also treated with a UV inhibitor which absorbs UVA and UVB radiation to further prevent the sun's harmful rays from reaching the skin. (Solarveil, 2003)

Also the way swimwear, sportswear and leisurewear are styled and worn has changed.

> When Nicole Kidman took a jog in the blazing sunshine in LA last week, not a square inch of her pale skin was left exposed. She wore a long-sleeved top, scarf and gloves, as well as a hat and sunglasses . . . Australians have the highest rate of skin cancer in the world and, as they know only too well, over-exposure to the sun's ultraviolet (UV) rays causes permanent damage to skin cells via burning, premature ageing or skin cancer. (Mendis, 2002)

Wearable Computers

Another allied field of research and development concerns not so much the development of clothing but adapting computer technology so that it can be worn, adopting some of the functional paradigms of clothing – comfort, ease of movement, adaptability to environmental circumstances. In the arena of new clothing technology, wearable computers and high fashion are representative of the different cultures which are present. Almost diametric opposites, they show how different the contributory cultures are, and how independent of each other. All the more fascinating then how computing is subtly beginning to encroach on clothing, and toys with the idea of fashion. Much of the research effort in this field has been concerned with bringing computer power and information technologies closer to the arena of daily work and tasks, particularly outside the environs of the office. 'Wearable technology' has much in common with other varieties of portable computing such as laptops, palm-held devices and so on but it provides the added advantage of delivering computer power in, for example, situations where the hands are not always free or in circumstances which are hazardous. The term 'wearable technology' is in general rather loosely applied, and often as much to *clothes that incorporate technology* as to *technology that is worn*. It is however worth pursuing the distinction between these two categories as they represent different cultural origins, ambitions and interests – clothes incorporating technology seem to be the goal of a wide variety of interested parties, including conventional purveyors of fashion and clothing. However the interest in technology that is worn (that which we might most properly call wearable technology) has been closely associated with the evolution of computing, particularly personal computing. With the turn of the millennium, and the progress of technology, this once straightforward dichotomy between the 'non-tekkies' and the 'tekkies' has started to blur. Take for example the corporate strategic approach of Philips who use the term *wearable electronics*:

> the ultimate dream is not to have easier tools: it is not to have to bother with tools at all! The step forward then is the integration of functions into objects that we do not feel clutter us, that are part of our life. The idea of integrating technology into clothing is therefore a logical step (Philips, 2003)

This broad-based view of convivial and unobtrusive technology – technology of all kinds – is appropriate to a corporation with many technological interests. A new era is heralded and the implication is that our technological world is about to undergo a major revision. Interestingly, the philosophical tenor of this statement shares similarities with the longer-standing technological optimism of science-fiction and computer buffs. What were once the wildest fancies and objectives of say, the academic research community, now seem plausible and converge with the interests of business.

> While wearable computers are empowering fashion accessories, clothes are still at the heart of fashion, and as humans we prefer to wear woven cloth against our bodies. The tactile and material properties of what people wear are important to them, and people are reluctant to have wires and hard plastic cases against their bodies. Eventually whole computers might be made from materials people are comfortable wearing. (Post and Orth, 1997)

Both of these statements sustain a humanistic view which gives priority to issues such as comfort and ease, issues which are readily identifiable with our notion of clothing. Compare them though with the traditionally 'harder', performance- and function-oriented language of the Xybernaut Corporation, provider of wearable computer systems who

> pioneered the research, development and commercialisation of wearable computer technology, hardware and related software. Designed for the worker who needs maximum mobility, portability and hands-free operation, the Xybernaut product line feature wearability, voice activation and full WINTEL compatability systems. Content is delivered before the wearer's eyes, where and when it's needed, without interfering with the full range of vision. (Xybernaut, 2003)

Products like these are undoubtedly an evolution of the PC, they are quite simply computers that you wear. They have precursors locked in both the conservative and the more romantic traditions of computing (see for example Steve Mann's website http://wearcam.org to get a full flavour of computer culture). The benefits of wearables are obvious and their market is in many senses secure. A number of universities, such as Carnegie Mellon, Massachusetts and Toronto, now even offer courses in wearable computing. Xybernaut's customers have included Federal Express and Bell Canada, and they have collaborated with Hitachi, IBM and Texas Instruments, confirming the industrial and business interest in them. The technology in its current form is attractive to companies seeking greater efficiency and productivity from their workforce.

For many at the forefront of technology, wearable computing is just one 'sign' heralding a new digital era, when a wide range of technologies and services will seamlessly converge, and in so doing will radically alter what we currently take to be daily normality (Rheingold, 2002, Lightman and Rojas, 2002). This new reality will be dominated by wireless mobile communications, allowing for example mobile hands-free connection to the Internet. If fully realized it will also create a data world in which our physical actions and behaviour, our possessions, and our computing and communication needs are all integrated. Tom Engibous, CEO and chairman of Texas Instruments, commenting on the relationship between communications, computing, wireless communications and the internet stated:

> The end users' experience will begin and end with communications. What happens in the middle is services and content . . . The mobile internet is . . . about real-time communications . . . that combine streaming video, audio, security, location-based services and mobile commerce . . . This will give people the ability to act on business, entertainment and pleasure anytime they want and anywhere they want. (Du Vergne Smith, 2001)

The story doesn't end with simply increasing access to the Internet or PC-based applications through the use of mobile or cell phones. Various new fundamental technologies are being established which will change the way we use computing and the ways we can communicate. Some of these technologies will have a profound impact on what we need and want to wear. For example the technology which underpins the integration of devices, from headset to automobile, is Bluetooth Wireless Technology (www.bluetooth.com). The logical outcome of this technology would be to create in effect a single physical network of consumer and work-based goods. Inclusion in this world of smart objects would be bound to become a necessity for the majority of us; we would have to wear something that integrated us. As much as we would have a new-found freedom to take our computing and communication functions with us wherever we chose, the price might also become that we have no choice but to take them. Mobile telephony provides solid evidence of this stick-and-carrot incentive which underlies the adoption of new technologies:

> more than half of American adults would, if given the choice, gladly carry around multiple wireless devices if that's what it takes to gain access to key communication and productivity tools. (Long, 2001)

Inevitably a tension arises between a practical, work-based or social need to carry devices and the way they (or we) look; issues of style, fashion and appearance naturally intervene. In an article for *Wired News*, Elisa Batista draws our attention to the cultural divide between the fashion world and the wearable technology world. En route she elicits some telling quotes from Scott E. Jordan of Scott eVest, 'I've encountered a lot of resistance from the mainstream apparel people . . . Then I got to Comdex . . . and I couldn't stock enough of them'; and also from Victor Chu, fashion technologist:

> It's become a battle between the cool people and the nerdy people . . . Fashion designers are driven by esthetics, looks and what is trendy. The electronics people are driven by functionality. (Batista, 2002)

Chu also makes some other points about conventional apparel retail issues – price, brand and so on – suggesting that the ordinary consumer might be strongly resistant to buying wearable technology. Others it seems are much more optimistic and it seems that the battle for acceptability has provoked a range of strategies to deal with the 'unfashionability' of 'nerdy geek-wear', these include:

- the integration of electronic components and circuitry with conventional clothing materials and processes, e.g. fabric and embroidery;
- making the technology look 'nicer' or 'fashionable';
- pretending or stating that the technology is (or almost is) fashion, e.g. using fashion marketing techniques or events.

Examples of these might include the fabric breadboard or 'smartkerchief' (Post and Orth, 1997); IBM's fascinating foray into digital jewellery (Bonsor, 2003); and Charmed Technology's very conscious use of the catwalk (www.charmed.com). Further technical issues to be resolved concern miniaturization and the problem of carrying power supplies, both of which contribute to the problems of equipment bulk and hardness. Of these, miniaturization is a conventional goal of computing and information technology and will undoubtedly progress. The issue of power supply is a more difficult problem but may not prove to be insoluble; for example; the work of Germany's Martin Rojahn, Markus Schubert and Michail Rakhlin who are developing silicon-coated synthetic fibres that generate electricity when exposed to light. Similar research is underway at Scotland's Herriot-Watt University (BBC News, 2002b). The future potential is for clothes that act as solar cells, providing energy from light; however one problem may lead to another:

> As far as fashion sense is concerned, colour shouldn't be a problem, explains Rojahn. Although the fibre is transparent, it can be made to take on different colours by adjusting the thickness of the transparent protective coating.
>
> 'Depending upon the thickness of the layer, it could be made to look blue, brown or greenish,' he says. So let's hope that either blue, brown or green is the new black. (abc.net.au, 2001)

We can see that the introduction of wearability as an issue in computer design has given rise to analogies and synergies with clothing, fashion, jewellery and various consumer-based portable technology markets – music, Internet, telephony and so on. Through these developments clothing for work will support many new work functions and requirements, particularly allowing our further integration with communication and management environments. When coupled with our already pervasive interest in portable technologies for leisure and private use we can see that the scene is set for a new relationship with technology. Curiously, the very newest of our technologies, those of communication and computing, might it seems, find their final form and home within some of our most ancient – textiles, clothing and jewellery. The simple logic and reason of this being that they all revolve around 'us'.

In many ways though, the current nature of computer-related clothing reflects the fact that the research community has identified and been exploring the creative 'space' that is smart (electronic) clothes for some twenty or more years – and high-technology businesses are finally poised to exploit it. However the traditional business and manufacturing communities of fashion and textiles have focused instead on other areas of fabric technology and clothing development – notably areas more readily adaptable to existing techniques of yarn, fabric and garment production. There is in this situation a very important issue: that a completely radical transformation of the nature of clothing, the pursuit of integral computing, might not only risk commercial instability in the sector but would also (most likely) demand extraordinarily new manufacturing technologies (new processes of fibre, fabric and garment construction). This would amount to a level of investment in plant, machinery, research and training that few companies would entertain. This tension between existing investment, financial adventure, resource development and consumer demand is likely to become the commercial battleground of fashion and textiles during the twenty-first century.

Body-centred Products

These may be defined as those

- that measure and/or monitor the state and condition of our bodies;
- that administer or dispense chemical and biochemical materials to our bodies;
- that modify the localized environmental condition around our bodies.

Typically much research in this area focuses on health- and medicinally-related uses of clothing and fabrics. There is also military research concerned with monitoring or sustaining the physical well-being of soldiers, pilots and so on. There is a broad continuum of body-centred applications including conventional and 'alternative' medicine; healthcare and therapeutic sectors; cosmetic and personal hygiene sectors. With regards to research and development, there are some differences of approach between the textile sector and the military and medical sectors. The textile sector has particularly focused on fabrics and yarns that incorporate various chemicals. The military and medical sectors, have also looked at using clothing to monitor the human body.

There are a broad range of outcomes for body-centred products that are applicable to the general consumer and fashion markets. These include products that

- have a deodorant effect;
- have improved wearability and comfort levels;
- reduce the need for washing clothes;
- reduce the amount or weight of clothes we have to wear;
- make us feel, psychologically, more secure;
- enhance or stimulate our moods.

Interestingly, and although it seems generally unannounced, there are also potential future risks in such products – the downsides of the list above; for example, depression, self-delusion, product addiction, overdosing and laziness! However products which contain vices and virtues in equal measure tend to do very well commercially.

As stated, the medical and military sectors have investigated monitoring the body. Much of this research is a particular case of wearable technology and involves embedding sensors in fabric or clothes that connect to computer systems. For such technology to be worthwhile it is necessary to create data-models not only of the biophysics of the body, but also of the body in action and the body wearing clothes. This kind of research is undertaken by organizations like the US Army Biophysics and Biomedical Modeling Division. The Division studies the effects of heat and cold, sweating, moisture retention and loss, and blood flow (USARIEM, 2002). Their research has obvious applications in the field of sport and sportswear. Sensors play a key role in such studies and sensor technology grows ever more sophisticated. For example the Southwest Research Institute, based in Texas, adapted a sensor

> routinely used in oil field exploration to develop a a seismic heart rate monitor for the U.S. Army. This device identifies a heartbeat quickly, through multiple layers of clothing. (SwRI, 2003)

Medically oriented sensor products that might lead to more consumer-based versions include Vivometrics' Lifeshirt and Sensatex's SmartShirt. Now on the market, Vivometric's Lifeshirt

'. . . reads every beat of your heart and also your emotional condition. We read, for instance, every sigh that you take, every swallow, every cough,' said Paul Kennedy, president of VivoMetrics. (IFAI, 2003)

Sensatex's shirt, uses technology originally developed by Sundaresen Jayaraman at the Georgia Institute of Technology, with funding from the US Defense Advanced Research Projects Agency:

> The idea is to monitor vital signs like heart rate and breathing for a potential market that runs from the infirm to triathletes. 'You basically throw on a shirt and your EKG is monitored,' says co-founder and CEO Jeff Wolf. The 'smart shirt' uses fabric woven with optical fibers to send and receive electrical impulses.
>
> Although it'll be years – if ever – before Wolf's designs show up on the shelves of Gap and Banana Republic (Dalton, 2001)

Philips, a company which is very active in 'mapping out' the relationship between technology, clothing and fabric, have provided an interesting conceptual example of how body-centred products need not be overtly 'medical' and can provide a platform for a more holistic approach to well-being:

> The cream kimono has a conductive embroidered spine at the back, which is able to disperse an electrostatic charge via the fibres on the inside. This creates a tingling sensation that relaxes the wearer. Inside the pocket there is a remote device with a number of different settings for the various levels of relaxation. Biometric sensors monitor the degree of relaxation and adjust the level of sensory stimulation accordingly. (Philips, 2003)

Not all 'reactive' or 'interactive' clothing will depend on electronics and sensors. The physical properties of fabric and other materials can be cleverly employed to trigger the release of heat, cold or substances. One example is the parka developed by Columbia Sportswear:

> The coat detects when the wearer's skin temperature has dropped and releases heat. The key lies in a layer of microscopic wax bubbles on the inside of the parka that capture and store body heat. When the wearer's body temperature falls below a certain level, the bubbles, which seek an equilibrium with their immediate surroundings, release the heat to warm the body. (Dalton, 2001)

Fabric reaction to body-heat now seems a standard technique for delivering a wide range of products. For example the Austrian company Palmer's Lingerie make tights that release vitamins and German scientists are developing a fabric that combats dermatitis (*TIME Europe*, 2002). Other fabrics are scented, antibacterial or antifungal (Powell, 2000), or produce insect repellent. These products are highly dependent on advances in textile and fibre engineering and are 'made from textiles fused with non-fabric substances such as ceramics, glass, carbon or plastic' (Tippit, 2000). One company at the forefront of these technologies is the South Korean company Hyosung Corporation. Hyosung not only produce the technically advanced MIPAN range of yarns but also explore applications. For example in their Active Wear range for fall/winter 2003–4, fabrics for the Messenger trekking outfits incorporate antibacterial and antifungal treatments; battery operated, heated, rechargeable electronic circuits; and heat is regulated by micro-capsules. Hyosung are also researching a new way of dressing '. . .with one single layer against the skin, whatever the weather' (MIPAN, 2003).

Social Products

These may be defined as those

- that incorporate personal leisure technologies;
- that incorporate intrapersonal communication technologies;
- that indicate or display social and physical mood, intention or state.

The underlying difference between the technology we use for work and the technology we use for leisure grows ever smaller. It is also possible to say that for many of us the worlds of work and leisure increasingly blur. However most of us now have set expectations of social technology: the personal technologies we own, that give us access to entertainment, our friends and families. The way such technology looks and the way we can interact with it are important when technology is personally owned, and in the public view such issues can become very important. Such technology succumbs both to general fashion and the fashion of personal portable technologies. We become concerned how multifunctional, compact, stylish, desirable, and expensive the technology is. It is of course possible to say that many companies may exhibit concerns about their image as well, and manifest them through the equipment they possess, but personal ownership increases self-identification with technology. From sneakers to MP3 player, the owner-user's identity and attitudes are publicly visible through their possessions. Personally owned portable technology thus stands apart from many of the other technologies mentioned in this chapter by virtue of the fact that already, quite clearly, it has established its own 'fashion' market.

The research and development of clothing that incorporates social technology is currently dominated by attempts to shift from 'carrying' personal technological items, such as music and telephone systems, to 'wearing' them. In effect integrating one sector of personal, fashionable, products within another. The logical conclusion of this technological path would be the effective 'disappearance' of these technologies as they become ordinarily incorporated in clothes. There are a number of reasons why such full integration might not take place. For example, the entrenchment of such audio-related systems within the paradigms of product design – in particular the world of discrete, desirable gadgetry – suggests full incorporation is several marketing eras away. There are also quite clear economic arguments against such a change – a significant marketing question is why incorporate technologies that already have every quality a retailer or marketeer would value? For example personal technology already exists in a market of high value-added products; there is a constant turnover of new products; product diversification is enormous. Integrating such technology with clothing would be to lose a large, separate market. There are also economic arguments from within fashion concerning: the potential extra cost of such garments; investing in new manufacturing techniques; the need for new workforces. Finally there are consumer concerns and views about aftercare, durability and gimmickry.

The question arises then: what do companies from Levi to Apple to Pioneer see that leads them to investigate new fusions of clothing and technology? What future opportunities are they pursuing? The answers to these questions are quite complex. Prediction and analysis will vary from company to company. More often than not corporate decisions about the future are based on the current activities and identity of a company. For many companies the fusion of technology and clothing 'enters' their existing market; provides access to another; and implies an initial proliferation of new products and markets. For example compare the range of consumer products and services associated with the personal computer in the early 1980s (about the time of its inception) with now. Companies might also be identifying strategic expansions, takeovers or alliances. They will also consider logical extensions of market share and product ranges. There will be opportunities for copyrights, patents and licensing. In the very new area of techno-fashion and fabrics, imaginable future returns on research investments are phenomenal even if immediate returns might be small. For a company, even to be prepared for a market change and to be ready to take advantage of it may be the reward for funding research. These general principles of business strategy play out in different ways in the clothing and technology sectors. For example clothing companies may be interested in new manufacturing techniques. However for fashion-based companies like Levi, the stakes are higher. Their brand image, so linked with iconic advertising and youth culture is also, necessarily, linked with the world of popular music. Companies like Levi now also need to be identified with a youth culture that revolves around mobile/cell phones, MP3 players, Internet chat rooms and gaming. To ignore the collision of fashion with technology essential to the 'the young' would be to risk losing brand associations and market position. In 2002 Levi joined forces with Philips to produce the ICD+ (Industrial Clothing Design) range incorporating portable technology. The line was not a commercial success and was discontinued, leading no doubt to a review of strategy. Undeterred, Philips have collaborated with Nike to produce perhaps a more straightforward system with a fashion/technology branding. The psa (portable sport audio) range of products can be seen at www.nike-philips.com.

For the technology companies, risks are of a different kind, for it is not only a battle of maintaining brand and position. Such companies risk not being players in the next generation of consumer technology. And if the next generation of technology is wireless and embedded in textiles and clothing it will prove to be far more pervasive than anything yet seen. For example the limited-edition Burton Amp Jacket, launched by Burton Snowboards and Apple in 2003. The jacket demonstrates how greater fusion between clothing and technology increases the opportunity to listen to music in otherwise awkward circumstances:

> The Burton Amp Jacket makes it effortless for snowboarders and other active users to control their music from the sleeve of the jacket without fumbling with zippers, gloves or pockets. SOFTswitch technology allows the iPod to be controlled through a soft, flexible, textile control pad integrated directly in the arm of the Amp jacket. Riders simply touch the control pad on the jacket sleeve to change songs or volume levels, while the iPod is held safely in the jacket's chest pocket. As the SOFTswitch keypad is a textile solution it enables the Burton Amp Jacket to be machine washable (when the iPod is removed.) (SOFTswitch, 2003)

Although not a full realization of integration, the jacket is a good example of what is realistically possible now. The jacket is the first application of research undertaken by the Wool Research Organisation of New Zealand (WRONZ) and UK electronic materials company Peratech Ltd who jointly formed and own Softswitch Inc. (10meters.com, 2002)

Extending the variety of situations within which we can use our technology is only one outcome of smart clothing. Our traditional use of clothes for dramatic effect, social display and signalling is that aspect of social and human behaviour which, arguably, has received the least attention from the new technologists of clothing. Ironically, it is also perhaps the area of technological innovation that would prove to be of most interest to many conventional fashion designers. In smart clothing there are potential consequences for altering the way we behave, the way we use technology and our cultural evolution. For example the result of technological convergence and miniaturization is that 'smartness' will become an attribute of many consumer goods. In an increasingly smart artificial environment our clothes will most likely become the 'remote' that helps us turn goods on and off and provides us with universal control. Whether automatic or manual this new capacity for control will change the way we interact with our own, and public or shared technology. In so doing we will almost certainly change the cultural norms of our interactions and relationships with others. The introduction of clothing into the equation of interactive technology seems to have had a profound effect on the perspectives of technology researchers. Clothing has brought with it the ideas of fashion, lifestyle and physical activities, transforming an earlier technology-driven perspective. An example is one of Philips conceptual forays into wearable technology – 'IN THE MIX':

> this outfit enables the DJ to step out from behind his turntables and move around the audience while continuing to shape the groove . . . using the outfit's wireless connectivity, the DJ and the audience can influence each other and their surroundings with light and sound. (Philips, 2003)

Even conventional physical behaviour might change. The 'Blue Wand', a pen-like device developed by researchers at the University of Karlsruhe in Germany, permits the control of multiple devices through pointing and gesture (Fuhrmann, Klein and Odendahl, 2003). One day perhaps, what once seemed the impossible power of magicians and wizards, might simply be achieved through our shirtsleeves.

One area of technological development that may unleash many new types of clothing product is that of visual display systems; in particular, at that point in time when display units are easily integrated with, or take on the characteristics of, fabric. Fabric integration and fabric mimicry present two quite different routes of solution and hence different likely outcomes. Integration seems to lead to specific visual forms that act as significant design elements that strongly inform a garment's concept:

> . . . a 'firefly' dress made of electricity-conducting organza, decorated with a spray of tiny, motion-sensitive lights which flicker with the wearer's every move. (Noonan, 1997)

Or for example the eye-catching pieces of American company Ani-Motion as worn by Robin Williams at the 2000 Academy Awards (Renzetti, 2000).

> ANI-Motion's patented process includes designing and fusing fiber optic threads onto fabric to create coats, hats, banners or other fabric-based articles that display three-dimensional animated graphics. (JADE, 1998)

The strongest future contenders for visual displays that mimic the properties of fabric are organic thin-film transistor technologies which utilize plastic substrates. This new technology does away with the need for glass and hence rigidity. The genesis of this technology suggests that initially its uses will be to extend the reach of the video and computer screen. It is possible to imagine other uses like active surface patterning, but these are very early days. However this has not stopped designers from speculating about the future, particularly the industrial design team at Lunar Design, who have toyed with the idea of e-paper, another potential solution for fabric-like displays.

> BLU explores the impact of e-paper and Bluetooth technology from fashion and brand perspectives. Displays composed of a matrix of microscopic beads pick up radio frequencies that orient the array into recognizable patterns. Capable of changing color and image, the garment itself becomes a street-level billboard. (Lunar Design, 2000)

Conventional computer displays have already entered the world of wearable technology. In Japan, fashion designer Michie Sone has collaborated with electronics group Pioneer Corp. to develop a padded white jacket incorporating a small computer screen (Mori, 2002). One future aim is to develop a foldable, washable display panel. Pioneer has been researching ultra-thin flexible displays since the early 1990s. They are one player in the tremendous competition to develop and mass-produce polymer and organic flexible displays (Braun, 2002).

> 'With high-caliber collaborators like DuPont, Sarnoff and Bell Labs working together, we are accelerating efforts toward commercializing moldable display devices with full-color video capability,' said Dalen Keys, research and development leader for DuPont Displays. (Mokhoff, 2002)

Interestingly display technology has the possibility of a new kind of 'miniaturization' by using technology that projects displays directly onto the eye. American company Microvision's concept product Microdisplay can 'scan a low-power beam of coloured light across the eye, creating the effect of viewing a full-size screen' (www.mvis.com).

Products which are a fusion of fashion and social technology, in many ways are liable to have a greater research and development impetus than work-related or body-centred products. The potential consumer market for such products is immense. The introduction of personal technology rather than putting up the cost of garments is ultimately far more likely to drive costs down or establish new pricing mechanisms. For example the initial costs of garments might be defrayed to the services and functions the garment permits. Further such services and functions will simply be an extension of existing technologies. In 2002 approximately half the US population owned a mobile or cell phone (Kharif, 2002). Unlike many other new clothing and fabric technologies, social technologies are already with us, established and accepted. The only 'problem' is thus how to incorporate them in fabric and garment.

The Prospect for Fashion

All generations remark on the 'speed' of their times and the rate of change. For the professional fashion community, the cycle of stylistic change is central to its self-definition as a creative and commercial community. For example fashion designers often like to think they are in a 'fast-moving' sector. It is a fundamental tenet of computer science that the introduction of computers into any system of work or organization does not simply accelerate that system but transfigures its nature. This principle might be extended to the introduction of any technology. It is therefore interesting to conjecture what are the fundamental transformations that are happening to fashion. Based on the many examples given in this chapter, we can be certain that the simplistic view of fashion as homogeneous – the fashion of the catwalk, the magazine, the catalogue and the shopping mall – will give way to many more definitions of it. Equally the fabrics and materials used to construct garments will start to harbour other dimensions, adding to handle, drape, colour and so on; our ability to know what the 'function' of some fabric or cloth is may ultimately be dependent on the 'signs' in the garment. Throughout our history, clothing and later fashion, have had, respectively, clear purposes and clear contexts. In general, the purpose and nature of clothing and fashion have changed very little since their inception. Prospects such as those of autonomous or robotic clothing, or clothing we are in some way 'uncertain' of, are truly radical departures from the past. Changing fundamentally the psychology of wearing and our belief that a garment or cloth is a singularity.

> The relatively straightforward assimilation of computer-aided design into the mechanistic aspects of fashion design has perhaps simulated an illusion that modern scientific and technological advances have not and cannot fundamentally alter the nature of fashion, that is to say its spirit and its internal culture and rationales. However what begins to emerge now is that there are other forces at work, in industry, culture and technology which radically alter the idea of what clothing is about, what it is for, how it might be made and why it might be made. (Gale, 2001)

The changes happening in fabric and clothing relate directly and integrally to changes in other industrial sectors. Fabric and yarn are drawing in the technologies of communication and computing, and clothing provides the connectivity and networks in which we, either as worker or consumer, are immersed. These changes create a series of new agendas for fashion and textile professionals, and new expectations for the consumer. As the technological vision of fashion and textiles grows ever more complex, the environment of future business will also become less predictable. Those who can intuit which is the best way for business to jump – either as investor, collaborator, manufacturer or retailer – will prove more useful than those who simply follow next year's predictions. Fashion and textile innovators will scan cultures, making sense of technology and seeing its sense and use in human behaviour. Fashion and textile professionals will not only have to deal with other sectors like computing, they will have to adopt or adapt the knowledge and practices of those other sectors. Each time some new dimension, product, practice or politics is added, the idea of what fashion and fabric is will be tested.

To understand that a fundamental change to fashion and textiles has begun is difficult. Partly this is due to the fact that there are so many different types of innovation and invention. Partly it is due to the fact that the impetus for these changes is often occurring 'outside' fashion and textiles. Also some of the changes represent tentative beginnings of much more dramatic future developments. Finally we can note that much of the primary research preceding the technological innovations has a functional perspective on clothing and fabric. Indeed its initial focus may not even be on clothing and fabric. The research is often driven by various types of metrics, ergonomics, and performance, and is primarily quantitative. This latter has tended to mean that the first waves of change occur primarily in the clothing sectors that share, in part or whole, this strong functional perspective – sportswear, workwear, lingerie and so on. An interesting question is then – what next? The answer is most likely dependent on two industries that began a process of technological convergence some time ago – computing and communications.

From the examples given in this chapter, it seems very likely that computing, communications, textiles and fashion are heading for a convergence, some might say a collision. It may of course take decades but the industrial intentions, particularly from the 'electronics side', are clear. The convergence is not simply about the problems of manufacture or product development. What is sure to follow is the meeting and perhaps clash of different industrial cultures. The electronics industries will see markets differently to fashion and textiles. They have different approaches to product design and retailing, they build on no historical clothing connection like textiles and fashion. Currently we see short-term research alliances between the two sectors. Soon we may see more permanent arrangements, and when the technical issues are resolved and markets clear, perhaps mergers and takeovers. What are the alternatives? That everything remains the same. That clothing does not become increasingly 'technologized' or that somewhere a line is drawn and clothing does not change. These alternatives seem counter-intuitive, our experience tells us that a technological path, once begun, rarely ends.

We might end where we began – the unpredictable world of tomorrow's looks, style and taste. If clothing is becoming X then what will fashion become? In spite of the changing material and functional nature of clothing, fashion itself will always remain in some way transcendent. If there is a difference between fashion and clothing, it is that fashion has never been solely concerned with pragmatism, ergonomics or even for that matter, making money. There is a difference between the business of fashion, the culture of fashion and the personal realm of our possessions. Neither is fashion trivially described as some cultural and social phenomenon. It is as much about the psychic process of self-revelation through dressing as it is about affirmation of our cultural identity; it follows no great logics. In these many senses the future of fashion is unpredictable. But in another way it is also certain: even if *Vogue* and haute couture were to disappear, the party would go on, and their replacements would be found. But most definitely there will be a new factor, the technological innovations now commenced in fashion and textiles. Part of the broad progress of our constructed physical and cultural world.

Bibliography

10meters.com (2003), 'On This Runway, It's the Fabric That Makes the Fashion Statement', *10meters.com*, 16 December, at www.10meters.com/wronz.html.

AAPN (1998a), 'How "Quick Response" Works in the American Apparel Industry', at www.usawear.org/qr.htm, American Apparel Producers' Network.

—— (1998b), Summary, at www.usawear.org/qr.htm, American Apparel Producers' Network.

abc.net.au (2001), 'Smart fabric to power palmtops', 13 April, at http://abc.net.au/science/news/stories/s276981.htm.

Agins, T. (2000), *The End of Fashion: How Marketing Changed the Clothing Business Forever*, New York: HarperCollins.

AICE (2002), 'Israeli Textiles and Apparel', at www.us-israel.org/jsource/Economy/eco7.html, The American-Israeli Cooperative Enterprise.

Aillaud, C. (1988), 'Emanuel Ungaro', *Architectural Digest*, September.

Alexander, H. (2001), 'Time to collect an Autograph', at www.telegraph.co.uk/fashion/main.jhtml?xml=/fashion/2001/01/17/efhussein17.xml.

—— (2003), 'Milan round-up: Italian renaissance', 7 March, at www.telegraph.co.uk.

Angell, T. and Barth (1983), 'Silicon Micromechanical Devices', *Scientific American*, April, 284(4).

Anson, R. (2002) 'Which Way for Western Markets: Quick Response or Lowest Cost?' *International Textiles*, August/September, 829.

ASPAC-TCIF (2002), Chairman's Summary, at www.meti.go.jp/aspac/material/taipei.html, Asia Pacific Textile & Clothing Industry Forum.

Bailly, J. (2002), 'Carlos Miele Sticks to His Roots', at www.fashionwindows.com/fashion/carlos_miele/S031B.asp.

Balestri, A. and Riccetti, M. (1998), 'The Rationality of the Fashion Machine', in G. Malossi (ed.), *The Style Engine*, New York: The Monacelli Press.

Barbieri, A. (2002), 'Fear & clothing', at www.theage.com.au/articles/2002/07/17/1026802705923.html

Bartlett, D. (2002), 'Can suits outsmart your competition?', at http://news.bbc.co.uk/1/hi/business/1836010.stm.

BASK (1997), 'DOWN', at www.bask.info/tech/down1.php, BASK Ltd.

Batista, E. (2002), 'Of Geeks, Fashion and Oxymorons', *Wired News*, 10 January, at www.wired.com/news/business/0,1367,49504,00.html.

BBC News (2000), 'Hynde's leather protest arrest', 10 March, at http://news.bbc.co.uk/1/hi/entertainment/672719.stm.

—— (2002a), 'Inflatable muscle suits for elderly', at http://news.bbc.co.uk/1/hi/health/2002225.stm.

—— (2002b), '"Solar cloth" offers moveable power', 23 May, at http://news.bbc.co.uk/1/hi/sci/tech/2000633.stm.

Beckers, H. L. (1992) in H. M. Strange (ed.), *Milestones in Management: An Essential Reader*, Oxford: Basil Blackwell.

Bedell, G. (2003), 'The changing face of the brand', *The Observer*, 19 January, at www.observer.co.uk/review/story/0,6903,877476,00.html.

Bender, A. (2003), 'Fashion and Consumption' at www.marquise.de/en/misc/fashion.shtml.

Blanchard, T. (2002), 'The style council', *The Observer*, 17 November, at www.observer.co.uk/magazine/story/0,11913,841548,00.html.

Bocock, R. (1993), *Consumption*, London: Routledge.

Bolton, A. (2002), *The Supermodern Wardrobe*, London: V & A Publications.

Bona, D. (2002), *Inside Oscar 2*, New York: Ballantine Books.

Bonsor, K. (2003), 'How Digital Jewelry will Work', at www.howstuffworks.com/digital-jewelry.htm, HowStuffWorks Inc.

Borem, A., Santos, F. and Bowen, D. (2003), *Understanding Biotechnology*, New Jersey: Prentice Hall PTR.

Braddock, S. and O'Mahony, M. (1999), *Techno Textiles: Revolutionary Fabrics for Fashion and Design*, London: Thames and Hudson.

Braddock, S. and O'Mahony, M. (2002), *Sportstech*, London: Thames and Hudson.

Bradley, B. (2003), 'Decked Out in Deco', at www.gomemphis.com/mca/style/article/0,1426,MCA_530_2195842,00.html.

Braun, D. (2002), 'Polymer and Organic Flexible Displays', at www.chipcenter.com/eexpert/dbraun/main.html, EE TIMES NETWORK.

Breward, C., Conekin, B. and Cox, C. (2002), *The Englishness of English Dress*, Oxford: Berg.

Brooks, D. (2001), *Bobos in Paradise: The New Upper Class and How They Got There*, New York: Simon and Schuster.

Burns, J. (2002), 'Fur fight won't raise hackels', *The Age*, 8 May, at www.theage.com.au/articles/2002/05/07/1019441497342.html.

Burns, L. D. and O'Bryant, N. (2002), *The Business of Fashion*, New York: Fairchild Publications.

Burt, D., Dobler, D. and Starling, S. (2002), *World Class Supply Management: the Key to Supply Chain Management with Student CD*, New York: McGraw-Hill Education.

Cailliez, V. (2003), 'Going to Extremes', *International Textiles*, February/March 832.

Calvin Woodings Consulting (1996), 'Lyocell Staple Fibre for Industrial Applications', at www.nonwoven.co.uk/TITampere96.htm.

Carman, J. (1966), 'The fate of fashion cycles in our modern society', in R. Haas (ed.), *Science, Technology and Marketing*, AMA Conference Proceedings.

Carpio, L. (2002a), 'Seamless', *International Textiles*, June/July, 828.

—— (2002b), 'Vintage Designs and Fabrics', *International Textiles*, October/November, 830.

Cartner-Morley, J. (2000), 'The latest must-have from Milan: Pucci cushions', *The Guardian*, 7 October.

—— (2002), 'Daahling, can you tell me the way to M&S?', *The Guardian*, 12 September, at www.guardian.co.uk/g2/story/0,3604,790608,00.html.

—— (2003), 'How to wear clothes', *The Guardian*, 29 March, at www.guardian.co.uk/g2/story/0,3604,790608,00.html.

Chang, W. and Kilduff, P. (2002), *The US Market for Technical Textiles*, at www.sbtdc.org/research/textiles.pdf, Small Business and Technology Development Center.

Chen, C. and Dan, N. (2002), 'Advances in Biochip Research and Commercial Development in China', at www.863.org.cn/english/Forum/3.doc, Hi-Tech Research and Development Program of China.

china.org.cn (2000), 'Army-Style Clothing Mothballed', *Beijing Review*, at www.china.org.cn/english/2000/Jul/232.htm.

Chisnall, P. (1994), *Consumer Behaviour 3e,* Berkshire: McGraw-Hill Education.

Claritas, (2003), 'Adding Intelligence to Information' at http://cluster1.claritas.com/claritas/Default.jsp?main=4.

CNN (2002), 'A glimpse of retail tech future at Prada', at www.cnn.com/2002/TECH/biztech/11/03/retail.tech.ap/index.html.

Colchester, C. (2003), *Clothing the Pacific*, Oxford: Berg.

Collins, J. (2003), 'Colour Challenge', *Drapers: The Fashion Business Weekly*, 25 January.

Conover, K. (1997), 'Clothing Materials: A totally (or near totally) subjective analysis of newer clothing materials for outdoor clothing', at www.pitt.edu/~kconover/Clothing%20Materials.htm.

Consumer Reports (1999), 'The Dress-Down Uniform: khakis', March, at www.consumerreports.org.

—— (2002), 'Finding jeans for you', August, at www.consumerreports.org.

Cotton Incorporated, (2003), *LifeStyle Monitor* - Spring/Summer 2000, at www.cottoninc.com/lsm15/homepage.cfm?Page=2445.

Cowey, P. (2002), 'Using Antimicrobials for Profit in the Textile Industry', *International Textiles,* May, 827.

Craik, L. (2000), 'Pucci', *The Guardian*, 10 March.

CTEI (2000), 'National Conference on Textiles Development', at www.ctei.gov.cn/textlib/Englishnews/00032401.htm.

Dalton, G. (2001). 'A Shirt that Thinks', at www.thestandard.com/article/0,1902,26999,00.html.

Dam, J. (1999), 'Issey Miyake', at www.time.com/time/asia/asia/magazine/1999/990823/miyake1.html.

Damhorst, M. L. (2002a), 'The Fashion Process', 11 April, at www.fcs.iastate.edu/classweb/Spring2003/TC165/notes/fashionx.pdf.

—— (2002b), 'Fashion Leadership Theories', 11 April, at www.fcs.iastate.edu/classweb/Spring2003/TC165/notes/fashionleadX.pdf.

Davis, B. (2003), 'Helmut Lang: Minimalism at its Best', at www.fashionwindows.com/runway_shows/ helmut_lang/default.asp.

Deeny, G. (2002), 'Fendi: Molto Moderno', at www.fashionwindows.com/runway_shows/fendi/MS031.asp.

—— (2003), 'Ralph Lauren Loosens Up for New Italian Flagship', at www.fashionwindows.com/fashion_designers/ralph_lauren/MF031.asp.

Deffeyes, K. (2003), *Hubbert's Peak: The Impending World Oil Shortage*, Princeton, NJ: Princeton University Press.

Desmond, J. (2003), *Consuming Behaviour,* Hampshire: Palgrave.

Dickerson, K. and Hillman, J. (1998), *Textiles and Apparel in the Global Economy*, 3rd Edn, Englewood Cliffs, NJ: Prentice Hall.

Diderich, J. (2003), 'Karl Lagerfeld clones himself on Paris catwalk', *World Environment News*, 10 March, at www.planetark.org/avantgo/dailynewsstory.cfm?newsid=20090, Reuters.

DNRE (2002), *Agriculture Notes: Ostriches*, State of Victoria Department of Natural Resources and Environment.

Dorner, J. (1975), *Fashion in the Forties and Fifties*, New York: Arlington House.

Du Pont (2001a), 'The Consumer/Retail difference: why choose LYCRA® brand?', E.I. duPont de Nemours and Company, at www.lycra.com/Lycra/difference/retail.html.

—— (2001b), 'The Consumer/Retail difference: why choose LYCRA® brand?', E.I. duPont de Nemours and Company, at www.lycra.com/Lycra/difference/retail.html.

—— (2001c), 'New in Consumer/Retail', E.I. duPont de Nemours and Company, at www.lycra.com/Lycra/news/retail.html.

Du Vergne Smith, N. (2001), 'Texas Instruments poised to ride the mobile Internet', *Tech Talk*, 14 February, at http://web.mit.edu/newsoffice/tt/2001/feb14/engibous.html, MIT News Office.

emergingtextiles.com (2003), 'US textile imports up 44% in December', Monthly Report, 21 February, at www.emergingtextiles.com.

Enokiworld (2003), '1980s Zoran Black Cashmere Sweater and Skirt', at www.enokiworld.com/goods/zorancashmere.htm.

Entwistle, J. (2003), 'Fashion as Culture Industry', at http://ist-socrates.berkeley.edu/~nalinik/newslett/n0004_entwistle.html.

ERGO (1998), 'Manufacture of holgraphic fabrics', at www.cordis.lu/ergo/home.html, European Research Gateways On-Line.

Erwin, S. (2002), 'Lighter Load is Cyber-Soldier Dream', *National Defense*, at www.nationaldefensemagazine.org/article.cfm?Id=112.

ESEB (2001), 'Genes, domestication and conservation: the impact of molecular studies', Symposium of the 8th Congress of The European Society for Evolutionary Biology, Aarhus, Denmark, at http://biology.aau.dk/eseb/symposia/23.html.

Europa (2002 a), 'Smart fibres protect their users – and their makers', at http://europa.eu.int/comm/research/growth/gcc/projects/smart-fibres.html, European Commission.

Europa (2002b), 'Overview of the Textile and Clothing Industry', at http://europa.eu.int/comm/enterprise/textile/overview.htm, The European Commission.

Farina, A. (2003), 'Clothing from Corn: DuPont develops innovative process to create polymer from renewable resources', at www.eurekalert.org/pub_releases/2003-02/d-cfc012903.php.

Fashion Bit (2002), 'Fendi', Fashion Bit: Italian Style Online, at www.fashionbit.com/fendi.asp, Bari: IBOL.

Fashion India (2002), 'At your Service – SEWA', at www.fashionindia.net/reviews/2002/feb/sewa.htm.

FFS (2003), 'A Healthy Part of a Vibrant Economy', at www.ffs.fi, Finnish Fur Sales.

Foster, L. (2003), 'Designs on Debenhams', *Drapers: The Fashion Business Weekly*, 25 January.

Freeman, H. (2000), 'Oversubscribed: Pucci's new boutique', *The Guardian*, 6 October.

—— (2003), 'Gongs and gags at the Oscars fashion parade', *The Guardian,* 24 March, at http://film.guardian.co.uk/oscars/story/0,12712,921085,00.html.

Frey, N. (1998), 'How to do it: An Interview with Paul Smith', in G. Malossi (ed.), *The Style Engine*, New York: The Monacelli Press.

Frings, G. (2001), *Fashion: from Concept to Consumer*, Englewood Cliifs, NJ: Prentice Hall.

Fuhrmann, T., Klein, M. and Odendahl, M. (2003), 'The Blue Wand as Interface for Ubiquitous and Wearable Computing Environments', at http://tm.uni-karlsruhe.de/~fuhrmann/BlueWand, University of Karlsruhe.

Gale, C. (2001), 'Design Dilemmas: The Impact of Industry, Culture and Technology on Fashion and Textiles', *The Fashion Future International Conference*, Taipei: Oriental Institute of Technology.

—— and Kaur, J. (2002), *The Textile Book*, Oxford: Berg.

Galindo-Meyer, C. (2003), 'Innovations: Hispanic Opinion Leaders' Role', at www.mcnair.berkeley.edu/uga/osl/mcnair/93BerkeleyMcNairJournal/CarmenGalindoMeyer.html.

Gallup (2003), 'The Gallup Organization', at www.gallup.com/help/about.asp.

Gap (2003), 'Ethical Sourcing Program', at www.gapinc.com/social_resp/sourcing/Beyond_the_Label.pdf.

GilbertZ (2000) 'World-Renowned Manufacturer St. John Knits to Implement Movex Fashion for Enterprise', Company Press Release at www.diamondtalk.com/forums/showthread.php?threadid=5598.

Global Sources (2002), 'Supply Chain Management: Collaborating for online solutions', at www.globalsources.com/MAGAZINE/FAS/0204/PECOMM4.HTM.

Godwin, E. W. (1884), *Dress, and its Relation to Health and Climate,* London: William Clowes and Sons.

Gray, K. (2002), 'Media Fashion Editors; Anna Wintour: "The Summer of her Discontent"', at http://fashion.about.com/cs/fashioneditors.

Groom, A. (2002), 'Pringle belles', at www.totalbusiness.org.uk/LS/luxury%20lifestyle/octnov02/058.asp.

Hagy, T. (2003), 'Christian Lacroix's Ball of Triumph', at www.fashionwindows.com/fashion_designers/christian_lacroix/hcs031.asp.

Handley, S. (2000), *Nylon: The Story of a Fashion Revolution: A Celebration of Design from Art Silk to Nylon and Thinking Fibres*, Baltimore: John Hopkins University Press.

Harris, J. G. and Davenport, T. H. (2001), 'Crouching Customer, Hidden Insight', CRM Project Volume 2, at www.crmproject.com/documents.asp?grID=170&d_ID=767.

Heisler, E. (2001), 'Corn Being Used to Produce Clothing and Other Textiles', *Greensboro News & Record*, at http://news.nationalgeographic.com/news/2002/07/0713_wirecornfabric.html.

Hello Magazine (2003), 'Pringle Ads Reveal Classic Side to Sultry Sophie', at www.hellomagazine.com/2003/01/23/sophiedahl.

Henahan, S. (1996), 'Bioengineered Spider Silk', at www.accessexcellence.org/WN/SU/spider.html.

Hillard, G. (1997), 'After a fashion: Hollywood stars attend Oscars show in style', CNN, 26 March, at www.cnn.com/SHOWBIZ/9703/26/oscar.fashion.

Hodson, H. (2001), 'Groomed for success', *The Telegraph*, 7 August, at www.telegraph.co.uk/fashion/main.jhtml;$sessionid$XD5JUQR5CD5DBQFIQMGCFF4AVCBQUIV0?xml=/fashion/2001/08/07/eflauder06.xml.

Hopkins, S. (1999), *The Century of Hats*, London: Aurum Press.

Horrocks, A. and Anand, S. (eds) (2000), *Handbook of Technical Textiles*, Cambridge: Woodhead and Manchester: The Textile Institute.

Horyn, C. (1999), 'Reviews/Fashion; Zoran, the Master of Deluxe Minimalism, Still Provokes', at http://query.nytimes.com/search/full-page?res=9F06E3D71F3BF933A15757C0A96F958260.

Hyman, H. H. (1960), 'Reflections on reference groups', *Public Opinion Quarterly*, Fall.

IFAI (2003), 'VivoMetrics' Lifeshirt Receives Market Clearance', at www.ifai.com, Industrial Fabrics Association International.

Industry Forum (2001), *Designer Manufacturing Handbook*, at www.industryforum.net.

—— (2002), 'Stevensons Garment Dyers', Case Study, at www.industryforum.net.

InfoManager (2003), 'Finnish Fur Sales deploys InfoManager Business Intelligence to provide the latest business information', at www.infomanager.fi/Web/Infomanager/europe/cases/ffs.html.

Integrity Publishing (2003), 'Exclusively Series; Las Vegas', St. John Boutique, at www.integritypublishing.com/ex_vegas_pages/stjohn.html.

International Textiles (2003a), 'Bayer Adds Essence to Textiles', *International Textiles,* February/March, 832.

—— (2003b), 'Hyosung Stretches its offer', *International Textiles,* February/March, 832.

JADE (1998), 'JADE and ANI-Motion Develop Fiber Optic Machinery that Lights Up the Clothing Industry', at www.jadecorp.com/jarch_anim.html, JADE Corporation.

Japan Information Network (2003), Focus 8: Japanese Consumers', at www.jinjapan.org/insight/html/focus08/consumption_of_goods/con03.html.

Jerrard, R., Hands, D. and Ingram, J. (2002), *Design Management Case Studies*, London: Routledge.

Jiang, L., Shuhong, L., Feng, L., Li, H., Zhai, J. and Zhu, D. (2002), 'Super-Hydrophobic Aligned Carbon Nanotube Films and Nano-

Fibers', at www.863.org.cn/english/Forum/4.doc, Hi-Tech Research and Development Program of China.

Kaul, S. (2000), 'Indian Fashion Going Places', *The Tribune*, 23 September, at www.tribuneindia.com/2000/20000923/windows/main7.htm.

Kharif, O. (2002), 'Dialling into Cellphone Chic', *BusinessWeek Online*, April.

King, C. W. (1963), 'Fashion adoption: A rebuttal to the "trickle-down" theory', in S. A. Greyser (ed.), *Toward Scientific Marketing*, Chicago: American Marketing Association.

—— (1964), 'The innovator in the fashion adoption process', in Smith, L. G. (ed.), *Reflections on progress in marketing*, Chicago: American Marketing Association.

Koolhaas, R. (2001), *Projects for Prada Part 1*, Milan: Fondazione Prada.

Kotler, P., Jain, D. and Maesinsee, S. (2002), *Marketing Moves: A New Approach to Profits, Growth and Removal*, New York: McGraw-Hill Education.

Kowalcyzk, P. (2001), 'Frenetic fashion cycle confuses consumers and stores alike', at www.newstribune.com/stories/022601/fea_0226010030.asp.

KSA (2002), 'Product Development - Charting a winning course', at www.kurtsalmon.com.

kuangmei.com (2002), 'The Healthy and Comfortable Fibre of the 21st Century: A Brief Introduction of Soybean Protein Fiber', www.kuangmei.com.

Kunz, G. (1998), *Merchandising: Theory, Principles, and Practice*, New York: Fairchild Publications.

La Ferla, R. (2001), 'Sober Yet Sleek, To Match The Times', at www.yeohlee.com/article5.html.

Lela (2003), '411', at http://chronicmagazine.com/burberry.html.

Lennox-Kerr, P. (2003), 'Innovations in Fibres & Fabrics', *International Textiles,* February/March, 832.

Lessona, L. B. (2003), 'Fashion Houses, Missoni', at www.made-in-italy.com/fashion/fashion_houses/missoni/intro.htm.

Levi Strauss (2003), 'What is Levi's® RED™?' in *RIVET: Selfridges – Bullring, Birmingham a CD prepared for the launch of the store RIVET.*

Lightman, A. and Rojas, W. (2002), *Brave New Unwired World*, New York: John Wiley & Sons.

Lipkin, R. (1996), 'Artificial Spider Silk: Scientists vie to synthesize the precious strands of the golden orb weaver', *Science News*, 9 March, at www.sciencenews.org/sn_edpik/ps_5.htm.

logolounge (2003), 'Trends: Fashion Logo Loyalty Declines Again', at www.logolounge.com/articles/default.asp?ArticleID=96.

Lohmann, B. (2000), 'Denim', at www.designboom.com/eng/education/denim2.html.

Long, M. (2001), 'Americans Say Yes to Multiple Wireless Devices', 10 March, at www.e-insite.net.

Lopriore, A. (2002), 'Check it out', *Metropolis*, 349, at http://metropolis.japantoday.com/HealthandBeautyarchive349/346/healthandbeautyinc.htm.

Lu, M. (2002), 'High-tech textiles coming into fashion', at http://publish.gio.gov.tw/FCJ/past/02101881.html.

Lumiere (1995), 'Langitude', at www.lumiere.com/fashion/95/12/lang.

Lunar Design (2000), 'Lunar's Blu Concepts' at www.lunardesign.com/portfolio/client_archive/blu.html.

lycra.com (2001), 'Experiments in techno fabrics and design', at www.lycra.com/Lycra/innovation/retail/spotlight_on_innovations/spotlight_on_innovations_1.htm.

Malossi, G. (ed.) (1998), *The Style Engine*, New York: The Monacelli Press.

Maneker, M. (2000), 'Just Suit Me', *New York Magazine*, 20 March, at www.newyorkmetro.com/nymetro/shopping/fashion/2455.

Marsh, G. and Trynka, P. (2002), *Denim: From Cowboys to Catwalk*, London: Aurum Press.

Marston, W. (2000), 'Future Tech: Wonder Wear', *Discover*, January, 21(1), at www.discover.com/jan_00/featwonder.html.

Martin, N. (1998), 'Vicinities: Fiber, Fabric, Clothing', in G. Malossi (ed.), *The Style Engine*, New York: The Monacelli Press.

Martin, R., Mackrell, A., Rickey, M., Buttolph, A., Menkes, S. et al. (1998), *The Fashion Book*, London: Phaidon Press.

McAuley, L. (2002), 'Canadian skiers lead way, in fashion, if not on slopes', at www.canada.com/sports/olympics/features/021402_fashion.html.

McCracken, G. (1990), 'Culture and Consumer Behaviour: an anthropological perspective', *Journal of Market Research Society*, January, 32(1).

McDowell, C. (1994), *The Designer Scam*, London: Hutchinson.

Mendis, G. (2002), 'Let's all do the Kidman cover-up', *Evening Standard*, 2 July.

MIPAN (2003), 'Active Wear: Magic Manga range', at www.mipan.com/eng/trend_info/2003_fall_active_01.html.

Missoni (2003), 'History; Biography', at www.missoni.it/eng/index.html.

MIT News (2002), 'Army selects MIT for $50 million institute to use nanomaterials to clothe, equip soldiers', 13 March, at http://web.mit.edu/newsoffice/nr/2002/isn.html, MIT News Office.

Miyake, I. (1978), *East Meets West*, Japan: Heibonsha.

Mokhoff, N. (2002), 'Trio to develop flexible, full-color displays', *EE Times*, 30 October, at www.eetimes.com/story/OEG20021030S0020.

Moore, C. M. and Burt, S. (2001), 'Developing a research agenda for the internationalization of fashion retailing', in T. Hines and M. Bruce (eds), *Fashion Marketing: Contemporary Issues,* Oxford: Butterworth-Heinemann.

Mori, A. (2002), 'In Tokyo, street fashion goes high-tech', *digitalMASS*, 6 February, at http://digitalmass.boston.com/news/2002/02/06/fashion.html.

NASA (2001), 'Aspen Systems Improves Aerogel Manufacturing Process', at http://technology.ksc.nasa.gov/wwwaccess/Stories/Facts/Aspen SystemsRevFS.pdf.

National Textile Center (2002), 'Micromachine Based Fabric Formation Systems: Objective and Relevance to NTC Mission', at www2.ncsu.edu/unity/lockers/project/ntcprojects/projects/F98-S12/objectiveand relevance.html.

NetLondon (1999), 'Sequin shortage threatens Millennium glitz', Net London.com News, 22 April.

Newman, C. and Kendrick, R. (1998), *Perfume: The Art and Science of Scent*, Washington, DC: National Geographic.

Newton, S. M. (1974), *Health, Art & Reason: Dress Reformers of the 19th Century,* London: John Murray Ltd.

Nexia Biotechnologies (2003), 'technology', at www.nexiabiotech.com/en/01_tech/index.php.

Nissan (2000), 'Autech Japan to Release Silvia Convertible', Press Release, 8 May, at www.nissan-global.com/GCC/Japan/NEWS/20000508_0e.html.

Nisshinbo. Co. (2000), 'The Power to Change, the Passion for Quality', at www.nisshinbo.co.jp/pdf/ar2000-no2_e.pdf, Nisshinbo. Co.

Noonan, E. (1997), 'Computerized clothing part of fashion's future', *Las Vegas Review-Journal*, 9 November, at http://lvrj.com/lvrj_home/1997/Nov-09-Sun-1997/business/6250660.html.

NTC (2002), 'The Role of Emotion in Success of Global Textile Product Retailing', Project No. I01 –A31, at www.ntcresearch.org/current/year11/yr11_proj.htm, National Textile Center.

Nystrom, P. (1928), *Economics of Fashion*, New York: Ronald Press.

Orecklin, M. (2000) 'A Sense of Style Beyond the Cutting Edge', at www.time.com/time/innovators/design/profile_chalayan.html.

Padgett, S. (2000), 'Fashion Forward: Hot Leather', *Las Vegas Review-Journal*, at www.reviewjournal.com/lvrj_home/2000/Oct-30-Mon-2000/living/14678794.html.

PageWise (2002), 'Vicuna wool', at www.allsands.com/Fashion/vicunas woolsca_rvz_gn.htm.

Parker, J. (1992), *All About Silk: A Fabric Dictionary & Swatchbook*, Fabric Reference Series Volume 1, Seattle: Rain City Publishing.

Parrinder, M. (2000), 'Move On', *'things' magazine*, winter, 11, at www.thingsmagazine.net/text/t11/pradasport.htm.

Pavitt, J. (2000), *Brand New*, London: V&A Publications.

Pearson, S. and Knudsen, D. (2003), 'Critical Trends and Emerging Solutions', at www.freeborders.com/company/press/coverage/03_31_03.shtml, just-style.com.

Pesch, M. (1996), *Techno Style: Music, Graphics, Fashion and Party Culture of The Techno Age*, Zurich: Edition Olms

Peterson, P. (1965), 'Some approaches to innovation in industry', in G. Steiner (ed.) (1965), *Creative Organization*, Chicago: University of Chicago Press.

Petrie, O. (1995), 'Harvesting of textile animal fibres', FAO Agricultural Services Bulletins – 122, at www.fao.org/docrep/v9384e/v9384e05.htm, Food and Agriculture Organization of the United Nations.

Philips (2003), 'New Nomads, an exploration of Wearable Electronics', at www.design.philips.com/smartconnections/newnomads/index.html, Philips.

Phillips, E. (1999), If IT Works, It's Not AI: A Commercial Look at Artificial Intelligence Startups, at http://kogs-www.informatik.uni-hamburg.de/~moeller/symbolics-info/ai-business.pdf

Popcorn, F. and Marigold, L. (2000), *EVEolution: The Eight Truths of Marketing to Women*, London: HarperCollins.

Post, E. and Orth, M. (1997), 'Smart Fabric, or Washable Computing', at www.media.mit.edu/~rehmi/fabric/.

Powell, C. (2000). 'a fresh start', *International Textiles*, February, 810.

Pringle, H. (2001), 'Secrets of the Alpaca Mummies', *Discover*, April, 22(4), at www.discover.com/apr_01/featalpaca.html.

Quelch, J. (1999), 'Global Village People' at http://backissues.worldlink.co.uk/articles/19021999195259/14.htm.

Quinn, B. (2002), *Techno Fashion*, Oxford and New York: Berg

Raymond, M. (2001), 'The making of a trend', in T. Hines and M. Bruce (eds), *Fashion Marketing: Contemporary Issues*, Oxford: Butterworth-Heinemann.

Renfeng, Z. (2003), 'New fur fashion trend spells big biz opportunities', at www1.chinadaily.com.cn/bw/2003-01-21/103175.html.

Renzetti, E. (2000), 'Fibre Optics Make Flashy Oscar Statement', *The Globe and Mail*, 1 April, at www.animot.com/news/040100academy awards.html.

Rheingold, H. (2002), *Smart Mobs: The Next Social Revolution*, Cambridge MA: Perseus Books.

Rickey, M. (2003), 'Welcome to the New World of British Fashion', at www.fashionwindows.com/fashion_review/london/S03_preview.asp.

Rivers, V. (2003), *The Shining Cloth: Dress and Adornment that Glitters*, London: Thames and Hudson.

Robson, J. (2002), 'All set for an Indian summer', *The Telegraph*, 21 May, at www.telegraph.co.uk/fashion/main.jhtml?xml=/fashion/2002/05/21/efash18.xml.

Rosen, E. (2002), *Making Sweatshops: The Globalization of the U.S. Apparel Industry*, Berkeley: University of California Press.

Salomon Smith Barney (2001), 'The Birth of Collaborative Commerce: A Closer Look at this Nascent Industry', at www.freeborders.com/industry/analysis.shtml.

Scheller, J., Gührs, K., Grosse, F. and Conrad, U. (2001), 'Production of spider silk proteins in tobacco and potato', *Nature*, 19(6).

Schneider, F. (1997), 'Arthur Anderson, Counting the cost', *Retail Week*, 24 July.

Seabrook, J. (2001), *Nobrow*, London: Methuen.

Sherwood, J. (2003), 'London fashion's dilemma: Are shows a 'media circus' or a way to showcase talent?', *International Herald Tribune*, 12 March, at www.iht.com/articles/89486.html.

Shiro, A. M. (1995), 'The Designer's Starting Point', *Women's Wear Daily*, 18 April.

Singleton, A. (2002), 'Cashmere - fiber of kings', Trade Partners UK New Products Press Release LPS 61, 18 July.

Sinha, P. (2001), 'The mechanics of fashion', in T. Hines and M. Bruce (eds.), *Fashion Marketing: Contemporary Issues,* Oxford: Butterworth-Heinemann.

Smith, R. (1999), 'Design Review: Inventive Garments Designed to Go With the Flow', *The New York Times*, 26 November, at http://query.nytimes.com/search/full-page?res=9506E5DE173FF935A15752C1A96F958260.

Smithsonian (2003), 'The Feather Trade & the American Conservation Movement: Feather Adornment', Virtual Exhibition at http://americanhistory.si.edu/feather/ftfa.htm, Smithsonian Institution's National Museum of American History.

Snead, E. (1997), 'Stone rocks fashion world by going gap', at www.usatoday.com/life/special/l96os062.htm.

SOFTswitch (2003), 'SOFTswitch technology enables Burton to release their Amp Jacket at MacWorld', at www.softswitch.co.uk/SOFTswitchNews.html.

Solarveil (2003), 'How does Solarveil work', at www.solarveil.com/info.htm.

Sones, M. (2002), 'Beauty, Feathers, Fur, and Fashion', at www.beautyworlds.com/beautyfeathersfashionfur.htm.

South African News (2000), 'Clothing Industry', *South African News*, 21(2), at www.southafrican-embassy.at/wirtschaft/trade.pdf.

South Beach Magazine (2003), 'Bal Harbour Shops: St. John/Galtrucco', at www.southbeach-usa.com/shopping/bal-harbour-shops/st-john-galtrucco.htm.

Stengg, W. (2001), 'The Textile and Clothing Industry in the EU: A Survey', Enterprise Papers No 2, at http://europa.eu.int/comm/enterprise/library/enterprise-papers/paper2.htm, The European Commission.

Stone, E. (2000), *The Dynamics of Fashion*, New York: Fairchild Publications.

Stone, J. and Farr, B. (1997), 'Iowa Textile and Apparel Industry News', 2(4), at www.iastate.edu/~tc-ext/PDF_files/v2n4.pdf.

Stuart, C. (2003), 'Nano-Tex's new CEO will seek the public eye, and to go public', *Small Times*, 21 January, at www.smalltimes.com/document_display.cfm?document_id=5344.

Sullivan, N. (1998) 'Far sighted: Mandarina Duck's full mental jackets', *Arena*, May, 78.

Sutton, S. (2002), 'Foreword' in S. Sutton (ed.) (2002), *The Social Psychology of Consumer Behaviour*, Buckingham: Open University Press.

SwRI (2003), 'Sensor Technology', at www.swri.edu/3pubs/brochure/d10/amd/amd01.htm, Southwest Research Institute.

Tactex (1988), 'taxtex controls inc. – technology', at www.tactex.com/technology.html, Tactex Controls Inc.

Taipei Journal (2002), 'High-tech textiles coming into fashion', 22 October, at www.taiwanheadlines.gov.tw/features/20021022f2.html.

Taipei Times (2002), 'Designer clothes for kids hit streets', *Taipei Times*, at http://taipeitimes.com/News/biz/archives/2002/07/28/158080.

TCFL (2002), 'TCFL 2012 - Global and Growing: Blueprint for a Positive Future', TCFL Forum Strategic Plan: Summary Report, Australian TCFL Forum.

TCSG (2000), *A National Strategy for the UK Textile and Clothing Industry*, Textile and Clothing Strategy Group.

Texprocil (2002), 'Development in Industry: Cotton and Textile Consumption in 1999-2000', 7 August, at http://texprocil/press/developmentindustry.htm, Press Release, The Cotton Textiles Export Promotion Council.

Textiles Intelligence (2002), 'Performance fabrics boost apparel market', *Textiles Intelligence*, Press Releases, 15 May, at www.textilesintelligence.com/til/press.cfm?prid=299.

TIME Europe (2002), 'Tech Watch', *TIME Europe*, 3 June, 159(22).

Tippit, S. (2000), 'Pardon me, that's just my jacket grumbling', MSNBC Living, 30 December.

TransAfrica Forum (2000), 'Clothing as a Cultural Expression: African Fashion', at www.transafricaforum.org/reports/clothing_issuebrief0600.pdf.

Twitchell, J. B. (2002), *Living it up: our love affair with Luxury*, New York: Columbia University Press.

UMKC (2000), 'Three gold sequins from Tutankhamun's tomb', *Echoes of Eternity* Exhibition, The Nelson-Atkins Museum of Art. Kansas City: University of Missouri at www.echoesofeternity.umkc.edu/Sequins.htm.

USARIEM (2002), 'Biophysics and Biomedical Modeling', at www.usariem.army.mil/bphysics/bmd.htm, U.S. Army Research Institute of Environmental Medicine.

Varley, R. (2001), *Retail Product Management: Buying and Merchandising*, London: Routledge.

Verbucken, M. (2000), *New Nomads: An Exploration of Wearable Electronics by Philips*, Rotterdam: 010 Publishers.

VF (2001), 'VF Corporation History', at www.vfc.com/pages/history.asp.

Voight, R. (1998), 'When Fashion Jumps Into Sports Arena', *International Herald Tribune*, 4 July, at www.iht.com/IHT/SR/070498/sr070498g.html.

Vossen, R. (2000), 'R&D, Firm size and Branch of Industry: Policy Implications', at www.ub.rug.nl/eldoc/som/b/98B43/98b43.pdf.

Walbran, S. (2002), 'Shanty Town Seamstresses Fuel the Fashion Industry', at www.changemakers.net/journal/02june/walbran.cfm.

Webb, B. (2001), 'Retail brand marketing in the new millennium', in T. Hines and M. Bruce (eds), *Fashion Marketing: Contemporary Issues*, Oxford: Butterworth-Heinemann.

Whitaker, B. (2001), 'An Arab Aesthetic', in *The Guardian*, 13 November, at www.guardian.co.uk/elsewhere/journalist/story/0,7792,592844,00.html.

White, N. and Griffiths, I. (eds.) (2000), *The Fashion Business: Theory, Practice, Image*, Oxford: Berg.

Wilcox, C. (2001), *Radical Fashion*, London: V&A Publications.

Williams, C. (2000), 'Do the Logomotion with me', *The Independent on Sunday*, 23 April, at www.cayte.com/fashion/logomotion.html.

Xybernaut (2003), 'Corporate Overview', at www.xybernaut.com/company/corporate/corp_over.htm, Xybernaut.

Yamanaka, N. (1987), *The Book of Kimono*, Tokyo: Kodansha International.

Yeohlee (2002), 'Designer Philosophy', at www.yeohlee.com/profilesnew.html.

Zaltman, G. (2003), *How Customers Think: Essential Insights into the Mind of the Market*, Harvard: Harvard Business School Press.

Zhou, W. and Gary, T. (2001), 'Synthetic Spider Silk Protein Production and Purification', at http://virtual.clemson.edu/groups/caeff/reuprog/reu/reu2001/Zhou_and_Gary_Abstract.html.

Index